Giambattista Vico
Keys to the *New Science*

Portrait of Giambattista Vico, from the Academy of the Arcadia in Rome.

Giambattista Vico
Keys to the *New Science*

Translations, Commentaries, and Essays

EDITED BY

Thora Ilin Bayer

AND

Donald Phillip Verene

CORNELL UNIVERSITY PRESS

ITHACA AND LONDON

First published 2009 by Cornell University Press
First printing, Cornell Paperbacks, 2009

Printed in the United States of America

Library of Congress Cataloging-in-Publication Data

Giambattista Vico : keys to the new science : translations, commentaries, and essays / edited by Thora Ilin Bayer and Donald Phillip Verene.
    p. cm.
  Translations, commentaries, and essays previously published in the annual New Vico studies, 1987–2006.
  Includes index.
  ISBN 978–0–8014–4733–4 (cloth : alk. paper)
  ISBN 978–0–8014–7472–9 (pbk. : alk. paper)
  1. Vico, Giambattista, 1668–1744. Principi di una scienza nuova. I. Bayer, Thora Ilin, 1966– II. Verene, Donald Phillip, 1937– III. Vico, Giambattista, 1668–1744. Selections. English. 2009. IV. New Vico studies. V. Title.
B3581.P73G414 2009
195—dc22

2008025321

Cloth printing   10 9 8 7 6 5 4 3 2 1

Paperback printing   10 9 8 7 6 5 4 3 2 1

Contents

Contents

Illustrations

Acknowledgments

All translations, commentaries, and essays are reprinted, revised, and edited from these issues of *New Vico Studies,* published by the Philosophy Documentation Center for the Institute for Vico Studies. The illustrations are reproduced from historical editions of Vico's works.

"Synopsis of Universal Law." *New Vico Studies* 21 (2003): 3–22.

"Definitions of the True and the Certain," from *On the One Principle and One End of Universal Law. New Vico Studies* 21 (2003): 50–51, 90–91.

"A New Science is Essayed," from *On the Constancy of the Jurisprudent. New Vico Studies* 23 (2005): 31–41.

"On Homer and His Two Poems," from *Dissertations. New Vico Studies* 24 (2006): 11–33.

"Vico's Address to His Readers, from a Lost Manuscript on Jurisprudence: Comment and Translation." *New Vico Studies* 19 (2001): 161–68.

"Vico's Reply to the False Book Notice, with a Translation of *Vici Vindiciae.*" *New Vico Studies* 24 (2006): 129–75.

"Vico's '*Ignota latebat.*'" *New Vico Studies* 5 (1987): 79–98.

"How All the Other Sciences Must Take Their Principles from This [Science of Divination]." *New Vico Studies* 22 (2004): 101–4.

"Vico's Addition to the Tree of the Poetic Sciences and His Use of the Muses: A Commentary." *New Vico Studies* 22 (2004): 105–12.

"Giambattista Vico's 'Reprehension of the Metaphysics of René Descartes, Benedict Spinoza, and John Locke': An Addition to the *New Science* (Translation and Commentary)." *New Vico Studies* 8 (1990): 2–18.

Acknowledgments

Special thanks to Molly Black Verene, associate editor of *New Vico Studies* and administrator of the Institute for Vico Studies, for suggesting this volume and for her work on its formulation and composition.

Abbreviations

A   *The Autobiography of Giambattista Vico.* Translated by Max Harold
Fisch and Thomas Goddard Bergin. Ithaca, N.Y.: Cornell
University Press, 1983.

FNS   *The First New Science.* Edited and translated by Leon Pompa.
Cambridge: Cambridge University Press, 2002.

NS   *The New Science of Giambattista Vico.* Translated by Thomas
Goddard Bergin and Max Harold Fisch. Ithaca, N.Y.: Cornell
University Press, 1984.

UL   *Universal Law.* In three books: *On the One Principle and One
End of Universal Law; On the Constancy of the Jurisprudent;* and
Dissertations. Translated by John D. Schaeffer. Books 1, 2, and 3
appear in *New Vico Studies,* vols. 21 (2003), 23 (2004), and 24
(2006), respectively.

Citations to *FNS* and *NS* are to the paragraph enumeration found
in the English translations and in most Italian editions.

Citations to *UL* are to book, part, chapter, and paragraph enumerations common to the translation and the Latin text.

Citations to classical works of Greek and Latin literature throughout are to the editions of the Loeb Classical Library of Harvard
University Press, using standard forms of citations and abbrevia-
tions of titles.

Giambattista Vico
Keys to the *New Science*

Introduction

Interpreting the *New Science*

Vico's Genetic Method

Giambattista Vico's *New Science* was published in two versions, one in 1725 and another in 1730. In his *Autobiography* Vico refers to these as the *First New Science* and the *Second New Science* (*A* 192). Prior to the *First New Science* Vico published his three books of *Universal Law* (1720–22). In his *Autobiography* Vico describes these three books on jurisprudence as a sketch of his "new science"— a first version of the *First New Science* (*A* 193).

Immediately after the appearance of the *Second New Science,* Vico began what would become several sets of "corrections, meliorations, and additions" that, as he notes in his *Autobiography,* can be incorporated into a third edition of his work (*A* 197). In 1735–36 Vico drafted a revised definitive text for a third edition that was given to the printer, with further annotations, in late 1743. Vico died in January 1744 while seeing this edition through the press. It appeared posthumously in July 1744. This third edition of the second version is what has become known to the world as Vico's *New Science*—its full title being *New Science concerning the Common Nature of the Nations* (1730/1744).

Nothing characterizes Vico's thought more closely than his use of the genetic method. In the preface to the English translation of Vico's *Autobiography* Max Harold Fisch writes that the work is "the first application of the genetic method by an original thinker to his own writings" (*A* v). As the founder of the modern form of intellectual autobiography, as well as of the philosophy of history,

1

Vico comprehends all human phenomena in terms of their origins and courses of development. To comprehend the genesis of something in the human world, as Vico says of his own life, is to grasp its causes, both natural and moral, and the occasions of fortune that affect it.

Most readers who are attracted to the *New Science* take what they wish from it, allowing it to become a source for their own thought, returning from time to time for rereadings of it as a whole or of its various parts. Our initial reading of Vico's work is enriched if we approach it through his own genetic method, if we explore certain parts of his other writings that are the background for the third edition of the *New Science*. The basis for such exploration can be found in passages from his theory of jurisprudence, his conception of his ideal reader, his response to the reception of the *First New Science,* and his additions to the *Second New Science* that do not appear in its English translation.

Many of the items crucial to our comprehension of the *New Science* have not until recently been available in English. Over the past decade and a half, the annual *New Vico Studies* has published translations, commentaries, and essays on textual issues that, taken together, provide the reader of the *New Science* with some valuable keys to its nature and background. The selections that follow are all from issues of *New Vico Studies.* The purpose of the present volume is to bring these together and to edit and introduce them in a manner that will prove useful to readers of Vico.

There are some repetitions among the selections and essays. Readers may wish to approach the contents of the volume not from beginning to end but to make use of the selections according to their own specific interests. Thus, every effort has been made to have each selection stand on its own.

No claim is made that this volume provides a systematic treatment of the background materials of the *New Science,* either within or without the development of Vico's thought; no single volume could accomplish such a task. The purpose of this volume is to offer some points of reference within Vico's own thought that may make central features of Vico's *New Science* more evident and strike some new chords in readers' consideration of it. With the appearance of these items in *New Vico Studies* and with the recent appearance of other translations of Vico's works, nearly all of Vico's works are now available in English (see appendix, "Vico's Writings in English Translation").

Vico's Method of Reading

In his *Autobiography* Vico describes a method of reading he devised while serving for nine years (1686–95) as a tutor to the children of the Rocca family, in their castle at Vatolla in the Cilento region south of Naples (*A* 120). In order to judge for himself the literary merits of Latin against the Italian, Tuscan tongue, he decided to study on successive days the works of the most cultivated writers of each. He read Cicero side by side with Boccaccio, Vergil with Dante, and Horace with Petrarch. He read the works of each three times: the first time to grasp each work as a whole, the second to comprehend the transitions and sequences of thought, and the third to collect fine turns of phrase and the author's manner of expression.

Although Vico does not say so, his method is a transposition of the first three principles of composition of classical rhetoric into a method of interpretation. Any composition requires the natural sequence of *inventio* (the amassing of materials pertaining to the subject matter to be discussed), *dispositio* (their arrangement into an order of thought), and *elocutio* (their formulation in language; Quintilian, *Inst. Orat.* 3.3.1). Each composition has content, order, and style. A complete reading of any work requires grasping each of these facets. By grasping each in turn the reader attains the basis to form a judgment of it, to interpret it. With this threefold method the reader remakes what the author has originally made in its composition.

Essential to Vico's program of reading was to read one type of work against the other. In this case—his study of poetics—it was to read the ancients against the moderns. Books are not to be read in isolation, but in comparison to each other. This comparative consideration of works gives a further dimension of interpretation. In his oration *On the Study Methods of Our Time* (1708/1709) Vico advocates a balance between the ancients, who excelled in the rhetorical probabilities of civil discourse and self-knowledge, and the moderns, who have mastered the certainties of mathematical reasoning and the discovery of facts through the experimental investigation of nature.

How might Vico's method of his own education and his conception of seeking a balance between the ancients and the moderns be applied to reading and interpreting the *New Science*?

The *New Science* (1744) may first be read as a whole. The work itself offers a guide to this reading in the "Idea of the Work," which is formulated as a commentary on the elements of the *dipintura*, the engraving of its frontispiece. In the opening line of the *New Science* Vico compares this engraving to that described in the text of the Tablet of Cebes, which was held in such high regard in Renaissance humanism. He notes that as the Tablet of Cebes offers a scheme of morals, the dipintura of the *New Science* offers a scheme of civil things. This tablet "may serve the *Reader* to conceive the *Idea of this Work* before reading it, and to bring it back most easily to memory with such aid as the imagination [*fantasia*] may provide him, after having read it" (*NS* 1).

In the "Idea of the Work" the whole of the *New Science* is presented in microcosm for the reader. In the last lines Vico writes, "to state the idea of the work in the briefest summary, the entire engraving represents the three worlds in the order in which the human minds of the gentiles have been raised from earth to heaven" (*NS* 42). To grasp this work as a whole, the reader must perceive how the worlds of the divine (the divine mind and the human mind understood as the divine element in man), the civil, and the natural intersect. The *New Science* is a book of wisdom, resting on the definition of wisdom as taken from the Greeks and expressed by Cicero: "Wisdom is the knowledge of things divine and human and acquaintance with the cause of each of them" (*Tusc.* 4.57). Human wisdom for Vico has two parts, civil and natural. The former is that in which the ancients excel; the latter is that over which the moderns have developed mastery.

Reading the work first as a whole prepares for the second reading, which concentrates on its arguments and transitions of thought. The aim of the first reading is not only to absorb the general features of the work but to locate the central idea or theme through which the author has made its contents coherent.

This central idea or theme serves as the ultimate principle guiding the specific transitions of the work.

Vico explicitly informs the reader what this principle is: "We find that the principle of these origins both of languages and letters lies in the fact that the first gentile peoples, by a demonstrated necessity of nature, were poets who spoke in poetic characters. This discovery, which is the master key of this Science, has cost us the persistent research of almost all our literary life" (*NS* 34). These poetic characters, he says, are imaginative genera or universals whereby the first figures of the gentile nations organized the particulars of their world. These genera are expressed in fables that tell first of gods and then of heroes. Vico writes, "the first science to be learned should be mythology or the interpretation of fables" (*NS* 51). The *New Science* depends upon the discovery of a new science of mythology that allows Vico to discover and present his new science of history of the common nature of the nations.

The heart of the *New Science* is book 2, "Poetic Wisdom," where Vico presents this new science of mythology. Book 2 is Vico's solution to Plato's ancient quarrel between philosophy and poetry that culminates in book 10 of the *Republic.* Plato's error was to fail to see that the poets and the philosophers are not contenders for a single form of wisdom. The ancient quarrel between the philosophers and the poets is resolved by the realization that there are two types of wisdom. That of the poets is the product of imagination (fantasia) found in the imaginative genera of the primal myths; that of the philosophers is the product of reason found in the intelligible genera of reflective discourse. Philosophic wisdom is generated from poetic wisdom; these two types of wisdom, once delineated, remain in a dialectical relation to each other that runs throughout the *New Science.*

The reader, when first looking into the table of contents of the *New Science,* can make little sense of its headings—the work appears to be eclectic, with headings concerning the universal flood, giants, divination, sacrifices, families, Roman assemblies, monsters, money, duels, astronomy, chronology, Homer, barbarism, providence, and so forth. But on finding Vico's statement of its master key the reader can begin to see how Vico's new science of mythology is the source for his new science of history. This science of mythology provides Vico with his "ideal eternal history" by serving as the basis of its first two ages, those of gods and heroes, which are the products of fantasia and precede the third age of humans, in which the pursuit of rational intelligibility dominates both society and thought.

The third reading focuses on turns of phrase, the passages in which the author excels in the use of language to the point of making what is said especially memorable. These are the moments in a work that achieve Longinus's rhetorical sense of the sublime: "A well-timed flash of sublimity scatters everything before it like a bolt of lightning and reveals the full power of the speaker at a single stroke" (*On the Sublime* 1.4). An example of what might be sought out in the third reading is perhaps the most quoted sentence in the *New Science:* "But in the night of thick darkness enveloping the earliest antiquity, so remote from ourselves there shines the eternal and never failing light of a truth beyond all question: that the world of civil society has certainly been made by men, and that its principles are therefore to be found within the modifications of our own human mind" (*NS* 331). Vico's "night of thick darkness" is reminiscent of Dante's "dark wood of error" in which he finds himself at the beginning of his quest in the *Divine Comedy* and from which he perceives the illumination of the truth he seeks. Vico has placed within this poetic statement an enthymeme, the favorite device of the orator: civil society is made by men; thus, its principles lie within our own human mind. The suppressed minor premise is Vico's famous principle—originally expressed in his *Most Ancient Wisdom of the Italians*—that the true is the made.

A second example of Vico's power of sublime expression is his characterization of the effects of the "barbarism of reflection" of the third age of ideal eternal history, the age of the human: "But if the peoples are rotting in that ultimate civil disease and cannot agree on a monarch from within, and are not conquered and preserved by better nations from without, then providence for their extreme ill has its extreme remedy at hand." He continues, saying that the barbarism of reflection is more inhuman than the barbarism of sense of the first age of ideal eternal history, the age of the gods. In the barbarism of reflection people "live like wild beasts in a deep solitude of spirit and will scarcely any two being able to agree since each follows his own pleasure or caprice." He notes that the barbarism of sense "displayed a generous savagery, against which one could defend oneself or take flight or be on one's guard, [but the barbarism of reflection,] with a base savagery, under soft words and embraces, plots against the life and fortune of friends and intimates" (*NS* 1106).

Vico describes this second barbarism in a manner similar to Dante's description of the lowest region of the inferno, in which we encounter sins that are not simply sins of the flesh or of the uncontrolled passions but those that destroy the social order itself: treachery committed against friends and relatives and against guests and hosts—the relationships of trust upon which civilized life depends.

Among Vico's more irenic passages is his tree of poetic wisdom (*NS* 367), which resonates with the long history of trees of knowledge, beginning with the biblical tree of the knowledge of good and evil, and his axioms 3 and 4 on the "conceit of nations" and "conceit of scholars" that are derivative of the ancient maxim that "man makes himself the measure of all things" (*NS* 120–28). Not all of Vico's turns of phrase depend upon a use of images. An example is his axiom 106, that Vico says could have been placed among the first of his axioms: "Doctrines must take their beginning from that of the subject matters of which they treat" (*NS* 314). This axiom guides almost any transition within the argument of the *New Science*. It is a clear declaration of Vico's genetic method. There is also axiom 66, which is a memorable gloss on his ideal eternal history: "Men first feel necessity, then look for utility, next attend to comfort, still later amuse themselves with pleasure, thence grow dissolute in luxury, and finally go mad and waste their substance" (*NS* 241). Here Vico's sense of luxury anticipates Jean-Jacques Rousseau's attack on luxury in the *First and Second Discourses*.

Vico's Science

The second aspect of Vico's reading program was to read works against each other. In his study of poetics, as mentioned above, he read the ancients against the moderns. The *New Science* balances its sources between classical and modern authors, just as Vico's list of his "four authors," as he calls them in his *Autobiography*, balances two ancients (Plato and Tacitus) with two moderns (Francis Bacon and Hugo Grotius; *A* 154). Vico's philological-philosophical method in the *New Science* adds another sense of reading works against each other. This method is the basis of his "new critical art," on which he asserts the *New Science* rests (*NS* 348).

This new critical art brings together the particular "certainties" of the life of nations that are the subject matters of philology—the customs, laws, languages, and deeds of peoples at war and in peace—with the universal "verities" of metaphysical and moral philosophy that proceed directly from the rational activity of the human mind and its meditation on the divine mind. The works of the philologists examine the results of human choice and authority that reflect the common or communal sense of each nation. The works of the philosophers put forth what can be established by reason. Vico's connection between philology and philosophy is also present in his four authors, in his combination of Plato the divine philosopher and Tacitus the historian, and of Bacon the philosopher of both common and esoteric wisdom and Grotius the systematizer of the laws of the nations.

Vico's title, *La Scienza nuova*, is intended to recall the titles of two other works, Bacon's *Novum organum* and Galileo's *Dialoghi delle nuove scienze*. Vico's new science advances a new instrument or logic by which to discover the truth of human affairs analogous to Bacon's new logic of induction to discover the truth of natural processes. Vico's first four axioms of the *New Science* parallel Bacon's maxims of the four idols, the tribe, den, marketplace, and theatre, through the awareness of which the mind readies itself for scientific investigations. Galileo's work first gave a basis for natural philosophy, which required a knowledge of the nature of physical motions. Vico's work first gave a basis for the distinctive human movements that comprise history. What Bacon and Galileo accomplished for the new science of nature Vico intended to accomplish for the new science of history—the science of civil wisdom. If the main part of Vico's title derives from Bacon and Galileo, the second part of his title mirrors the subtitle of Grotius's *On the Law of*

War and Peace. On the title page of its 1646 edition, below the title is "Wherein are set forth the law of nature and of nations."

Few writers are as straightforward as Vico in stating for the reader the key to their works, as Vico does in his statement that the master key to his science is the discovery of poetic characters or imaginative universals. Even fewer writers are as clear as he is in explaining the proof of their work. In his section on "Method" Vico writes, "Indeed, we make bold to affirm that he who meditates this Science narrates to himself this ideal eternal history so far as he himself makes it for himself by that proof 'it had, has, and will have to be'" (*NS* 349). Here Vico shares the term *meditation* with René Descartes' *Meditations on First Philosophy,* but he differs on what meditation entails. Meditation for Descartes is the deduction of first principles, these principles being established as indubitable by the application to them of the logical law of noncontradiction. The model for meditation in Descartes' sense is mathematical reasoning. For Vico, to meditate (*meditare*) is to narrate (*narrare*). The model for meditation in Vico's sense is the fable that relates a primordial truth (*vera narratio*).

The original form of narration is the art conveyed by the Muses, who, as Hesiod wrote, "sing of what was, is, and is to come." Vico glosses this line of the *Theogony* (36–39) in his statement of the means of proof of his new science. Vico's gloss adds the principle of necessity to the Muses' sequence of beginning, middle, and end. The proof of the new science is for its readers to make it for themselves as what "had, has, and will have to be" (*dovette, deve, dovrà*). Vico's aim, unlike Descartes' aim of logical certainty, is a knowledge *per causas.* Vico's new critical art aims at the true narration of the development of nations. We can be convinced of this truth if we can remake for ourselves what Vico has made in his narration of the *New Science.* As Vico claims, "history cannot be more certain than when he who makes the things also narrates them" (*NS* 349).

The giants, who take the first step toward their humanization as founders of families after the world has dried out, over a period of two centuries, from the universal flood, call out the name of Jove by speaking back in imitation of the sound of the first thunder: "these interjections of Jove should give birth to one produced by the human voice: *pa!*, and this should then be doubled: *pape!*" (*NS* 448). Jove is the first imaginative universal and, as Vico says, every nation has its Jove. The Jove experience causes these first humans to have the first thought through their natural power of fantasia and apprehend the thunderous sky as Jove. This fear of Jupiter Tonans makes them run into caves and, out of modesty and shame, to form marriages. The Jove experience is not generated by the giants from their terrestrial experience; it is thrust upon them. It comes as an epiphany, a break in being. Those among the giants who can produce the first name can then make sense of all their experience by associating the name of a god with each thing in the world. From this original experience all of history is made. The gentiles are no longer living in nature; they slowly develop a second nature, the world of culture or history, generated from their own human nature.

It remains for human beings, having made history, to make a knowledge of history. Vico's statement concerning the proof of his science implies that there must be a starting point, a first principle from which this knowledge can be made. This first principle is metaphysical. The new critical art that brings philology together in a balance with philosophy requires a beginning that is wholly topical and occurs as an epiphany in the knower. This epiphany, required for man to make a knowledge of history, is analogous to the Jove experience from which history itself is initiated.

Jove may be called a collective imaginative universal in that the primordial power of fantasia is that of bringing together the particular instances of thunder into a single, repetitive meaning. Thunder can be brought to mind again and again by uttering the name Jove. The human sound of *pape* mediates the immediate perceptions of thunder and allows the first humans to grasp thunder as an object. Vico's "ideal eternal history" can be called a recollective imaginative universal in that it recalls all the separate histories of the nations as one common pattern of three ages. There is no proof in a logical or Cartesian sense of this first principle. It is the result of an epiphany on the part of those who look upon history and suddenly see that all events repeat themselves and that the lives of all nations follow a necessary sequence in which they are born, rise, and fall within the great body of history.

Once the knower has this insight, Vico's critical art can come into play to verify and give content to this single principle of genesis.

The *New Science* is often seen as a work of philosophy, and indeed Vico seems on occasion to regard it as such. Strictly speaking, the *New Science* is not a philosophy, nor is it a history. Vico is neither philosopher nor philologian. Vico is a new scientist; the knowledge Vico claims in the *New Science* is different in kind from either philosophy or philology because it is made up of both.

The new scientist claims that he has a knowledge of human things, playing upon the ancient notion mentioned earlier, that wisdom is a knowledge of things divine and human. To have a knowledge of human things requires that we have some knowledge of divine things or we could not tell the difference between them. Vico claims a knowledge of the divine in the sense that he claims his science shows what "providence has wrought in history" (*NS* 342). Ideal eternal history is providential order realized in history. As the first human beings, by uttering the name Jove, become makers of history, the first knowers, by uttering the name *providence*, become makers of the new science of history. The *New Science* offers a natural theology based upon the principles of history rooted in human nature, not upon the principles of physical nature.

If these remarks offer a beginning point concerning the possibilities of reading and interpreting the *New Science* they have served their purpose. Vico says that each of the ancients was a complete university and that now we require a curriculum taught in various subjects by various people to attempt to accomplish what is in whole in the thought of any one of the ancients. The *New Science* attempts to restore this ideal of the complete university. If its reader were to follow out all the sources and lines of thought that the *New Science* contains it would be a complete education.

The Structure of This Volume

The selections in part 1 of this volume offer some insights into the origination of the *New Science* in the three books of Vico's *Universal Law*. Vico's earlier *Six Inaugural University Orations* on pedagogy (1699–1708/9) express his commitment to the Socratic ideal of self-knowledge and its grounding in civil wisdom. Vico sees civil wisdom as revived in the humanist tradition of the Renaissance as becoming lost in the rise and dominance of Cartesianism with its identification of knowledge with the ideal of certainty embodied in the mathematical method of thought. The reader of the *New Science* must keep in mind that throughout his career Vico was a professor of Latin eloquence, which meant that he taught the principles of classical rhetoric as they applied to forensic oratory. Vico finds civil wisdom actualized in Roman law as presented in the *Digest* and Justinian's *Institutes*. He accepts the presupposition of the *Digest,* that what the Greeks called *philosophia* the Romans called *iurisprudentia.*

The key to Roman law is the *ius gentium,* that part of Roman law that is common to the systems of law of all peoples. This is distinct from the *ius naturale* that Vico understands as the natural law of the philosophers, which is an ideal of reason, and from the *ius civile* that varies from nation to nation and is based on human choice and authority distinctive to each nation. The conception of the ius gentium suggests to Vico the principle of the common nature of the nations, not as a static commonality but as the common pattern of the three ages of his ideal eternal history shared by all nations in their rise, development, and fall. Throughout the *New Science* Vico's constant reference point is Roman law.

Although Descartes projected a morals based on his metaphysics and physics, it being the final branch in his tree of knowledge described in the prefatory letter to the *Principles,* he was never able to produce it beyond the ethical discussions in his correspondence with Princess Elizabeth. One might imagine connecting morals to mathematical method—Benedict de Spinoza's *Ethics* is the example—but one cannot imagine employing Descartes' method as a guide to jurisprudential reasoning or as a means for speaking in the law courts. Descartes, having in his *Discourse* excluded the forms of humanistic knowledge from the principles of right reasoning, cannot recapture them in a new, rationally certain form. Vico intends, in his *Most Ancient Wisdom of the Italians Unearthed from the Origins of the Latin Language,* to demonstrate the defects inherent in Descartes' metaphysics. Descartes attempts to generate first principles by a process of logical supposition joined with hypothetical doubt. Vico attempts to generate first principles by returning to the original meanings of words through which the Latin peoples—and, before them, the Greeks and the Etruscans—constructed reality.

In the *Most Ancient Wisdom* Vico advances his well-known dictum: *verum esse ipsum factum* or *verum et factum convertuntur,* that the true is the made or that the true is convertible with the made. He refers to this principle only once in the *New Science* and then only indirectly and not by name (*NS* 349), although Vico's notion of making—that human beings make history—runs throughout the *New Science*. Not to be overlooked in relation to the *New Science* is Vico's companion principle, the interrelation of *verum* and *certum.* His best statement of this is in chapter 82 of the first book of the *Universal Law: certum est pars veri*—the certain is part of the true. This relation runs throughout jurisprudence: that any particular, positive, certain law based on legislative authority must also have the authority of law itself. It must be a particular reflection of what is just, right, and reasonable.

In the second book of the *Universal Law* Vico includes a chapter in the form of an outline, with the title "Nova scientia tentatur" (A New Science Is Essayed; *UL* bk. 2, pt. 2, chap. 1). In it and throughout the *Universal Law* Vico develops connections between the philological and the philosophical that issue in his philosophical-philological method of the *New Science.* In the third book of the *Universal Law* Vico lays the groundwork for his discovery of the true Homer in the *New Science.* Here Vico begins to establish his claim that Homer is the mind of the Greek people themselves—a part of Vico's science of mythology.

As he works his way from the *Universal Law* to the versions of the *New Science,* Vico searches for a theory of jurisprudence that will confront the errors of the seventeenth-century natural-law theorists: Hugo Grotius, Samuel von Pufendorf, John Selden, and Thomas Hobbes. Vico realized that they cannot give an adequate account of the origin of the law. Vico realized there must be an understanding of how the law arises through custom, and to accomplish this a philosophy of law must be grounded in a philosophy of society. The law cannot be simply a rational structure occurring through a covenant that produces society. Law and society must be understood as a single process of development. A nation is a birth, and it lives out a course of life in the way that anything human is born, matures, and declines to its end.

Part 2 of this volume provides perspective on the reception of Vico's *First New Science*. From Vico's letters on the lack of recognition of the *New Science*—especially those to his friend Father Giacco and to Abbé Esperti, his agent in Rome—and from his fascinating reply to the false notice of the publication of the *First New Science* one can grasp how strange his ideas seemed to other scholars. His one fear, as Vico states at the end of his *Study Methods*, was to be alone in wisdom. How alone Vico was in his own time is evident from the very fact of the false book notice.

Part 3 of this volume supplies the reader with discussions of the iconography of the *New Science,* along with two main additions Vico made for its third edition. Much of his fairly extensive sets of "corrections, meliorations and additions" are reworkings of particular paragraphs. The two additions that appear in part 3, along with the "Practic of the New Science" that is readily available at the end of the Cornell Paperbacks edition of the Thomas Goddard Bergin and Max Harold Fisch translation of the *New Science,* present the passages of greatest philosophical significance that do not appear in the English translation. The essay on the *impresa* and its inscription, "Ignota latebat," concerns the icon added to the title page of the 1744 edition of the *New Science* that portrays the nature of the modern metaphysics of René Descartes and John Locke, criticized in Vico's addition of the "Reprehension" and that is set against the figure of Dame Metaphysics in the dipintura of the frontispiece.

PART 1

Background of the *New Science* in the *Universal Law* (1720–1722)

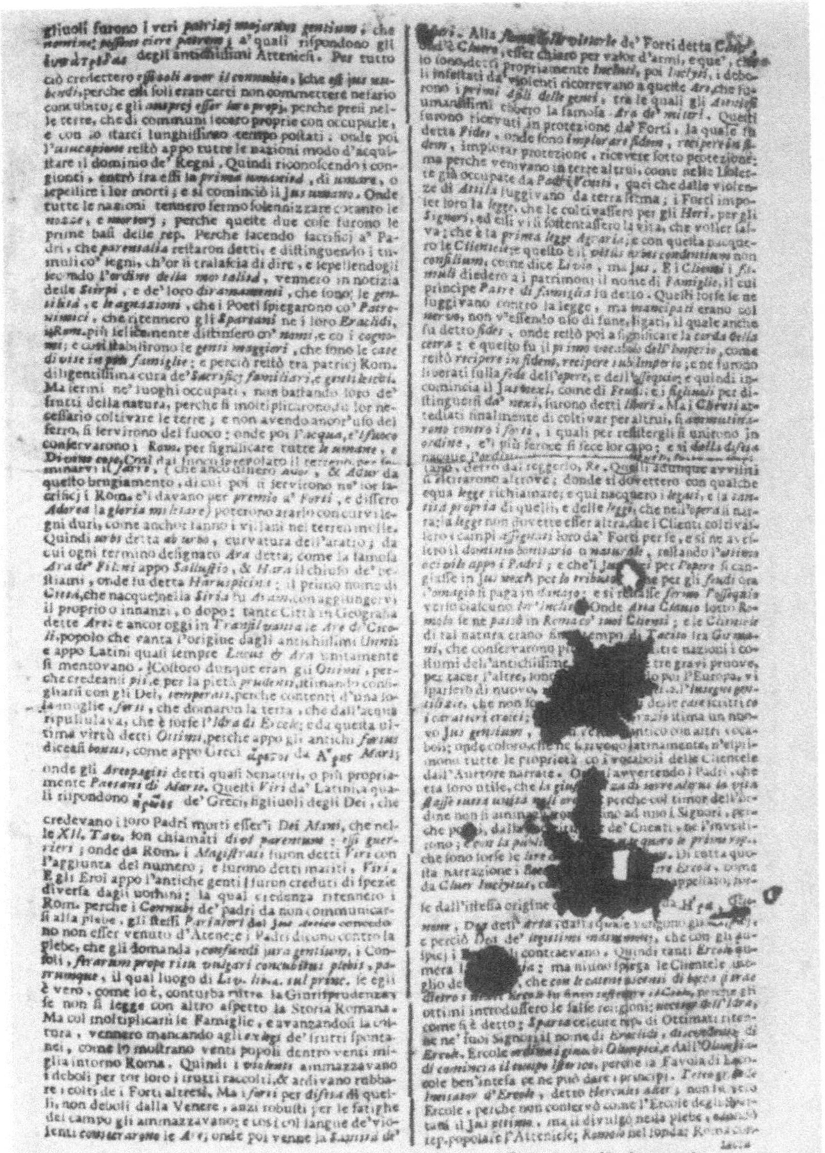

Figure 1. Page from *Sinopsi del diritto universale.*

Synopsis of Universal Law

Translation by
DONALD PHILLIP VERENE

In the 1720s, prior to the first version of his *New Science* (1725), Vico published three volumes in Latin grouped under the general Italian title *Il diritto universale*. To announce this work, Vico had printed four densely written pages in Italian that are untitled but are commonly called *Sinopsi del diritto universale*. This synopsis of Vico's work on *Universal Law* appeared in July 1720. The first volume, *De uno universi iuris principio et fine uno* (On the One Principle and One End of Universal Law) followed in September. Between August and September 1721, Vico published the second volume, *De constantia iurisprudentis* (On the Constancy of the Jurisprudent). In August of the following year, Vico published a third volume, *Notae in duos libros*, containing notes on the first two volumes and supplementary essays or "dissertations."

The most problematic term in Vico's writings on universal law is *ius*. This translation agrees with Alan Watson, in his translation of the *Digest*, that "ius cannot be exactly translated from Latin to English." Watson retains ius, but pairs it in English with "law," connecting it to "right" only in instances where it applies to specific conditions and individuals. I have followed this procedure, which accords with Thomas Goddard Bergin and Max Harold Fisch's explanation in the introduction to their translation of the *New Science:*

> We must begin by reminding the reader of a constant source of confusion and misunderstanding in English translations from the legal literature of continental Europe. English uses the one word

"law" in two very different senses for which European languages have distinct and contrasting terms: Latin *ius* and *lex*, Italian *diritto* and *legge*, French *droit* and *loi*, Spanish *derecho* and *ley*, German *Recht* and *Gesetz*. The second term of each pair properly denotes enacted law, law which has been *made* law by the authority of some lawmaking body, at some time and place; therefore by will. The first term of each pair denotes the legal order, law, structure, or system, conceived as, ideally at least, a rational whole; law, therefore, by reason. The distinction is between what is law because it has been so decided and what is law because it is in itself straight, right, or reasonable. (*NS*, E4)

Synopsis of Universal Law

Giambattista Vico, at the beginning of the month of March of the present year 1720, has, in Naples, given to the presses of Felice Mosca a Latin work in one volume in quarto, divided into two books—the first titled *On the One Principle and One End of Universal Law*, the second *On the Constancy of the Jurisprudent*—in which he seeks to establish a principle through which all divine and human erudition can be demonstrated.

And, putting forth two definitions—one of the true, which is *quod rerum ordini conformatur* [that conforming to the order of things], the other of the certain, which is *conscientia dubitandi secura* [consciousness free from doubt] and taking as lemmas only five metaphysical truths, he demonstrates that from the order, through the order, and in the order of things man knows the true, and that from the idea of order three things follow:

1. God is,
2. is infinite mind,
3. that thus in us, as a result of the sciences, as from Him, through Him, and in Him are the principles of things.

Hence he argues, regarding the nature of God, that He is *nosse, velle, posse infinitum*, [infinite knowledge, will, and power], from which he demonstrates the nature of man, that he is *nosse, velle, posse finitum, quod tendat ad infinitum* [finite knowledge, will, and power that tends toward the infinite].

From which he demonstrates the principles of sacred history:

1. Adam was created by God,
2. of a perfect nature,
3. by his own fault corrupted; and, consequently he demonstrates the principles of Christian theology.

By way of all this he concludes that the natural pleasure that perfect man had in contemplating the eternally true was in corrupt man changed into a force that produces truth for us through the pain of the senses. This force of the true he determines to be human reason in corrupted nature, and to be the source of the virtues intellectual as well as moral; and the foundation of the latter to be the humility of the human spirit, the form of which is love, and the author and the end of all things to be God. Such are the principles of Christian morality.

He makes of virtue three parts—prudence, temperance, and fortitude—that regulate the three parts of man: prudence, intelligence; temperance, caprice; fortitude, force; and that human reason embraced by the will is virtue insofar as it combats cupidity, and this same virtue is justice insofar as it gauges utilities. And thus from the three parts of virtue he brings forth three rights or reasons: dominion, liberty, and tutelage [i.e., guardianship, security]. From prudence, or just choice of utilities, comes dominion; from temperance or moderation of the self's will and things pertaining to it comes liberty; from fortitude, or moderated force, comes tutelage, and these three parts of justice are the three sources of all commonwealths and all laws.

Hence he shows the just to be in nature, because that which is equal when measured is just when chosen; and the two measures arithmetic and geometry, that are the norms made use of by the two kinds of justice, commutative and distributive, are in nature, because they are truths on which everyone concurs.

Hence he demonstrates that due to their nature there exists among men a truly just society—that is, *aequum bonum*, of equal utility—that consists of *ius naturale immutabile* [immutable natural law]; everyone everywhere concurs about such a society. And that the Skeptics—Epicurus, Machiavelli, Hobbes, Spinoza, Bayle, and others—claim man to be sociable because of utility, brought to it through need or fear, because they were not aware that the causes of things are other than the occasions of them; utilities may themselves change, but the equanimity of them is eternal; and the temporal not being the cause of the eternal, nor the corporeal able to produce the abstract, utility is the occasion through which the idea of equality, which is the eternal cause of the just, is awakened in the mind of man.

Having established the ius naturale immutabile, he makes of it two parts: one dependent on the will, which gives substance to all of voluntary law and consists of liberty, dominion, and tutelage of this and that; the other dependent on an eternal reason, which provides just measure to liberty, dominion, and tutelage, and provides them with the eternal form of the just. And these two parts are called by the ancient interpreters *ius naturale prius* [prior natural law] and *ius naturale posterius* [posterior natural law] and are the same as the *prima naturae* [prime nature] and *naturae consequentia* [consequent nature] of the Stoics, and that which is *prius* takes the shape of *ius immutabile* [immutable law] through that which is *posterius*. Because it could be forbidden, for example, that a man defend himself and be obliged to endure wrongs; but it could never be the case that he would not be allowed by nature to defend himself against such.

Having established one principle of laws and of jurisprudence—reason—he passes to the other, which is authority, and shows that authority is the form of the certain, as reason is the form of the true; so that authority is part of reason, in the same way that the certain is part of the true: whence tyrants should be endured, who also are an ordination of God, because even under them, one has the certain, the consciousness that does not doubt the state, which for that reason should not be disturbed.

Hence he relates the origin and progress of authority, and shows the first authority to be that called "of nature," that he defines as *sua cuiusque humanae naturae proprietas: nosse, velle, posse, et quidem posse tum animo, tum corpore, quia utroque constamus* [the unique property of human nature: knowledge, will, and power, and indeed power of spirit and body, because we are constituted

of both] by which man *est in omni natura mortali summus* [is ultimately the sum of his mortal nature].

From this was born the authority that is called "of reason" and
that he defines as *sua cuiusque proprietas disponendi de re tua ut velis,
vivendi ut velis, tuendi te et tua si velis* [the unique property of disposing of things that are yours as you will, of living as you will,
and of defending yourself and what is yours if you will]. This form
of authority, in solitude and in the state of lawlessness, is called
"monastic" authority, by which man *est in solitudine summus* [is
supreme in solitude] and by *iure superioris* [superior right] can
kill anyone who commits violence. Whence he infers duels to be
the first judgments in the state of lawlessness and that Brennus
[leader of the Gauls] did not respond falsely to the Romans—that
the first law that was born in the world was made by violence—but
he omitted the most important point: violence dictated from a
better nature.

Hence the *ius gentium* [law of the gentes] is born, which he defines as *ius violentiae* [law of violence] and he divides into the *ius
maiorum gentium* [law of the greater gentes] and *minorum* [the
lesser]. He shows that the first is the law of private violence in the
lawless state, and from this are born the families, in addition to
another form of commonwealths, that he shows to be that of the
clienteles that in ancient history can be seen scattered all over the
Occident—above all in Gaul, Germany, Britain, Spain, Italy, and
finally Greece—from which then come to be born the commonwealths of the optimates under the names of "kingdoms" in Italy
and in Greece, of "principalities" in the rest; and Romulus imi-
tated the greater gentes and ordered his commonwealth according to this form. This was not noticed; it was believed in good faith
that the first commonwealths were absolute kingdoms; that they
themselves elected the kings on the basis of their robustness and
dignity of appearance; and that, in this rough and unrestrained
liberty, as if they had a science of good taste, everyone could agree
upon the most robust and most beautiful.

It is not thus to be denied that there were heroic kings. But
it is claimed that the principles of all profane history were lack-
ing because of the ignorance of the true principles of poetry; he

proves poetry to be the first history of the gentiles and thus it must be the torch of the law of the gentes. Suspending for a little the credit to antiquity—that the first priests were theologians and with their theology founded the commonwealths—he formulates three questions:

1. The nature of men is thus made by first attending to necessity, then to comfort, and finally to pleasure. Is it possible that poetry is born prior to all the arts of comfort and of pleasure, all of which are needed for the commonwealth (all agree it is still questionable whether it is born for utility or for pleasure); might it not be born from some necessity?

2. The same nature of men is also made first through awareness of all the things that touch them through the senses, then through customs, and finally through abstract things; and the history of the philosophers proceeds according to this order because first are the physicists; then Socrates called morals from the heavens, and finally came Plato and the other divines. How is it that matters were reversed in the uncultured world—that Orpheus sang to the beasts, Amphion to the stones about the nature and the powers of the gods whence they tamed the animals and united the stones into cities?

3. Children understand only particulars; whence even the most ingenious of them only know how to explain themselves in terms of similarities. How is it that in the childhood of the world all of a sudden there were men who understood the commonwealths, in which are the universals of human institutions?

From all such he proves that the origin of poetry was neither pleasure nor comfort but necessity, which the first fathers had in order to teach to their offspring the examples of the ancestors. And the humane gentes—because ingenious, in this poverty of languages, like ingenious children, instead of genera, of which they were incapable—were led by nature to form images, which are the first characters of language, from which later letters, "characters," are articulated. And such were the fables of the Greeks and, for example, the hieroglyphics of the Egyptians. And, because children retained words most easily in memory when enclosed within certain measures, there not yet being writing, the fathers spoke to them by singing.[1]

He discovers this origin of poetry: that the theology of the poets must be presumed not natural but civil; and indeed, mythology must explain the fables by means of this perspective such that the fabulous time is not different from the obscure time but is the history of it, and this must give us the principles of historic time. Accompanying this meditation are the following facts—indeed, certainties:

1. The first city mentioned in all profane history is Cumae, located in Italy.[2]

2. The first architecture is the Etruscan, because it is the most unrefined, the most simple, and the most solid, like that of the Egyptians.

3. The Roman art of deploying battle lines, in the judgment of Livy, is better than the Greek, putting it before the Macedonian phalanx; and this art is not the daughter of geometry and arithmetic, whence it can be said that the Romans also had it from the Etruscans.

4. Certainly from the Etruscans they learned haruspices, which is recognized as the most ancient species of divination.

5. There are no nations that surpass the Romans in the majesty of their togas, their insignias, and their triumphs; these things they certainly have from the Etruscans.

6. When Athens and Sparta were small towns, the Etruscans in Italy had a very powerful kingdom that gave its name to the sea from Maremma to as far as the Strait of Messina.

---

1. "This is emended in the course of the work in chapter 12 ('On the Origin of Poetry'), book 2, part 2, where it is proved that not reflection but nature brought the first men to song, when they began to found humanity; whence it came about that, there not being writing, descendents with song preserved in memory the things of the ancestors" [manuscript note of Vico]. See *UL* bk. 2, pt. 2, chap. 12, esp. par. 41.

2. "This stands fully proved in book 2, part 2, chapter 4 of the *Notae*" [manuscript note of Vico]. See *UL* bk. 3, chap. 4, pars. 44–45; cf. *UL* bk. 2, pt. 2, chap. 1, par. 4 ("2960 [1043 BCE] The City of Cumae is founded"); cf. *FNS* 239 and *NS* 757.

7. Italian philosophy is more ancient and more learned than the Greek, to say the same as Plato in the *Timaeus,* whence he admonished his own for knowing little of antiquity.

8. Romulus had dared to found his city thus in the middle of the powerful kingdom of the Etruscans and a great number of other small regimes; and the Roman populace under their kings, in 250 years, laid waste to more than twenty peoples among these and did not extend their empire more than twenty miles, according to St. Augustine (*City of God,* book 3, chapter 15); and it had to continue another 250 years to subjugate all of Italy; in the middle of such powerful and fierce peoples they needed to remain under the protection of the ius gentium and not to make war unless attacked.

9. By an evident proof (that, because it is long, is here omitted) he demonstrates that the Latins have preserved more vestiges of the infancy of their language than the Greeks: because the Athenians emended the laws every year, and the Spartans, prohibited by Lycurgus to write them, spoke of them always in the language of the present.

10. The *ius nexi* [nexian law, law of bondage] certainly was not transported from Attica to Rome, because before the Law of the Twelve Tables, the fathers cruelly exercised it on the plebeians, and because of this they revolted. And, too, Theseus with the law *De nexo soluto forti sanate* [On the strong and sound freed from the bond] at the end of the heroic times founds the liberty of the Athenians; and the Romans, finally after three hundred years of their commonwealth, referred to it in the Twelve Tables.

From all these facts he concluded that the Romans strongly preserved the customs of the greater gentes, upon which Romulus founded the commonwealth and that because of this custody they alone can provide us the certainty of the origin, as the succession is not interrupted in profane history.

Hence, returning to the order already begun, he proposes the definition of *ius civile* [civil law] in the manner of Gaius, with which *omnes populi partim suo proprio, partim communi omnium hominum iure utuntur* [all peoples have laws part of which are proper to themselves and part of which are in common with all other peoples].

Two axioms:

First: Voluntary law has for its torch the history of either things or words.

Second: A certain rule of interpretation is that words must be taken in their proper signification; if not, trouble may follow.

Three postulates:

First, that on account of all this he reasons that men in the obscure time must have acted by these principles, and if sacred history does not tell us otherwise, and much more if it assists us, let us grant that they so acted.

Second, that the ius civile being a mixture of ius gentium and what is particular to itself, which in Roman law is found to be uniform with that which is narrated of how men in the obscure time acted, it is granted to be *de iure gentium* [from the ius gentium].

Third, that speech, either in prose or in verse, and much more in verse than in prose (since the first profane authors were poets), was suited to the things narrated in the obscure time, properly signifying them, and that later its signification of them came to be improper. As, for example, it is more proper to say *usurpare trinoctium* [to seize for one's own use the space of three nights], of the wife who for three nights denies herself to her husband and of herself in relation to him *usum surripit* [privily to have taken away use], than to say *usurpare,* meaning "to interrupt the possession by calling into question the possessor." And more proper, for example, is the poetic locution *sanguis circa praecordia fervet* [the blood boils in my heart] than *irasci* [enraged] of the prose writers. This is a way of speaking through characters, through images; but in speaking through abstract genera, blood, heart, and boiling are made into one word, *ira* [rage, ire].

By means of these principles he relates that, after the Flood, Noah and Shem, his son, keeping to the true religion of God the creator, preserved in the state of nature the memory of the sciences and the arts that were before the Flood, so that after the Babylonian confusion of languages all the arts of civility remained, not lost but perpetuated in memories. Whence soon the monarchical form of government was born and remained firm among the Chaldeans, and, by way of the neighboring countries soon was introduced by the descendents of Ham, another son of Noah, into Syria and Egypt, for this reason Tacitus said *suetum regibus Orientem* [the Orient is accustomed to kings]. And there soon came about a species of divination, called "magic," and even though false, it was certainly more learned than the auspices that those in the Occident used, but which would have had need of a long series of centuries of observations in order to become a science. But of Japheth, third son of Noah who went lawlessly into the far Occident, divesting himself of the true religion, whence he was believed to be Iapetus [one of the Titans, father of Prometheus], it developed that his descendents little by little became completely impious, thus highly ignorant and almost brutes.

The earth was partitioned among the sons of Noah in the year of the world 1656. Rome was founded in 3250. This will be the period, then, of the obscure time of Italy—1594 years.

Then, these lawless and impious men, vagabonds roving wherever talent took them through this great forest of the world, lost all humanity, with uncertain language, dissolved into a brute and uncertain and because uncertain, often nefarious lasciviousness, and wasting away in idleness caused by the abundance of fruits that nature gave them, in the manner of wild beasts, all alone, not recognizing their own, left their dead above the ground unburied.

A few of better disposition, contemplating the sky in this idleness, from the motions of the stars believed it animate and that it spoke with lightning. From which in auguristic science the verb *contemplari* [to behold, contemplate] is derived from the regions of the sky, that were called *templa* [open places in the sky] and that the augurs designated as places to observe lightning flashes, or the flights of birds (*contemplari* the Greeks called θεωρειν [to observe, contemplate], *meditari deum* [to contemplate the deity]).

He shows that they, believing the sky to be god, being ashamed of their venal imprudence in the face of the sky (whence later purity related to making sacrifice was called *castitas* [chastity]), hid themselves, each taking for himself a woman in places where there was no illumination, called *luci* [sacred groves, also an open place in a wood], never mentioned by the Latins without some reference to religion. And in order to remain firmly where they would have abundance of water, observing that birds made nests near to springs, they followed them as their guide into the mountains because there springs arise most;[3] and from this originates the religion of water (the gods themselves swore by Styx, deep water); and indeed nature made them find sites in strong places, which from the word πηγη [a spring (Latin, *pege*)], *fons* [fountain], *pagi* [villages; *pagus*, a place with fixed boundaries] they were first called.

From Greek Διος [genitive of Ζευς], from Latin *Dius* [a deity; *diu*, by day] is the word *Diespiter* ["*Dijovis*"; "Father of Day" (*dies*, day)], as Jove was called, and the sky and all such that is of the sky was called *Dium* [*sub Jove*, under the open sky].

And, believing the birds to be heavenly animals, they founded divination by the auspices. And so, first of all among them divine law is born, which was absolutely called from the beginning *ius* [law], the same as what the Greeks call διαιον, and because of the beauty of pronouncing it they later added the κ, making δικαιον [just, lawful], as Plato relates [*Cratylus*, 412d–e]: but the Latins better said *Ious* [Jove], whence perhaps comes the oblique *Iovis* [Jovian]. When human law is born, the attribute "divine" is added to the first law.

The poets made of all this a character, Jove, and assigned to him the eagle and lightning, the two things most observable in their divinity; and the Romans called all the great birds *aquilas* [eagles] as though it meant *aquilegas* [discerners of water] (wherewith he proves the first laws to have had this name) and they were esteemed as divinities of the Roman Empire.

---

3. "And this too is corrected in the *Notae* to the first book, chapter 149 [*UL* bk. 1, chap. 149, par. 2] and in the course of the work in book 2, part 2, chapter 20, in the paragraph *De matrimoniis* [On marriages; *UL* bk. 2, pt. 2, chap. 20, par. 17], where it is demonstrated that the first men founded humanity without any reflection, but, guided by the auspices, they were brought to establish themselves in high places near to springs" [manuscript note of Vico].

Then in places of stability—from which perhaps they were called *heri* [heirs, owners], *signori* [nobles, masters], and perhaps thereafter said to have *"haereditas" ab "haerendo"* [heirship from holding fast] that corresponds to Theseus of the Greeks and was called *a* θεσει [thesis] "position"—by employing certain women, and only under certain protected conditions, they became certain fathers; and in addition acquired certain economic authority with which they founded imperial paternity wherewith the fathers are the heads of the families.

And he proves that they themselves held the *ius vitae et necis* [the right of life and death] over the children of the family—from which comes the line of proper inheritance and through it living instruments of acquisition—and among the greater gentes the father's authority was exactly that which the Romans later claimed properly their own. And these children were the true patricians of the *maiorum gentium* [greater gentes] who *nomine possent ciere patrem* [could name their fathers], to which corresponded the εὐπατριδαι [class of aristocrats] of the ancient Athenians.

They held that they alone had marriage, which *est ius nubendi* [is the right of nuptials], because they alone were certain not to commit nefarious intercourse, and that the auspices were properly theirs because the auspices were taken in lands, that they made theirs by occupying them in common, and by remaining in residence on them for the longest time; whence later usucapion remained for all the nations the mode of acquiring the dominion of kingdoms.

Hence, by recognizing relatives, the first humans come to inhume and bury their dead, and, thus, began human law. Whence all nations firmly supported the solemnizing of nuptials and funerals, because these two things were the prime bases of the commonwealths. So that making sacrifices to the fathers came to be called *parentalia* [festival in honor of dead relations], and marking the graves with signs that will not be discussed now, and burying them according to the order of their mortality, they came to note the lines of descent and their branches; these are the lines of nobility and the agnations that the poets explained by means of patronymics, that the Spartans retained in their Heraclids, and that the Romans more successfully distinguished by means of names and surnames. And thus the greater gentes were established as houses subdivided into families, and for this reason there remained among the Roman patricians the most diligent care of domestic and noble sacrifices.

But, once firmly established in occupied areas, the fruits of nature not being enough for them, because of their multiplying numbers, it was necessary for them to cultivate the lands. And, not as yet having use of iron, they availed themselves of fire; thereafter the Romans have held water and fire to signify all human and divine things. They scorched the land with fire in order to sow spelt (that they called *ador* [spelt] and *adur* [to set fire to] from this burning, which afterward the Romans employed in their sacrifices, and they gave it as a reward to the brave for military glory, saying *adorea* [a reward of valor, originally consisting of grain]), thus being able to plow it with hard carved wood, as peasants still do in soft terrain. Hence, *urbs* [a walled town, city] called *ab urbo,* from the curvature [*urbum*] of the plow: whence every bounded space was called *ara* [altar], like the famous "Altar of the Philaeni" according to Sallust, and *hara* [pen] the enclosure for cattle, hence *haruspicina* [divination (*haruspicium,* the inspection of victims in divination)]. The name of the first city to be born in Syria was Aram; other cities were named by adding this to the proper name either before or after it—many cities in geography are called *are* [*area,* a ground, an open space, clearing], and still today in Transylvania there is the "are of the Szeklers," a people who boast of an origin from the most ancient Huns; and by the Latins *lucus* [a wood or grove sacred to a deity] and *ara* are almost always mentioned together.

These people, thus, were the best because they believed themselves pious and, because of this piety, prudent, placing great value on seeking advice from the gods; temperate, because they were content with one wife only; strong, because they dominated the earth, that was repullulated with water (which is perhaps the Hydra of Hercules); and from this last virtue they were called the "best," because according to the ancients *fortus* [strong] is said to be *bonus* [good], just as according to the Greeks αριστοι [victorious, best ruling] is from Αρης, "Mars" [god of war], from which the "Areopagites" were said to resemble senators or, more specifically, to be countrymen of Mars.

These were called *viri* [*vir*, a man, man of courage, principle, or honor, one who deserves the name of a man] by the Latins, to which corresponds ηρωες [heroes, warriors, free men] by the Greeks, "sons of the gods," who believed their dead warrior fathers to be the gods of the underworld, that in the Twelve Tables are called *divi parentum* [the gods of the parents]: whence magistrates were called *viri* by the Romans with the addition of a number [e.g., *triumviri*, a board of three holding office together, a triumvirate], and husbands were called *viri*. And the heroes according to the ancient gentes were believed to be a different species of men; this belief was retained by the Romans, because the marriages of the fathers were not imparted to the plebeians; they did not concede that the Attic law had parity with the Roman such as to have come from Athens; and the fathers declared themselves against the plebeians, who asked them *confundi iura gentium* [to extend the law of the gentes]; the consuls held that *ferarum prope ritu vulgari concubitus plebis patrumque* [marriage between plebeians and patricians would be nearly as vulgar as coupling in the manner of beasts]. This passage in Livy (book 4, beginning), if it is true as such, upsets all jurisprudence, if the history of Rome is not read from a new perspective.

But with the multiplying of families and the advancing of cultivation, those outside the law came to lack the spontaneous fruits of nature, as shown by the presence of twenty peoples within twenty miles around Rome. Hence, the violent killed the weak to take from them the fruits of nature they had collected and they dared even to rob the crops of the strong. But the strong, not weak from venery, as well as robust from work in the fields, killed them in order to defend themselves; and thus with the blood of the violent consecrated the clearings, from which later comes the sanctity of the walls.

Attracted by the fame of the victories of the strong—called *cluer* [splendor of arms], whence is *cluere* [to be named, esteemed], "to be resplendent in the valor of arms," and those who are such are properly called *incluti*, then later *inclyti* [illustrious]—the weak, ravaged by the violent, retreated to these clearings, that were the first asylums of the gentes, among which the most humane Athenians had the famous "Altar of the Dispossessed." These were received in protection by the strong, which were called *fides* [faith, fealty], whence there is *implorare fidem, recipere in fidem,* "to implore for protection," "to receive in protection." But, because they were arriving in the lands of others, as in the little islands already occupied by the Venetian fathers who because of the violence of Attila fled from terra firma, the strong imposed on them the law that they must cultivate the land for the *heri,* for the signori, and could there sustain the life they wished to preserve. This is the first agrarian law, and, with this, the clienteles are born. And this is the *vetus urbes condentium* [the old claim of the founders of cities] not the *consilium* [counsel], as Livy says, but *ius* [the law]. And the clients, the *famuli* [those bound in domestic servitude], gave to the estates the name of family, the prince of which was called paterfamilias.

These clients, if they fled from their masters against the law, were mancipated with sinew—that is, tied, rope not being in use; this sinew also was called *fides* [the binding of the body is like the incorporeal bond or cord of fidelity], which later remained to signify the string of the lyre. And this was the first word of dominion, which remained in *recipere in fidem* [to receive in trust or protection], *recipere sub imperio* [to receive under dominion, power, authority]. And they were freed from them through the faithfulness of work and through obedience, and hence commences the *ius nexi* [law of bondage] as of feudal tributes. And the sons, to distinguish them from the *nexi* [bound] were called *liberi* [free].

But the clients, finally growing weary of cultivating crops for others, mutinied against the strong, who, in order to resist them, unified themselves into an order, and they made the most fierce among them their chief; and, thus, from the need for defense is born order, that was then called "civil," under a captain, so called from "to rule" [*reggere*], *re* [king]. They, however—the dispirited— withdrew elsewhere, from which they had to be recalled by means of some equitable law, and now were born the ties and the soundness proper to them and to the laws, which is related in the book. The law could not have been other than that the clients cultivated for themselves the fields assigned them by the strong, and so they would have bonitarian or natural dominion over them, in contrast to that of the best or civil dominion that rested with the fathers, and that the ius nexi through work is changed into ius nexi through tribute (whence is perhaps the saying "the tithe of Hercules")[4] as, now for the fiefs homage is paid in money; and, so, obedience toward each illustrious one of them would remain firm. Whence Atta Clausus [progenitor of the Roman house of Claudia] under Romulus moved to Rome with all his clients; and the clienteles of such nature existed until the time of Tacitus among the Germans, who preserved more than all other nations the customs of the most ancient gentes. Of this there are at least three weighty proofs: inundating Europe, the Germans spread anew

1. duels by way of tournaments,
2. gentile insignia, which were none other than the names of their houses written in heroic characters,
3. and feuds, which [Hugo] Grotius considers a new *ius gentium,* but which in fact is the ancient one put in other words—whence those who wrote of it in Latin express all the properties of it by means of the vocabulary of the clienteles as this author relates.

Now here, the fathers, knowing that it was useful to them to take another's life by just force, cautiously all united in an order, and because of fear of this order the clients did not kill even one of the nobles, for of the multitude of the clients, few collided with it. And by means of public violence the first commonwealths were born, which are perhaps present on the lyres of Orpheus and Amphion.

Out of this whole narration the poets created the character Hercules, as from *cluer, inclytus,* so from "glory of Juno" [*Heras kleos,* glory of Hera (Roman, Juno)] he was called Ηρακλης [Heracles]; hence perhaps ηρως [hero], came from the same origin as Ηρα [Hera]; Juno was goddess of the air [αηρ; *aer*], from which comes the auspices, and thence goddess of legitimate matrimonies,

---

4. This brief parenthetical remark on the "tithe of Hercules" is a marginal note in Vico's handwriting, added in one of the two known copies of the *Synopsis.* See G. B. Vico, *Opere,* vol. 2, pt. 1 (Bari: Laterza, 1936), 15.

which in accordance with the auspices the strong contracted. Hence, mythology numbers many Hercules; but none explains the clienteles better than the Gallic Hercules, who with chains issuing from his mouth is pulling the nexi after him. Hercules was imagined to support the sky, because the patricians introduced false religions; he was slayer of the Hydra, as it is said. Sparta, celebrated commonwealth of the optimates, retained for its nobles the name of the Heraclids, descendents of Hercules. Hercules orders the Olympic games; and from the Olympiads historical time begins, so that the fable of Hercules, properly understood, can provide us the principles of it. Theseus, great imitator of Hercules, called *Hercules alter* [the second Hercules], was not the true Hercules, because he did not preserve, as did the Hercules of the Spartans, the ius of the patricians, but divulged it to the plebeians and founded the Athenian popular commonwealth. Romulus, in founding Rome, consecrated the great altar to Hercules, and the Romans adopted him as the god of oaths.

Thus, by investing public violence with civil power, civil authority was born, whence it is supreme in the commonwealths; and the necessity of force passed into the necessity of civil reason; but certain images of true violence remained. Mancipation, the form of nearly all legal actions, consisted in the civil consignment of a knot, a sign that the lands were in the dominion of the aristocrats; vindication was a simulated use of force; the conditions that were proved to be the ancient forms of repression were changed into provisos and denunciations; and usurpations into discrete citations. And this he claims to be what Justinian calls, in the proem of the *Institutes, antiqui iuris fabulas* [the fables of the ancient law]. The agreements thus remained firm, which proves well, in terms of origin, an ancient simplicity, as can be observed well in rustic peoples, who have a highly religious use of words in promises and in oaths—which is found in the unfortunate and pitiable vows of Theseus and Agamemnon. And these were thus the agreements from which they introduced to all an ancient civil law, completely rigorous, as can be seen from those of Sparta and of Rome. And this was the ius gentium with which the lesser gentes were founded, and the peoples were signified; for example, *gens romana* [Roman gens]; and thus many houses that are divided into many families are united in a single community, such that in the beginning the peoples were the sole signori, as today the Venetian Signoria is.

In this form of commonwealth, because of its own nature, that was born in order to defend itself from the plebeians, the optimates preserved for themselves in secret and *in latenti* [in concealment] as Pomponius said, the science of divine and human things—namely, of the laws. This is the heroic wisdom that Horace claims in the *Art of Poetry* to be the first poetry, the founding mother of the commonwealths, because, since the optimates alone introduced it, they alone had the science of heroic language, which among the Chaldeans is that of magic characters, among the Egyptians that of sacred characters, called "hieroglyphics."

This heroic language was the *fas* [divine law] of the gentes; it was certain language, because it was the language of the laws; later, "gentes" designated entire nations of many peoples who speak a common language; how these second languages were born is related in the work. From such the Romans called *fasti* [court days, festivals], the days during which judgments are rendered; and the formulas by means of which these were considered, the ancients called *carmina* [songs, poems]. The aristocrats were the scholars of heroic literature, within which they preserved heroic wisdom, the foundation of which was that human souls are immortal; it is almost a tradition of the human race not to esteem the body, because bodies could be touched but the images of the ancestors could not. This is the theology of the poets, who described souls as *imagines humanae maiorum* [images of human ancestors].

Hence the Romans established through a metaphysics of the laws the division of things into corporal and incorporeal, those that are touchable, those that are in the intellect—this he proves to be the proper philosophy of Roman jurisprudence. And the Romans also acted, as well as they could, to preserve heroic literature by defining words from the nature of things, such that *testamentum* [testament, will] for example, might practically be called *testatio mentis* [witness of conscience], not coming, as the grammarians claim, from *testamen* [evidence, proof], accompanied by the elongation of the syllable.

He shows that once more among the civil powers there were disagreements (because among those holding greatest power the monastic law returned) and duels (that which the ancient Romans called wars), and in each people without one having knowledge of another the laws of the clienteles were preserved, and learned from a common civil law (because the hospices were introduced later); by the divine law of the gentes they recognized:

1. the declaration of wars,
2. that declarations could not be made apart from civil authorities,
3. the sanctity of ambassadors,
4. the burial of the dead,
5. the need for rational justification of reprisals,
6. mancipations taught them through the justice of wartime occupations,
7. that the vanquished gentes were not true peoples, but clients [*famuli*] of the victorious people, who the Romans with mansuetude later called *socii* [subject peoples],
8. the bonitary dominion remaining with the vanquished, the optimal dominion passing to the strong,
9. the ius nexi that produced for them an outline of slavery,
10. of manumission,
11. of patronage with its proprieties,
12. of allotment,
13. of works,
14. of subservience.

With the founding of the commonwealths, the heroes of private just force ended, and the heroes of public just force began, heroes of wars; those wars that were the most clamorous were most memorable, and established for the Greeks the beginning of historical time from the Trojan War. Since poetry began as being partly true, partly fabulous, since it began as being partly for necessity, partly for pleasure, it indeed was born from the nature of ingenious men in the ignorance of genera. Whence in those rudest of times Homer arose, great father of poetic inventions, who no one else ever in the learned world could equal, because in the world of the philosophers men become accustomed to conceive of things in terms of genera and to speak of them in terms of abstractions.

On the basis of all of the above, he affirmed that the *ius gentium,* if properly translated into Greek, would be called δικαιον ηρωϊκον [heroic justice]; but the Latins call it *ius optimum* [law of the best] having the significance of *ius fortissimum* [law of the strongest], whence later it remained among the Romans having the significance of *ius certissimum* [the most certain law].

After the birth of both forms of the ius gentium Rome was founded, and when Romulus, who founded it, through the law of the best, died he was numbered among the gods. And as the law of the best was named from Jove, *Ious optumus* [Jove the best], so in similar manner by Quirinus [i.e., Romulus] the law of the best was called *quiritium* [Quirites, citizens of Rome], from the spear [*quiris*], weapon of the heroes, that then was retained by the Spartans, commonwealth of optimates, and the Romans, who used for particular weapons throwing-spears, which were the heaviest spears. Whence Minerva [goddess of wisdom], armed with a spear, is the same as Bellona [goddess of war], heroic character of the fathers, and they together are the intellect [*mens*] and the valor of warfare. Thus *ius quiritium romanorum* [law of the Roman Quirites] is the law of the Roman spears, of the Romans armed with spears, of the fathers united in order, who in meeting together were addressed principally by the title of Roman majesty, calling them *quirites,* a name that outside of the assemblies was not given to anyone.

Servius Tullius took the ius nexi from the fathers, connecting it to tribute, and ordered that it be paid by the clients, and by them according to the census. But the fathers thereafter, by oppressing the plebeians with usury, in a certain way retained it and slowly with the Law of the Twelve Tables they imparted it to them, but the ius nexi, remaining on its feet on account of usury, was finally dissolved with the Petelian Law, through which it remained only in relation to *noxa* [injury, an injurious act], or damage.

Roman history indeed narrates the strident custody of dominion, that the fathers held over the Roman lands, and hence over the auspices, the nuptials, the magistrates, and the priesthood, against the plebeians; all these things are part of the law of the best and, consequently, of the ius quiritium, which Roman history shows was the cause of public virtue and justice and thus of Roman grandeur, and it shows that the Romans alone founded jurisprudence born from the custody of the formulas of legal actions, that therefore were called a species of *ius civile*, as indeed Pomponius notices, because all the rest was ius gentium that the Romans made civil for themselves not with invention, but with custody.

This alone was capable of demonstrating the true origin and uninterrupted progress of all profane history. That before everything was chaos or confusion of the lawless, from which came heroes and men; and the heroes, of celestial origin, founded the false religions, because they derived them from the auspices and from the earth gods were born; the heroes by means of the auspices made themselves fathers, whence came the patricians, and from these the signori; from men came the clients, who were united in two communities in the aristocratic commonwealths, optimates and plebeians; finally came the empires, founded by means of the virtue of the few, either by diffusing themselves all into the free commonwealths or being reduced to one ruler in the monarchies.

On the basis of such principles he brought to view in all of their most important parts both Roman history, from the aspect of its laws, and jurisprudence, from the aspect of the orders of the commonwealth, with its mutations then mixing with the civil order that is proper to the optimates, with the natural order that is proper to liberty and kingdom, and that, since the free republic, vigorously upholding the praetorian law, which with a reverence for the civil law followed the natural order, was practically an interpreter through which ancient civil law, fixed around the Law of the Twelve Tables, passed into the new civil law of the imperial constitutions, based wholly on natural equity. Thus, according to the eternal design of divine providence in disposing of the things of empires it occurred that, when Constantine granted peace to the church, all the world was governed by an empire, which regulated itself by a form of law already compatible with Christian religion, and jurisprudence acquired the principle *De summa Trinitate et fide catholica* [On the highest Trinity and the

Catholic faith (the first title in the *Imperial Constitutional Codex*)],
which is the beginning and the end of jurisprudence and of religion. And in a science in which there is all of divine and human
erudition, demonstrated according to the principles of Christian
jurisprudence, the constancy of the jurisconsult to act justly must
be firmly based.

The True and the Certain

From *On the One Principle and One End of Universal Law*

Translation by
JOHN D. SCHAEFFER

The philosophical problem that Giambattista Vico finds in the law is the relationship of the true (*verum*) and the certain (*certum*)—that is, the connection that exists in the law between the law as rational and universally valid and the law as positive, historical (the product of human will deriving validity from authority as present in particular societies). He expresses this connection in the prologue and in chapters 82 and 83 of the first book of his *Universal Law, On the One Principle and One End of Universal Law*. The distinction between the true and the certain, as well as their necessary connection, is the basis of Vico's philosophical-philological method in the *New Science*. Philosophy aims at rational universal truths, and philology studies what is produced in society by acts of human will and authority. In axiom 10 of the *New Science* Vico claims: "Philosophy contemplates reason, whence comes knowledge of the true; philology observes that of which human choice is author, whence comes consciousness of the certain" (*NS* 138).

From the Prologue: Definitions of the True and the Certain

[30] "True" and "certain" are two words that must be distinguished, just as everyone distinguishes what is false from what is merely doubtful.[1] Indeed, falsehood is as far from the doubtful as

1. Vico has a footnote here: "Just as we set forth in the first book, 'On Metaphysics,' of our *On the Most Ancient Wisdom of the Italians Unearthed from the Origins*

the certain is from the true. If these two things are not carefully distinguished, given that many true things are doubtful, it might appear that a thing can be certain and doubtful at the same time. On the other hand, since many false things are held to be certain, they might be held to be both false and true.

[31] Truth arises when the mind is in conformity with the order of things; the certain arises when consciousness is secure from doubt. That which conforms to the order of things is called reason. Thus, if the order of things is eternal, reason is eternal, from which it follows that truth is eternal. But if the order of things is not permanent in every place for everyone or everything, then reason will have only probable knowledge of things and achieve only a degree of verisimilitude in cases requiring action. As truth rests on reason, so the certain rests upon authority, whether of the senses, called αὐτοψία [seeing with one's own eyes] or on the words of others, which is called "authority" in particular. From both of these persuasion is born. But authority itself is a part of reason: for if the senses are not deceived and the words of others are true, then we are persuaded of the truth. If, on the other hand, the sense impressions or the words are false, we will also be persuaded of falsehood. "Prejudices" should be attributed to all such false persuasions.[2]

Chapter 82
True Law and Certain Law

[1] The reason of the law is that which makes the law true, and the true is the proper and perpetual concomitant of necessary law.

The certain is part of the true.

[2] The certain is a proper and perpetual attribute of positive law, but the certain is nevertheless a part of the true, as in the definition

---

of the Latin Language." See the trans. of Lucia M. Palmer (Ithaca, N.Y.: Cornell University Press, 1988).

2. Vico comments in *UL* bk. 3, note 4, "Just as authority generates persuasion, so reason, when it has the character of necessity, generates knowledge [*scientiam*]. Reason that does not have the force of necessity generates opinion."

of civil law by Ulpian we cited above.[3] Lawgivers seize that part of the truth and make it certain by means of their authority because men may not be able to hold to it merely from a sense of shame. This is the rationale of Ulpian's definition. Thus, in all legal fictions that ground all positive law—for the natural law is both true and noble—there is to be found a truth dictated by reason. Thus we have the well-known passage from Ulpian: "The law is harsh, but it is written," by which he means, "The law is certain, but does not contain the whole truth." In other words, there is some reason that does not permit the law to conform entirely to the truth.

Chapter 83
The Certain Is from Authority, the True from Reason

[1] Thus you may conclude that the certain is from authority just as the true is from reason, and that it is not possible for authority to be completely in conflict with reason, for then there would be no laws but monstrosities of laws. Thus we can easily understand what Julian declared: "It is not possible to give a reason for everything established by our ancestors."[4] You can compare this with Neratius's comment on Julian in the same vein that "otherwise many things established by lawgivers that are certain (*not 'true'*) could be overturned."[5] Both say that it is inappropriate to demand that natural reason support authority.

Authority is part of reason.

[2] One should require a civil rationale from authority—that is, a common utility that must necessarily support each law, even

---

3. "Ulpian defines civil law as 'what is neither totally different from the natural law nor what completely accords with it, but which partly adds to it and partly subtracts from it'" [*UL* bk. 1, chap. 77]. This is Vico's paraphrase of *Digest,* 1.1.6.

4. "It is not possible to find an underlying reason for everything which was settled by our forebears." *Digest,* 1.3.20.

5. "Accordingly, it is not right to go ferreting after the motives behind the things that are settled as law. To do otherwise is to subvert many present certainties." *Digest,* 1.3.21.

when the legislators articulate the natural law.[6] We indicated as much in our dissertation *On the Study Methods of Our Time.*[7]

Civil reason is part of natural reason.

[3] When civil reason articulates public utility, it is in that instance a part of natural reason. It is not the whole of reason, however, because even though civil reason dictates that each utility be accorded to all equally, nonetheless sometimes some people are treated inequitably.

---

6. "Public law is concerned with organization of the Roman state, while private law is about the well-being of individuals. Our business is private law. It has three parts, in that it is derived from the law of nature, of all peoples, or of the state." *Institutes of Justinian*, 1.1.4.

7. Giambattista Vico, *On the Study Methods of Our Time*, trans. Elio Gianturco (Ithaca, N.Y.: Cornell University Press, 1990), 67.

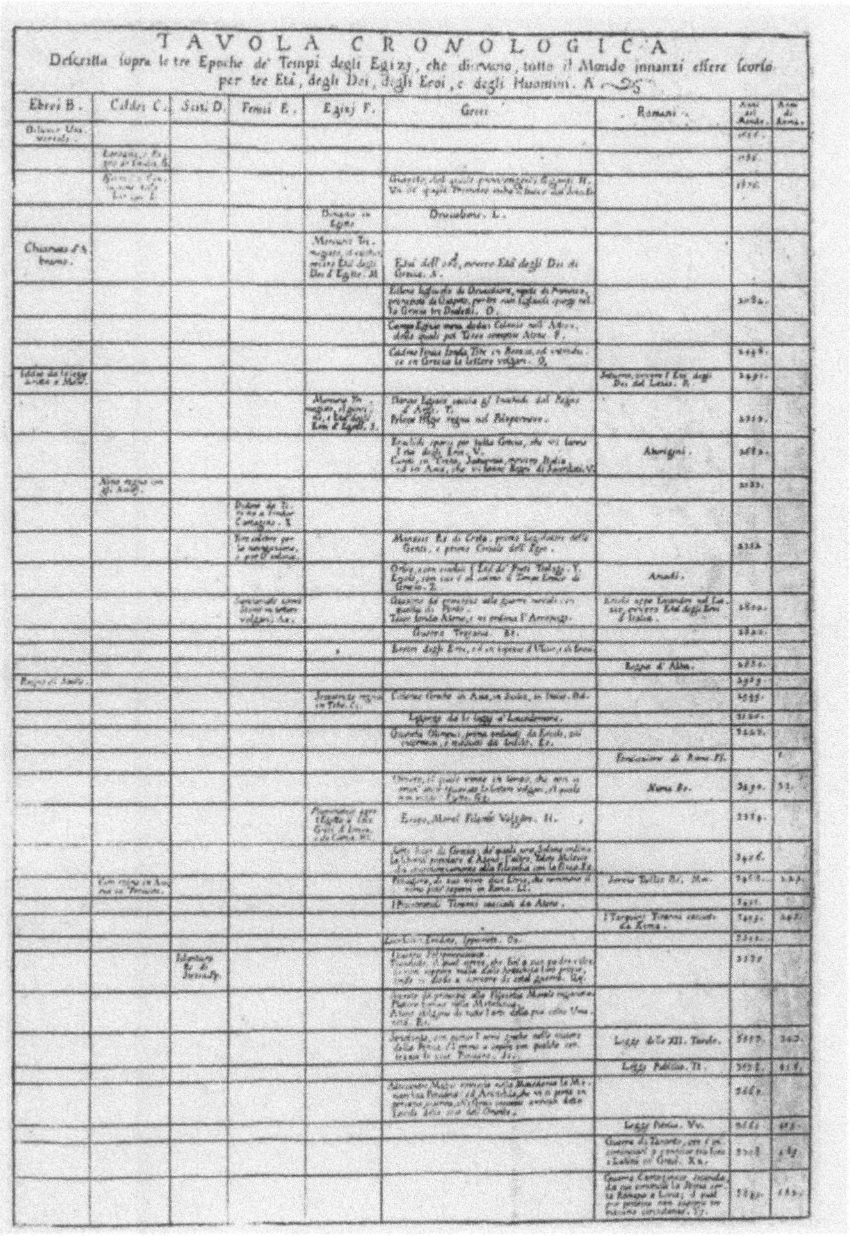

TAVOLA CRONOLOGICA

Descritta sopra le tre Epoche de' Tempi degli Egizj, che dicevano, tutto il Mondo innanzi essere scorso per tre Età, degli Dei, degli Eroi, e degli Huomini.

Ebrei B.	Caldei C.	Sciti D.	Fenici E.	Egizj F.	Greci	Romani	Anni del Mondo	Anni di Roma

Figure 2. Chronological table from the 1744 edition of the *Scienza nuova*.

A New Science Is Essayed

From *On the Constancy of the Jurisprudent*

Translation by
JOHN D. SCHAEFFER

The second book of Giambattista Vico's *Universal Law, On the Constancy of the Jurisprudent,* is divided into two major parts. The first is "On the Constancy of Philosophy," and the second is "On the Constancy of Philology." Vico begins this second part with a sketch of a "new science" that will be based on a reconception of philology. He introduces it as follows:

> The two sources of all that is knowable: intellect, will. As man consists of intellect and will, so whatever man knows comes from the human intellect or the human will. Thus whatever is termed 'knowable' is to be referred either to the necessity of reason or to the authority of the will. Philosophy establishes the constancy of reason: let us attempt to make philology establish the constancy of authority, following the path by which we said authority was a part of reason.

The chronological table that follows is a first sketch of the chronological table in book 1 of the *New Science* (1730/1744). The dates are based on the biblical ages of the world. Vico's use of Marcus Terentius Varro's divisions of time, which follow the chronological table, is the basis of his "ideal eternal history" in the *New Science*. He comments that Varro "divided the times of the world into three: a dark time, corresponding to the Egyptian age of the gods; a fabulous time, corresponding to their age of the heroes; and a historic time corresponding to their age of men" (*NS* 52). Except for his work on the Latin language, Varro's writings are lost. Vico's source for Varro's three ages of history is the little-known work of the Roman grammarian Censorinus, *De die natali liber* (Natal Day), in which these ages are mentioned and attributed to Varro.[1] The occasion of Censorinus's little book was the birthday, in 238 CE of a prominent Roman, Q. Caerellius.

Chapter 1
A New Science Is Essayed

What is philology?—Philology has two
parts: the history of words... and the
history of things.

[1] Philology is the study of discourse and concerns itself with whatever deals with words while recounting their history and narrating their origin and progress. It classifies them according to the various stages of the language, so as to grasp their proper and figurative meanings and their usage. But, since the ideas of things are depicted in words, philology must first look to understand the history of things.

Its auxiliary arts: epigraphy,
numismatics, chronology—
The extensive work of the philologist
is a necessary service to the state.

[2] Thus, philologists follow their calling when they write commentaries on commonwealths, the customs, laws, institutions, branches of learning, and artifacts of nations and peoples. They attend with great care to epigraphy, numismatics, and chronology, that they may be able to provide weightier evidence concerning ancient times. The purpose of this study is to explicate all writers of learned languages, whether orators, or philosophers, or even historians, but especially the poets. Thus the commonwealth receives this great benefit: it can interpret the ancient language of its laws and religion.

[3] But before we treat of historical matters, it helps to present a chronological table that is accepted by all, that we might show what is relevant to establishing our historical principles.

1. Censorinus, *The Birthday Book,* trans. Holt N. Parker (Chicago: University of Chicago Press, 2007), sec. 21.

From *On the Constancy of the Jurisprudent*

[4] 1656 after the creation of the world.	The Flood.
1657 [2346 BCE]	The division of the earth among the sons of Noah.
1656–86 [2347–2147 BCE]	The birth of astrology among the Chaldeans. Nimrod or Nembrot: the Babylonian confusion of tongues and the foundation of the first Assyrian kingdom, the Chaldeans. The four dynasties of Egypt: of Thebes, This, Tanis, and Memphis.
2082 [1921 BCE]	The call of Abraham.
2448 [1555 BCE]	(1) The Egyptian Cecrops is said to have founded twelve small colonies in Attica, which later united to form Athens. Hellen, the son of Deucalion, founds a kingdom in Thessaly and the Greek people. (2) The Phoenician Cadmus leads a colony to Greece and founds Thebes in Boeotia. (1) is proof of Egyptian power; (2) of Syrian power.
2491 [1512 BCE]	Law given to Moses.
2553 [1450 BCE]	(1) Danaus the Egyptian seizes the kingdom of Argos from the Inachids.
2682 [1321 BCE]	(2) The Phrygian Pelops, son of Tantalus, founds a kingdom in the Peloponnesus. (1) is a second proof of Egyptian power; (2) a second proof of Asiatic power.

The Greeks considered everything prior to this time a Dark Age.

2737 [1266 BCE]	Ninus, the son of Belus, founds the second Assyrian kingdom, the Medes.
2752 [1251 BCE]	Tyre famous for its seafaring and colonies. An argument for Asian power. Minos flourishes, the first lawgiver of the gentile peoples.

	The heroic age, the time of Orpheus, Hercules, Jason, Castor, Pollux, and the Argonauts.
	Theseus founds the kingdom of Athens.
	During this age the Aborigines rule Italy.
2820 [1183 BCE]	The Trojan War.
	Wanderings of Ulysses and Aeneas; then the kingdom of Alba.
2909 [1094 BCE]	Hebrew kingdom founded under Saul.
	Throughout this time the Athenians abandon monarchy and are ruled by a false theocracy.
2949 [1054 BCE]	Attic and Aeolian peoples send colonies to Ionia, or Asia Minor. An argument for Greek power.
2960 [1043 BCE]	The city of Cumae is founded.
3033 [970 BCE]	Four Egyptian dynasties are succeeded by the single dynasty of Thebes.
	The Egyptian Sesostris is thought to have flourished around this time.
3089 [914 BCE]	Hesiod flourished.
3113 [890 BCE]	Dido of Tyre founds Carthage. Argument for Phoenician power.
3119 [884 BCE]	Homer flourished.
3120 [883 BCE]	Lycurgus gives laws to Sparta.
3223 [780 BCE]	The Olympic games, instituted by Hercules and suspended for a long time, are restored.
	Here begins a historic time for Varro.
	At this time Italy was a wild forest, and the Latin kings, believed to be descendants of Aeneas, reigned at Alba.
3250 [753 BCE]	Rome is founded in the year of the world 3250, during the sixth Olympiad, 430 years after the capture of Troy.
40 AUC [714 BCE]	Under Numa, colonists sent to Italy from Corinth and other Greek cities are said to have established Croton, Tarentum,

	and the other cities of Magna Graecia. An argument for Greek power.
82 AUC [670 BCE]	While Tullus waged war with Alba, the powerful kingdom of the Etruscans flourished in Italy, giving its name to the entire southern sea from the shore of Etruria to the Straits of Messina.
84 AUC [668 BCE]	The Egyptian king Psammeticus opens Egypt, until now closed to foreigners, to the Ionians and Carians.
138 AUC [616 BCE]	According to Herodotus (book I, chapter 95), this marks the beginning of certain Egyptian history. Tarquinius Priscus, according to Florus, carries to Rome all the ornaments and insignia of conquered Tuscany that blazed forth the grandeur of Roman rule later when it was preeminent.
156 AUC [598 BCE]	The Seven Sages of Greece flourish. Of these sages, Thales is the first natural philosopher; Solon establishes Athenian liberty through his laws.
218 AUC [536 BCE]	Cyrus founds the third Assyrian kingdom, that of the Persians.
226 AUC [528 BCE]	About this time philosophy and mathematics flourish at Croton, the school that Pythagoras left during the seventieth Olympiad.
241 AUC [513 BCE]	Shortly thereafter, the Pisistratid tyrants are finally removed from Athens, and the city regains its freedom. In 244 AUC [510 BCE] Rome casts out its kings and tastes liberty for the first time.
303 AUC [451 BCE]	While Athens is enjoying the fullness of liberty, and Attic refinement blossoms everywhere, and Socrates is adorning the country with its most distinguished leaders and philosophers—Plato, Xenophon, Alcibiades—the Law of the Twelve Tables is enacted at Rome.

353 AUC [401 BCE]	Xenophon, consummate general and a philosopher, on the campaign that penetrated into the heart of Persia, was the first Greek to learn the truth about Asian institutions, and according to Jerome's *Commentary on Daniel*, he was the first to give a true account of it.
475 AUC [279 BCE]	The Romans, now famous in all Italy and a great sea power, become known to the Greeks through the injuries they received from the Tarentines.
535 AUC [219 BCE]	Second Punic War. Livy professes to write a true history of Roman affairs, beginning with this time period; and yet, though he writes a sublime and detailed account of Hannibal crossing the Alps into Italy, whether Hannibal came over the Cottian or the Pennine Alps he does not know.

What is history?

[5] History is the witness of time.

Varro's divisions of time.

[6] Until now, three periods of time have been enumerated, following Varro: the dark age, the mythical age, and the historical age.

[7] Until now, a history of the dark age seemed hopeless, and because a history of it was hopeless, the age is dark.

Division of the mythical age in accordance with our principles.

[8] The history of the mythical or heroic age can be divided conveniently into two parts; the history of the greater gentes and that of the lesser gentes. The history of the mythical age of the greater gentes should extend all the way up to the time that Hercules established the Olympic games, the Greeks' most celebrated epoch, for it tells the story of the twelve gods of the greater gentes.

Why has mythology, the first history of things, been so unfruitful up to now?

[9] But the mythology of these fabulous times was not thought to concern the customs and commonwealths of that fabulous period as much as the nature of the gods, so that the common people would be ignorant of divine affairs. This is the reason, after the course of so many centuries, it is excusable that their mythology is so uncertain, so contradictory, and thus completely fruitless.

[10] The history of the mythical age, which concluded with the founder of the Olympic games, includes the Argonauts. The following age narrates the rest of the fables that took place after Hercules was taken into heaven; it embraces the Trojan War, the wanderings of Ulysses, and the landing of Aeneas in Italy. We call these the mythical times "of the lesser gentes," but the learned properly call them "the heroic age."

The laziness common to all scholars.

[11] The more suspicious scholars differ strongly about whether the events of that period truly happened, and whether the heroes truly existed as they were portrayed. I am indeed amazed that those scholars blessed with good memories, who know by how many years Hercules preceded Theseus and Theseus Nestor, patiently accept these chronological monstrosities. They accept that Theseus was the same age as Amphitryon, whose wife was the mother of Hercules, and at the same time that Theseus was inspired by the glory of Hercules, and performed such famous deeds imitating him that Plutarch recounts that he was called "a second Hercules." They number Orpheus among the Argonauts, and must convince themselves that the Greek people suddenly went from being wild beasts tamed by Orpheus with the music of his lyre to achieving such a high level of culture that they knew about shipbuilding and navigation and the long routes over the Aegean and Pontic seas to Colchis. And they put that same Orpheus into the era of Castor and Pollux, the brothers of Helen; so that within a single human lifetime the Greeks went from living like beasts to having a commonwealth so powerful that they

could fight a war on both land and sea and overturn the richest kingdom in Asia.[2]

The error of the learned in every age:
That poetry was born intentionally,
and that poetic speech intentionally
differed from common speech.

[12] Moreover, until now everyone has thought that poets invented the fables from their own—almost divine—imagination, and that they invented a poetic language for themselves by their own art. From this two things follow. One, if Homer, the father of all poets—and, as Plutarch laughingly calls him, of all philosophers as well—had arisen out his own imaginative power and composed only by his own art when philosophy was at the crudest level, why, after humanity had been graced with all the arts of philosophy, was there no one who could later even come close to him? It is simply incredible that anyone could become as great as Homer simply by his own efforts. And this raises a question that disturbs pious minds: Could the various peoples each have been overwhelmed by its own particular flood, and did some of each people survive by chance in the high mountains and thus preserve the antediluvian wisdom? This question, which presumes that the world is eternal, must be answered by the Christian philosopher.

The reasons why principles of history
are wanted.

[13] The second conclusion that follows is this: If poetic inventions and poetic speech arise from the special imagination and art of poets, and if languages are the witnesses of history, then poets cannot provide testimony about the common customs and commonwealths of the entire heroic age. Therefore, just as the facts about the dark age are unknown, so the facts about the heroic

2. Vico writes in *UL* bk. 3, note 4, "But in what sense the Trojan War and the expedition of the Argonauts, as well as the journeys of Perseus into Ethiopia, Hercules into Spain, and Bacchus into India are true, will be explained in chapter 12 of this part of book 2: 'On the Origin of Poetry' which speaks 'Concerning the transformation of the first words'" [*UL* bk. 2, pt. 2, chap. 12, pars. 11–35].

age are false. But all serious authors, Plato being the most preeminent, constantly cite the poets as witnesses of remotest antiquity.

[14] The beginnings of historical times are very few, and lie scattered around like a pile of ruins from the ancient world. For example, there is Tanais, who set out from Scythia and subjugated all the East and even Egypt. And likewise there is the famous Sesostris the Egyptian, who drove the Scythians out of the East and even subjugated a great part of Europe and Africa. Herodotus testifies that he saw the monuments of these conquests scattered throughout Asia. And yet both of them, like Hercules, brought nothing back home except the glory of having conquered the world.

> *The beginnings of profane history*
> *are irreconcilable with those of sacred*
> *history—Roman history shows that the*
> *beginnings of profane history, as they*
> *have been formulated up to now, are*
> *false—And that the law of the nations*
> *[*ius gentium*] supports Roman history.*

[15] If these things were true, they would prove, along with the Chinese, the enormous age of the world. The Christian philosopher must not disguise this claim, but must completely disprove and refute it. This will be easy to accomplish, because of the truth we have learned from Roman history. The Romans came to know about other foreign peoples through the injuries they suffered from them, and foreign peoples came to know about the Romans through the wars the Romans waged to avenge those injuries; and the punishments of war were always captivity and slavery. And so with the founding of the first communities on earth began that custom that persisted for an extremely long time—namely, that the peoples dwelled in isolation from one another without any communication, as the Tarentine war sufficiently teaches. It was fought 475 years after the founding of Rome. Although the Romans were from the same small peninsula of Italy and had subjugated most of it, and were now the masters not only of the northern but the southern seas, the Tarentines refused to allow the Roman fleet to land and insulted them saying, in the words of Florus, that they "did not know who they were or where they came from."

The Greeks were ignorant of antiquity.

[16] The Egyptians deny us the possibility of tracing the beginnings of profane history from the Greeks, for when the Greeks were boasting that they were the first founders of humanity, the Egyptians corrected them with a witty pun, "The Greeks have always been children." Thus, Plato, in the *Timaeus,* took advantage of this incident of the Egyptian priests to note how ignorant the Greeks were of their own antiquity. And Aristotle in his *Politics* reproaches the Greeks for telling fables about Assyrian history, tantamount to saying that they were ignorant of the history of the greatest empire on earth. Ptolemy lists a long series of Assyrian kings, of whom the Greeks were completely ignorant. But why would not the Greeks be ignorant of the Assyrians for a long time, for they learned of them neither through peace nor war, and it was the most ancient custom of peoples to learn of one another either through war or alliances of friendship?[3]

The imagination of the Greeks took great delight in falsehoods.

[17] But why do we think the Greeks had knowledge of foreign affairs when they knew practically nothing of their own ancient history? For how many fables adorn Plutarch's Theseus, with whom Greek history takes it origin? Therefore, before we published the synopsis of this book in Italian, we listened not only calmly but eagerly to that line from the satirist:

Beware of what the lying Greeks say in their history.[4]

[18] Rome, moreover, was founded a long time after even the lesser gentes; and the Romans long preserved that custom, which

---

3. Vico writes in *UL* bk. 3, note 5, "These arguments are confirmed by the weighty authority of Polybius who writes in his *Historia,* book 2, chapter 37, that the Greeks learned of Asian affairs through the wars of Alexander the Great, just as the Romans learned of African affairs through the Punic wars."

4. Vico writes in *UL* bk. 3, note 6,

How far does the vanity of Greek history go?

In addition to the authority of Polybius to which we referred above, there are two irrefutable arguments that prove that not only were the Greeks ignorant of

Sallust relates in the *Conspiracy of Catiline:* "They preferred to perform noble deeds that others might praise them than to tell the accomplishments of others."

> *The writers of history deny in word*
> *what they admit in fact: that history*
> *does not have its principles—What*
> *could they be?*

[19] Thus it must be concluded that profane history does not yet have its principles, even though books with impressive titles have been written on the subject. The writers on historical matters say as much when they admit that profane history has neither certain origins nor a certain sequence. If this were not true, then the events of the dark age would have been brought to light, and the events of the heroic age would have been distilled from the fables; and if we knew these things, we would know the causes from which the events of the historical age were born.

> *Etymology has been weak up to now:*
> *Why?—The first argument of*
> *weakness—The second argument.*

[20] And this is another conclusion, an objection with which we confront all philologists: Until now their etymology has been

---

Asian affairs, as Polybius says, but were also culpably ignorant of their ancient history. The first argument comes from the Trojan War, the most famous epoch in all profane history, and the second from Homer, the father of all Greek learning. The Greeks were so shamefully ignorant of both of these facts that all their most learned writers judged the Trojan War to be fiction. And the opinions about Homer, such as what his native land was and when he lived, were so innumerable and irreconcilable that estimations of the time he lived differed by five hundred years. For this reason all Greek events that happened up to the time of Homer should be deemed unreliable, for we will show from Homer himself that Homer lived 460 years after the Trojan War, in the time of Numa. Thus, everything that Herodotus, the father of Greek history, narrates about the five hundred years after the Trojan War, not only about foreign peoples but about the Greeks themselves, should be received as entirely fictional. You could extend this argument to the period that extended after Homer and with the same judgment because the Greeks were ignorant of both Homer's country and his time period. You should conclude from all these things that no history of profane antiquity is more certain to us than Roman history.

The line of poetry is Juvenal, *Satire* 10.174.

weak, otherwise etymology would have provided us with the true origins and progress of words, if history could have told us the certain origin and sequence of things. As a result, philologists frequently—from a similarity in the sound of a single syllable or even a single letter, and some sort of resemblance between the things represented—imagine that they have related the origins of Latin words, for example, by deriving them from Greek or Hebrew or some other distant tongue. But it did not occur to them that those sounds that naturally had to be the first words in the Latin language had nothing in common even with the nearby Greek—not pronouns, not even interjections. In other words, the Latin and Greek peoples used different sounds to express fear and sorrow, joy and wonder, and similar disturbances of the passions. For the more learned grammarians of the Greek language claim that the word Διός is a more recent Greek word.

The two errors of all philology—First: that the poets used words improperly.

[21] Hence those absurd beliefs of all philologists: that prose speech determines a word's proper meaning—for example, *nasci*, to be born; *vivere*, to live; *mori*, to die; *videre*, to see; *audire*, to hear; *timere*, to fear; *irasci*, to be angry; these are proper meanings of prose; the equivalent expressions of the poets, on the other hand, are improper: *in luminas oras ede*, to come forth into the shores of light; *caelestes ducere auras*, to breathe the heavenly breezes, or *spiritum regere artus*, the spirit guides the limbs; *animam in auras recedere*, the soul returns to the air; *rem oculis usupare*, to seize a thing with the eyes; *auribus haurire vocem*, to drink speech with the ears; *gelu per ossa currere*, a chill runs through the bones; *sanguinem fervere circa praecordia*, the blood boils around the heart.[5] And then,

---

5. Vico writes in *UL* bk. 3, note 7:

> *The poetic expression is the proper meaning; the vulgar expression is the improper.*

The proper expression is the one that cannot be applied with equal propriety to meanings other than the one of which it is the characteristic expression, such as "the blood boils around my heart," an expression that cannot signify any other passion but anger. But people can with equal propriety substitute "to hope" [*sperare*] for "to fear" [*timere*]

on the contrary, they maintain with wonder, and truly, that poets are much more ancient than writers of prose, as if in the time of Homer, and even more of Hesiod, or even Orpheus in the heroic age, the Greek peoples spoke a language that much later was used by the writers of prose speech. Whereas among the peoples, especially seafaring peoples who carry on trade with foreigners, languages, even within a span of five hundred years, would change so much that they would seem entirely different.

The second error: Homer, Hesiod, Orpheus spoke their own peculiar language.

[22] With the equal perversity they agree on these two contradictory beliefs: First, that the poets spoke "in a different language," to quote Cicero, than the people, and likewise that Homer, Hesiod, and Orpheus spoke their own proper language rather than the language of the common people; second, that the poets were the first founders of commonwealths. But if the poets took savage brutes living in the forests and fashioned them into a civil society, why did they use a language so distant from the common one that grammar was created primarily to explain their meaning?

If usage so will it, in whose hands lies the judgment,
the right and the rule of speech. [Horace, *Ars Poetica*, 71–72]

Terence uses this meaning in the *Andria:* "What you fear [*speras*], I will easily repel" [2.3.].

And Vergil later employs this antique usage: "I could fear [*sperare*] so great a pain" [*Aenead*, 4.419].

Here is the reason: A poetic expression is composed out of the specifically proper characteristics of things and describes those things in terms of their most striking properties. But expressions in prose discourse abstract from these properties one word, like a genus. For example, from blood, boiling, and heart, it forms "anger" [*irasci*]. But genera by their very nature are common, not proper. Thus, whoever speaks in terms of genera can never speak properly about things. Hence it is a fact that the vulgar languages are a great impediment to philosophers in trying to distinguish the true nature of things.

In this note Vico is exploiting the double meaning of the term *proper* to show that poetry's employment of specific sensual meanings is more proper—that is, more unique—than the "proper" meaning of words that has been formed by abstracting generalized significations.

A serious doubt: Has the true origin of poetry been unknown until now?

[23] Two things, very contradictory and yet very true, put me in serious doubt whether poetry's true origin has not been hidden and unknown up to now.

Why do philosophers avoid the studies of philology? Are they right?

[24] And for all these reasons I, who during my life have always taken more delight in reason than in memory, thought that the more I knew about philology the more ignorant I seemed to be. And so not without cause did René Descartes and [Nicolas de] Malebranche say that it would be unsuitable for a philosopher to spend too much time or effort on philology. But if this statement were not accepted with moderation, bearing the names of such great authorities, it would clearly lead Christian states to ruin. For the laws in each part of the divine book were given to us in other languages, those of the Old Testament in Hebrew and other Eastern languages, those of the New Testament in Greek; and the laws in the *Corpus of Justinian Law* in Latin, and these are illuminated by the *Basilica* and other books on Eastern law written in Greek. Theology and jurisprudence are based in large part on knowledge of these languages, and translators have none of the credibility of the original authors.

It is a worthy task for a Christian philosopher to reduce philology to the structure of a science—Why Plato's Cratylus *ultimately failed.*

[25] And so those two preeminent philosophers, had they been more concerned about the glory of the common name "Christian" rather than with the private glory of philosophers, the study of philology would have progressed so that the philosophers might see whether it was possible to subsume philology under the principles of philosophy, following the impressive example of Plato, who tried to do this in the *Cratylus*. But Plato's results were unhappy, because he didn't know the certain language in which

the first laws had been introduced, for this was the language of the age of the poet heroes, who were the first to found commonwealths with laws. And he did not know this language because at Athens the laws had long been articulated in a modern language because they were changed every year by the *nomothetes*.

The attempts made by Julius Caesar Scaliger, Sanchez, and Schoppe are more witty than true.

[26] The acute philosopher Julius Caesar Scaliger, followed later by [Francisco] Sanchez and [Caspar] Schoppe, studiously inquired about the sources of the Latin language by means of philosophical reasoning, but the reasoning was extracted from Aristotelianism, which originated many centuries after languages were first established, nor can Aristotelianism be considered a philosophy of the entire human race, since it was not even accepted by the other Greek philosophical sects.

[27] Therefore, we have decided in this book to discuss the principles of humanity, a task undertaken with piety even if not promising success. The study of humanity is philology, and by taking irrefutable arguments from the nature of fallen man, we may bring philology under the rules of science.

On Homer and His
Two Poems

From the *Dissertations*

Translation by
JOHN D. SCHAEFFER

The third book of Vico's *Universal Law* contains, in addition to notes on the first two books, a series of short *Dissertations*. In his *Autobiography* Vico says he "read both the poems of Homer in the light of his principles of philology"; and by certain canons of mythology that he had conceived, he gives these poems an aspect different from that which they have hitherto borne, and shows how divinely the poet weaves into the treatment of his two subjects two groups of Greek stories, the one belonging to the obscure period and the other to the heroic, according to Marcus Terentius Varro's division (see the headnote to "A New Science is Essayed"). These interpretations of Homer, along with the canons of mythology, he had printed in quarto by Felice Mosca in the following year, 1722, with the title *Notes by Giambattista Vico on Two Books, One "On the Principle of Universal Law," the other "On the Constancy of the Jurisprudent"* (*A* 160). Vico's discussion of Homer is the basis for book 3 of the *New Science,* "Discovery of the True Homer."

Chapter 4
On Homer and His Two Poems
(Selections)

Proof of Homer's age.

[12] There are major disagreements about the exact time of Homer's life: one opinion has him living at the time of the Trojan War—that is, about sixty years after Theseus founded Athens.

Another opinion holds that he lived about 460 years after the Trojan War—that is, at the time that Numa was king of the Romans. I hold for the second opinion on account of Homer's portrayal of Greek culture, humanity, luxury, decadence, frauds, and liberty. Also, according to this second opinion, Homer would not have been able to travel to Egypt because he lived before Psammeticus, when Egypt was closed to foreigners.

[13] You should infer two extremely important corollaries from this discussion.

In Homer's time no vernacular
language was written.

[14] Written vernacular language does not occur among the Greeks until the time of the sixth or seventh Olympiads. In fact, in all of Homer's works letters are mentioned only once, when Proetus wrote to his father-in-law asking that Bellerophon be executed. Homer makes it plain that this writing was in the form of σήματα—that is, signs traced in heroic characters [*Iliad* 6.168].

Poetic traditions before and after
Homer are corrupt.

[15] Poetic traditions, or fables, that came to Homer were corrupted after being passed on for so many ages, and after Homer they continued to be corrupted because Homer himself never committed his poems to vernacular letters, but after being preserved as memorized songs, they were only written down in the vernacular after a long time, as Josephus says.

On the changes in meaning of
the first words.

[22] The fables, invented long before the time of Homer, tell how Hercules carried off the golden apples from Hesperia and how he led away the oxen of Cacus. Atlas in Mauritania supported the heavens upon his shoulders until Hercules succeeded him in this labor. In Ethiopia Perseus set Andromeda free. The fables tell the story of the Argonauts' expedition to Pontus and of Bacchus's victories in India. And they say that two famous and ancient cities, one in Egypt and one in Greece, were both named Thebes.

[23] I hope to bring a shining light, based on our principles, to bear on these ancient matters that have been obscure until now. I can do so if one admits two truths that we have established already.

[24] I. Homer flourished five hundred years after the age of the heroes (I accept the chronologists' definition of the heroic age; in fact, we have defined it as reaching to the time of Homer).

[25] II. In Homer's time writing in the vernacular language had not yet been invented.

[26] Given these facts, we can judge of the Greek fables with at least as much gravity as we judge of the antiquity of our own cities, which have come down to us through many centuries of crude illiteracy. The illiterate believe such things completely, but people with more ingenuity judge them to be false, or at least true with a high degree of falsity.

Axioms of philology.

[27] I assume that the principal cause of this effect is that the first words changed in meaning from their original signification, a change that necessarily took a long time. Before we can even speak of this, it is necessary to establish these two things:

[28] I. Any profane knowledge that we have about the whole ancient world has come to us through the Greeks and in no other way.

[29] II. In the beginning words were born among the Greeks when they inhabited a small area of the globe. Then the words were diffused more widely as the Greek peoples were diffused.

[57] Homer was ignorant of origins because the meanings of the first words had changed. Thus, he confused his presentation of the two poems. When told in the correct order, they clearly recount the universal history of the dark time. They narrate the wanderings throughout the Mediterranean region, the asylums, of clientship founded by the first agrarian law, of the plebs rising up in the agrarian revolts, of kings or fathers, the first order established on earth, and then of the establishment of heroic kingdoms or aristocratic commonwealths. Then they would tell of the wars and plundering in which the heroic kingdoms engaged against each other. Then they would tell of just wars—that is, solemnly declared wars. When relating foreign wars, they would tell how

alliances were based on friendship because of similarity in name, tribe, or language. Finally they would tell of the civil wars waged between the Optimates and the plebeians over sacred marriage and political power—and tell of the plebeians' defeat. Thus the plebs, to escape the rage of the victors, committed themselves and their fortunes to the sea and became wanderers of the seas, thus creating colonies in remote lands.

Homer, according to our account
of the origins of poetry, would have
seemed to his audience to be telling
probable stories.

[58] Therefore, since the poet heroes, and I judge Homer to be among them, were the historians of the deeds and events of the dark time, as we discussed in our refutation of Varro's three ages, they must have narrated things that seemed true to the common people—that is, opinions suited to those of their listeners so that they might believe them. According to the origin of poetry that we have developed above, and not in accord with any other account, Homer narrates things that are completely suited to his age. We will now enumerate these briefly.

The gigantic bodies and strength
of the heroes.

[59] In the beginning the heroes had huge bodies and the strength of giants, such as Polyphemus. These heroes were more ancient than the warrior heroes, and the fact that Homer's audience believed in them shows that the tradition of the giants had endured among them.

The impossible religion of the gods was
credible to Homer's audience.

[60] From the story of the giants flows that religion in which the gods and goddesses are present to the Homeric heroes, sometimes openly, sometimes disguised as someone else, sometimes known, sometimes unknown. The poets used this religion as a kind of perpetual machine [*machina perpetua*] to sustain and resolve their stories. The first peoples who had founded the gentes

after hearing the thunder were so dominated by that false religion that everything that they saw, heard, or remembered they believed to be gods because their fantasy had already been affected by vice. Finally, as the power of the fantasy diminished, some thought that the gods had appeared to them; others did not.

The gods were honored because of their power.

[61] They still honored the gods because of their power. Thus, in several passages in Homer Jupiter is held to be the king of the gods because his strength is greater than all of them as shown preeminently in the fable of the chain. Thus, in Homer's time it was easy to persuade the common people that Diomedes, with the powerful assistance of the goddess Minerva, could inflict wounds on Mars and Venus, since Minerva herself had wounded Mars with a stone and humiliated Venus during a conflict between the gods [*Il.*5.335, 855; 21.404, 424]. And Achilles did not fear a fight with Apollo, if only he could have strength equal to the god's [*Il.*22.20].

Why were unjust laws considered just in Homer's time?

[62] On the basis of this religion the heroic law was considered just. Achilles thought that there could be no law that applied equally to men who were unequal. When Hector came desiring a treaty, Achilles told him, "Between men and lions there can be no treaty, nor can wolves and lambs reach a mutual agreement" [*Il.* 22.261]. This opinion of justice is congruent with the first commonwealths, for we have demonstrated they were aristocratic commonwealths in which the plebs, because they were weak, and the heroes, because they were strong, did not share in the same equal rights. This legal position obtained among the Romans until the Law of the Twelve Tables, as we have stated at the conclusion of this work.

Why are Homer's gods and heroes so crude?

[63] To this we must add that the people of Homer's time were still extremely crude because of the barbaric conditions of their

feral origin, and so they looked to the gods as being made in their own image. Thus they were convinced that the gods argued and fought with each other without ceasing, such as the contest between Mars and Minerva in which Mars called Minerva a "dog fly" [*Il.* 21.394]. But what kind of behavior could they not attribute to the gods when they see Agamemnon and Achilles, the former a king and the latter the greatest of heroes, calling each other "dog"? [*Il.*1.225]. Even when Greek humanity was more cultivated, this insult was scarcely used for the vilest slaves, as the writers of comedies testify. So they also would approve of that divine fight in which Minerva strikes Mars with a large rock (although in Homer it is a heroic spear) and then thrashes and strips Venus, and Juno punches Diana [*Il.*21.489].

Whence the famous ferocity of the heroes?

[64] Homer's listeners greatly admired the ferocity of the heroes, which the heroes had maintained from their cruel and bestial origin, even though in our own more merciful times we would attribute it to wild and barbaric people. Not mentioning other examples, there is the episode in which Achilles was so enraged that he threatened the old king because of one word he said imprudently about his love for Hector whom Achilles had killed. Priam, most happy before and most wretched now, came alone to Achilles to confide in him alone. Since he was a suppliant he was received with hospitality, an old man, yet Achilles said he would cut off his head under his own roof [*Il.*24.556]. Achilles even wished that, after he was dead, his household gods would be propitiated for the loss of Chryseis by the blood of a royal Trojan maiden whose throat would be cut over his tomb.

Whence the vindictive style of Homer?

[65] This vindictive custom pleased people in Homer's time, and to this pleasure we must also attribute his description of bloody battles, deadly duels, and the various and many spectacular cruel slaughters. Because of this vindictive style, especially in the *Iliad*, we consider Homer sublime.

From the *Dissertations*

In Homer's time the law of the gentes
was still inhuman.

[66] The barbaric customs of the Greeks in the Homeric age
are proved decisively by two things. The first, that the Greeks did
not yet have the custom of burying the dead of their enemies. You
can read in several places that Homer's heroes threatened their
enemies that, when defeated and killed, they would leave them
to be devoured by dogs and crows [Cf. *Il*.22.261]. Thus there is
a sharp battle over Patroclus's corpse, and Priam wishes to have
the body of Hector returned [*Il*.17; 24.477–691]. The second reason is the inhuman custom, still not abandoned by the Greeks, of
using poisoned arrows. Ulysses went to Ephyra to find poison in
which he could dip his arrows.

Why were the Homeric heroes
emotionally unstable?

[67] What does it mean that, when the heroes, and the gods as
well, are moved by powerful feelings, they are immediately calmed
by a simple speech or even by a single word, and assume a spirit
contrary to the previous one? Are they not like children, weak in
mind and more changeable than women in their opinions?

... Or extremely difficult?

[68] But then, on the contrary, no reason is able to induce
Achilles to relent from his anger and give much needed help to
the Greeks who are perishing at their ships. Such a difficult character today would be called a country boor.

... Weak in spirit? And limited
in mind?

[69] The same thing applies to the Homeric heroes for whom,
when they are passive in spirit, or when they are greatly excited by
other passions, or while they are speaking or doing something entirely different, something sad, will chance to come into their minds
and they immediately are overcome by grief. On the opposite side,
when they are afflicted with pain and sadness, as Ulysses was when he
spoke to Alcinous, then eating and drinking makes them forget all
their past woes. Both are characteristics of a very short attention.

... *Or slow of mind?*

[70] To this defect one should also attribute the custom of the Homeric heroes of talking to themselves as if to someone else—seen above all in Ulysses while he survived his wanderings. The heroes carry on such deliberations about things that a more intelligent person would judge to be unworthy of such thought. This argues even more that they had slow minds.

Homeric expressions come from crude and unstable minds.

[71] These expressions will illustrate the well-known crudeness of mind that prevailed even into Homeric times: "the sacred force of Antinous understood"; "the sacred strength of Telemachus spoke out," as if their minds were not their own and unknown to them [*Ody.*18.34, 60]. They said "minds" and "souls" instead of "mind" and "soul" because to such crude people each thought was one mind and each decision was one soul, and so it seemed to them that there were many minds combined in one intellect and many souls combined in one will. In the same way, they said "breasts" and "mouths" instead of "breast" and "mouth" because they thought that each feeling always needed a different breast, and for every countenance a different mouth was always required. And they said "prudences" and "fortitudes" because they did not understand that many remember "the bed, the dinner, the fight" instead of "I think" about them because memory and fantasy overwhelmed them. They would say "to think in one's breast," "to feel with the heart," because they could neither feel nor understand anything unless they were excited by passions. And the comparisons, which in Homer are incomparable to anyone else's, are almost always taken from animals (which [Julius Caesar] Scaliger turns into a criticism of the poet), which proves conclusively that at this time the imagination of the Greek people was crude.

Homer's silly old wives' tales were accepted in his own time.

[72] The people of Homer's time demonstrated their crude nature by easily accepting as true what now appears to us as silly old wives' tales, particularly as found in the *Odyssey*. They accepted

them with the same supreme credulity with which the heroes accepted all the marvelous stories told to them by people they did not know—as happened to wandering Ulysses when he spoke to whatever people he was among.

Why is Homer the greatest of poets?

[73] In an age when people were crude, Homer flourished as the greatest poet. According to our account of the origins of poetry, he was the greatest of poets simply because he flourished in an age of crude peoples when the Greeks were outstanding in sensation, fantasy, memory, imagination, but with little reason or judgment. Thus, *Homer would never have been so great if he had not often nodded.*

On the ancient wisdom recovered from the fables.

[74] Therefore there is no need for the learned, who want to join their own reputation to that of the prince of poets, to intrude their stupidities into the supreme wisdom of Homer's strange and unusual utterances.

Why was philosophy concealed from the common people? Whence the acroamatic [oral teachings] and esoteric teachings?

[75] The philosophers, the chief of whom was Pythagoras, felt differently about divine things than the blind common people did. They would have come into grave danger if their ideas on divine philosophy became known. They could be called atheists, as Socrates was, and be convicted of violating religion. So they carefully concealed their wisdom from the common people, and communicated its highest secret wisdom only among themselves. Publicly they taught the duties of civic life. Hence comes that famous division of teachings, one the acroamatic or acousmatic— that is, what was transmitted orally to listening disciples who were already initiated into the sacred philosophy. From this comes the saying "to listen to the philosophers" instead of "to work at philosophy." Other teachings were exoteric or cyclic because they

were produced for the common (profane) people in a cycle of lectures.

The rationale for Pythagorean silence.

[76] Hence Pythagoras carefully examined those who wished to become his followers. He made them remain silent for five years. Then he took care to introduce them to philosophy through his own learned listeners. Finally, those who seemed most worthy he admitted to his own inner sanctum to listen to him personally.

Whence Pythagorean symbolism?

[77] In Pythagoras's time, vernacular writing had not yet been invented, as we demonstrated above from Philo, so he must have preserved his philosophy either by heroic characters, or symbols, or in a song full of enigmas and mysteries that his disciples called "golden." Philolaus first revealed the Pythagorean philosophy in vernacular writings, but even though he wrote in the vernacular, the language remained incomprehensible to the common people, as the utter obscurity of the few remaining fragments testifies. Therefore, since vernacular writing had not yet been invented, and since reverence for, or fear of, civil religion had seized the philosophers, they thought it appropriate to clothe this secret philosophy in pleasing fables, if there were any that could be so used. Thus, when they discussed this occult wisdom, they would seem to the common people to be speaking in the usual language of, and with the proper respect for, popular religion. It is also true that they would have to create some new fables if there were no existing ones that could be adapted to the secret wisdom. Plato and the Stoics worked up many fables, the most famous of which are those about the phoenix and the destruction of the world by fire, and about the aged prophetess, Fate.

Why were the philosophers also poets?

[78] It is therefore far from the truth that the first philosophers tried to unearth ancient and secret wisdom from the fables, so that they themselves buried their wisdom and teachings in the fables of the poets. This error was the result of the philologists being ignorant of the true origins of poetry. On the one hand,

they thought Homer was an incomparable poet because of the sublimity of his stories and the grandeur of his language; on the other hand, they noticed he was guilty of many great blunders. Since they were unable to reconcile these, they concluded that the blunders must contain supreme wisdom. And so, from Plato even to our own time there has burned the desire to unearth ancient wisdom from the fables of the poets (and this indeed was one of the desires and projects of the great Verulam) [Francis Bacon, *Of the Wisdom of the Ancients* (1609)].

Vico's Address to His Readers from a Lost Manuscript on Jurisprudence

Translation and Commentary by
DONALD PHILLIP VERENE

Vico's Manuscript

In the Villarosa collection of Giambattista Vico's manuscripts in the National Library in Naples there is an autograph of two sheets of paper, written on three sides in Latin, with the title "Ad Lectores Aequanimos." I have examined these pages, which are written in Vico's characteristically legible hand in neat lines. These pages are recognized as written in 1720 as part of a draft, now lost, of the *Universal Law*. In July of the same year Vico published the pamphlet "Synopsis of Universal Law," announcing the two books of his work on jurisprudence, and in September the first book appeared, *On the One Principle and One End of Universal Law* (see the translated text of the "Synopsis" and translated excerpts from the *Universal Law*).

The definitive published text of "Ad Lectores Aequanimos" appears in *Varia. Il De mente heroica e gli scritti latini minori,* edited by Gian Galeazzo Visconti, volume 12 of *Opere di Giambattista Vico* of the Centro di Studi Vichiani (1996). The "Ad Lectores" was published first by Giuseppe Ferrari in 1837, who erroneously thought it to be part of Vico's lost commentary on the *Law of War and Peace* of Hugo Grotius, which Vico mentions in his *Autobiography* (*A* 155). Fausto Nicolini and Benedetto Croce have demonstrated that it is instead part of a first draft of the *Universal Law*. Visconti suggests that this draft was likely done by Vico as an expansion of his inaugural University oration of October 18, 1719. The text of this oration is lost, but Vico briefly summarizes it in his *Autobiography*

(*A* 156–57). This oration of 1719 announces the basic themes of the *Synopsis* and the *Universal Law*. Visconti further suggests that Vico may have developed this probable expansion for publication of the 1719 oration, in a manner analogous to that of *On the Study Methods of Our Time* (1709), which was delivered in a shorter form as the inaugural oration for October 18, 1708 (*A* 146). The published version of the *Study Methods,* Visconti notes, ends with a *commiato,* a postface, in which Vico takes leave of the text proper, reflecting on his role as its author and addressing the reader as to how the work is to be approached and understood. This commiato was evidently not part of the oration as delivered in 1708 and very likely was added in the published version in response to criticism that had arisen. At one point in it Vico addresses the reader as "Aequanime Lector."

Vico likely developed his ideas in the lost draft on jurisprudence as an enlargement of his study of Grotius. His mention of Grotius in "Ad Lectores" supports this and is probably what led Ferrari to think it part of Vico's lost commentary on Grotius. Visconti points out that the *commiati* of the two orations are very different in approach. That of the *Study Methods* is modest in tone, urging the reader to consider the truth of what has been said and asking the reader's indulgence. Vico even expresses his personal uncertainties and fears, saying that his greatest apprehension has always been to be "alone in wisdom," a kind of solitude, he says, that carries with it the danger of becoming either a god or a fool.

In the "Ad Lectores" Vico is just the opposite. He is combative, forceful to the point of being abusive, challenging the reader to accept the clear truth of his principles, and refusing to consider criticism. The "Ad Lectores" itself remains very much a draft. Vico likely would have rewritten and polished it if he had published it.

In the "Ad Lectores" Vico speaks of seven principles he describes as metaphysical that are in the lost manuscript. Visconti points out that Vico synthesizes seven principles in the *Scienza nuova prima* (1725). In book 2 Vico says there are three principles of humanity: divine providence, marriage, and burial. In book 3 he says there are three principles of a language common to all nations: poetic fables as a first form of thought, an etymology common to all languages, and the fact that there are Latin words not of Greek origin. The seventh principle concerns the natural law of the gentes as connected to Vico's conception of the nature of the first humans. With these principles Vico goes beyond the jurisprudence of Grotius and the seventeenth-century natural-law theorists. These principles, of course, became part of the *New Science*.

Although Visconti does not mention it, the other place where Vico devotes space to addressing his reader is at the end of the "Idea dell'opera" of the 1730 edition of the *New Science* (these remarks are deleted from the 1744 edition). Vico addresses the "young reader" in terms of seven points. His tone is almost paternal, or at least of kind teacher to pupil. His concern is not to combat criticism but to give direct, useful advice, seeming to presuppose that his readers will be equable. His third point here is the same as that in the "Ad Lectores," that the young reader must come prepared with a sufficient body of varied learning and scholarship or he will not understand, but Vico does not include the warning not to accuse him of obscurity in his writing, made in the "Ad Lectores." His sixth point calls attention to the fact that the ideas expressed are of a wholly new kind, the same point that he turns into a challenge to the mature scholarly reader in the "Ad Lectores."

Vico's claim to "newness" is a claim he makes in all his works. It can be found in the *Study Methods,* concerning his pedagogical thesis of balancing the ancients against the moderns; in the *Most Ancient Wisdom of the Italians,* concerning his metaphysics based on etymology; and in the *Universal Law,* concerning the nature and beginnings of Roman law and law in general. In the *New Science, new* becomes part of the title.

Vico's claim in the first paragraph of the "Ad Lectores," that the jurisconsult cannot rightfully judge unless he has meditated all of the law, is a theme expressed in the *Universal Law,* especially in the second book, *On the Constancy of the Jurisprudent.* In the "Ad Lectores" Vico speaks only of meditating all of the law in the sense of *lex,* positive or made law. In the *Constancy of the Jurisprudent,* Vico gives the jurisconsult the burden of mastering the law in both its senses, as *diritto* (as a product of reason) and as lex (as a product of legislative authority).

Vico's reference, in the second paragraph of the "Ad Lectores," to *ius gentium naturale,* becomes the *diritto naturale delle genti* of the

New Science, the key to Vico's conception of a "law of nations." By adding *naturale* to the Roman *ius gentium* (that part of Roman law that the Romans claimed to be part of all other systems of law) Vico combines *ius gentium* with *ius naturale* (the conception of law as a rational ideal that Vico calls the "law of the philosophers") and formulates the idea of an actual natural law, a universal sense of law originating directly from human nature and concretely functioning in the life of all nations.

Vico may have not published the pages of the "Ad Lectores" because he thought it imprudent, the same reason he did not send a copy of the *Vici Vindiciae* (1729; see the translation, herein) and a letter he wrote to Burkhard Mencken, president of the Leipzig Academy of Sciences, concerning the malevolent book notice of the *First New Science* which had appeared in the Leipzig *Acta Eruditorum.* In the last section of the *Vici vindiciae* Vico addresses the reader ("Ab aequanimo lectore petitio") in an irenic tone, saying that he researched the *Scienza nuova* of 1725 for twenty years, consulting all possible works in order to contribute to the doctrine of the natural law of the gentes. He did include the letter to Mencken in his *Autobiography (A* 190). It might in particular be imprudent to include an attack on the reader in his work on jurisprudence, because he had hoped to use the work to aid his advancement to a university chair. But he did personally like these remarks well enough to retain them in manuscript.

The force and approach of Vico's remarks to his critics match well Vico's portrait of himself at the end of the continuation of his autobiography of 1731: that he was "choleric to a fault," that "he would inveigh too violently against the errors of thought or scholarship," and that he would withdraw to his desk "as to his high impregnable citadel, to meditate and to write further works which he was wont to call so many noble acts of vengeance against his detractors" (*A* 199–200).

Vico's Dilemma

Vico's challenge to his readers, in the "Ad Lectores," to be fair and equable in their approach to his work on jurisprudence, is put in the form of a constructive dilemma. The scheme of such a dilemma, in logical symbolism, is:

$$(p \supset q) \bullet (r \supset s)$$
$$p \lor r$$

$$\therefore q \lor s$$

The first half of the first premise in Vico's dilemma is the inference that "if the reader is an erudite *youth* (Y), then failure to comprehend the work will be due to an *inability* to comprehend with ease authors in truly difficult subjects (I). Thus Y implies I: ($Y \supset I$). The second half of the first premise is the inference that "if the reader is an *expert* in every kind of erudition (an accomplished, mature scholar) (E), then failure to comprehend the work will be due to an *unwillingness* to accept principles that are absolutely new (U). Thus E implies U: ($E \supset U$). These two inferences ($Y \supset I$) and ($E \supset U$) can be conjoined: ($Y \supset I$) $\bullet$ ($E \supset U$).

The second premise of the dilemma is stated first by Vico in the order of his remarks: Either "the reader is an erudite youth" (Y) or "the reader is an expert in every kind of erudition" (E). Thus Y or E: ($Y \lor E$). Therefore, Vico claims, the failure to comprehend his work will be due either to "an *inability* to grasp a work of this difficulty" (I) or "an *unwillingness* to accept principles that are absolutely new" (U).

Thus I or U: $\therefore$ ($I \lor U$).

$$(Y \supset I) \bullet (E \supset U)$$
$$Y \lor E$$
$$\therefore I \lor U$$

There are three ways to respond to a dilemma by "going between the horns," by "grasping it by the horns," or by constructing a counterdilemma. Vico has incorporated into his presentation of this dilemma his answer to any attempt at rebuttal. To go between the horns of a dilemma is to reject its disjunctive premise. This requires the production of a third option (or more). Vico has established the disjunct so as to preclude this possibility because his alternatives are exhaustive. Of the two types of potential readers, one may have sufficient erudition to comprehend the work; the other actually possesses fully developed erudition. A reader who does not in principle have sufficient erudition is not a relevant reader; such a reader cannot be brought into the argument's "universe of discourse." Vico makes no claim to be writing a popular work for everyone who can read. Thus, any relevant reader will be one or the other of Vico's two types. Vico's alternatives are logical contraries. A disjunctive premise is unassailable when the alternatives exhaust the possibilities.

To grasp the dilemma by the horns is to reject the first premise, which is a conjunction. Since both halves of a conjunction must be true for the conjunction to be true, to reject a conjunction requires denial of only one of its parts. If we attempt to deny that inability to comprehend works of this magnitude is the cause of the erudite youth's failure at comprehension, and that the cause is instead the obscurity of Vico's writing (and hence his thought), we will not fare well. The partially erudite youth is by definition in no position to make such a judgment, for on what ground could the youth judge? Language that contains knowledge of things divine and human—namely, wisdom—may at first appear obscure, particularly to the inexperienced. But it is in fact profound and cannot be otherwise, for there is no simple statement of the highest matters. Great works become evident in their thought only when we attain to their level.

If we attempt to deny the second half of the first premise—that concerning the reader expert in every kind of erudition—we can do so, Vico claims, only by formulating an even more parsimonious set of principles and complete system of the subject matter than his work presents. In order to deny this half of the premise, the expert can refute Vico only by joining in his project and carrying its truth to a higher perfection. Otherwise, Vico claims, the critic-reader will be reduced simply to pointing out inconsistencies through single arguments and citing scattered pieces of counterevidence from other works. Neither of these practices can refute a total system of thought. The scientific way to put this is: Only theories refute (replace) theories; facts as such do not refute theories, nor do single arguments about inconsistencies.

Vico's potential critic, if he or she does not want to enter the service of Vico in an attempt to refute him, is left with the possibility of a counterdilemma. Counterdilemmas are rare. To be successful one must accomplish a reductio ad absurdum on Vico's position through a second dilemma, using the elements of Vico's dilemma. The possibility of a successful counterdilemma, could one be conceived, is remote because of the strength of Vico's disjunction of the two types of readers. What would be the counter-figures to these two types of readers that would then produce an absurdity? Should one be tempted to waste time on the extraordinary means of a counterdilmema, Vico offers the advice to be well and serene. These are states of body and mind that encourage an equilibrium of thought. Made to choose between the two alternatives of Vico's disjunct, Vico's adversary is "impaled on the horns of the dilemma."

Vico is a thinker who places *ars topica* ahead of *ars critica*. The topical approach to ideas is one of equilibrium, to attempt fairly to grasp what the thinker has said, to enter into his accomplishment. It has the ideal of *pensare insieme*. Ars critica can come into play profitably, in Vico's view, only after the work is thoroughly grasped. To read a major system of thought from the standpoint of ars critica from the beginning is to stand outside it and never to be in a position truly to reap its potential benefits. It is to reason in the dark from the start and to see at best by lamplight what can be seen only face-to-face through the doctrine's own source of illumination.

Rhetorically a dilemma lends itself to irony. In the "Ad Lectores" Vico is not only logically combative with his potential critic, he is ironic. Vico's figure of the erudite youth implies not simply the young but the aspiring and honest reader; it typifies the "caitiff semilearned or pseudo-learned" of the end of the *Autobiography* (A 199), and those who would feign learning with empty erudition, those of whom Vico speaks in the third *Inaugural University Oration*. This is the scholar who decides "we do not know what Vico means," and concludes that Vico's work is obscure because, in fact, such a scholar is unable to think about what Vico thinks about. Vico's figure of the person of erudition of every kind is the scholar who is accomplished, but only within the confines of a current state of knowledge. Such a scholar will not consider the truth of what is absolutely new, because it seems too strange, too far from fixed opinion. This is the reader-critic who, without poetry or piety, takes critique as an ideal, a good in itself. Vico criticizes the critic in advance and finally offers the advice to stop trying to discredit in one way or another what is said and try to see whether there might be something to these odd ideas.

Finally, it is an old trick, both legal and literary, to abuse the opponent or the reader, making them feel obliged to show that what the advocate or the author thinks of them is not true. Vico lets his readers know that they probably will not be able to understand it, either because they are too unprepared or too provincial in their thinking. Nothing else will bring a reader more quickly into a difficult work.

To the Equable Readers

"Equable reader," I call you at the end of the work; in fact I do not believe worthy of the name "reader" anyone who would not have read from beginning to end in a continuous and methodical way these books [i.e., the parts of Vico's work] that offer a rigorous treatment of their subject matter; nor do I consider "equable" anyone who would pass judgment without having attentively meditated all of the law (the jurisconsult will accuse such a person not only of inequity, but also of incapacity to be a suitable part of human society). Thus, you who have read these books, either you are an erudite youth or a person most expert in every kind of erudition.

If you, O Reader, are an erudite youth, I ask you to consider whether you are able easily to comprehend the authors of metaphysics, of theology, of moral and civil customs, of language, of history, of Roman jurisprudence, and above all the *Law of War and Peace* of Hugo Grotius—that is to say the natural law of the gentes; and in case you might not have comprehended what I write, I ask you to be careful not to attribute darkness and fogginess to me as a defect characteristic of my manner of writing.

If instead, O Reader, you are a person most expert in every kind of erudition, I ask you to consider only these two things: first, if

I have decreed erroneous principles; second, if I have deduced blasphemous conclusions from such principles. But in case I may have done these two things well, you do not comport yourself with equity if you disapprove of conclusions that arise by a rigorous method from true principles simply on the ground that they are absolutely new; and above all, if they do not meet your approval only because they do not occur in common use, then as it is your right to judge as you wish, so it is also mine; I have certainly made no use in these books of oratorical panderings to induce the minds of persons to accept my opinion.

But in case you decide to attack my claims, I ask you to do combat with me with equal weapons, as powerful men do when they come together, and to see if from other very few true principles (mine are seven in total, and so simple, because they are metaphysical principles that in order for one to know them it is sufficient only to be human [i.e., they derive directly from human nature]) you are able to put together in one system, more easily and more happily by a different method, more truth than I have worked out in the universal history of the gentes—in poetry, in philology, in moral and civil doctrine conforming in an absolute manner to Christian jurisprudence; only in this way will you show that my system itself falls and crumbles. If instead you would attempt with inconsistent arguments and with citations employed here and there from books, even if very numerous and even if imparted to memory more than comprehended, to bring down my doctrine, pardon me, I ask you, whether I would be obliged not to respond to you; in fact, your manner of argumentation itself, not my arrogance, will impose silence on me, because your argumentations would likely be just those that I have demonstrated are false in the Third Part of My General Treatment as not having been in accord with my principles.

Try to be well and interpret, for me and for you, serenely and favorably this, my doctrine.

PART 2

Reception of the
First New Science
(1725)

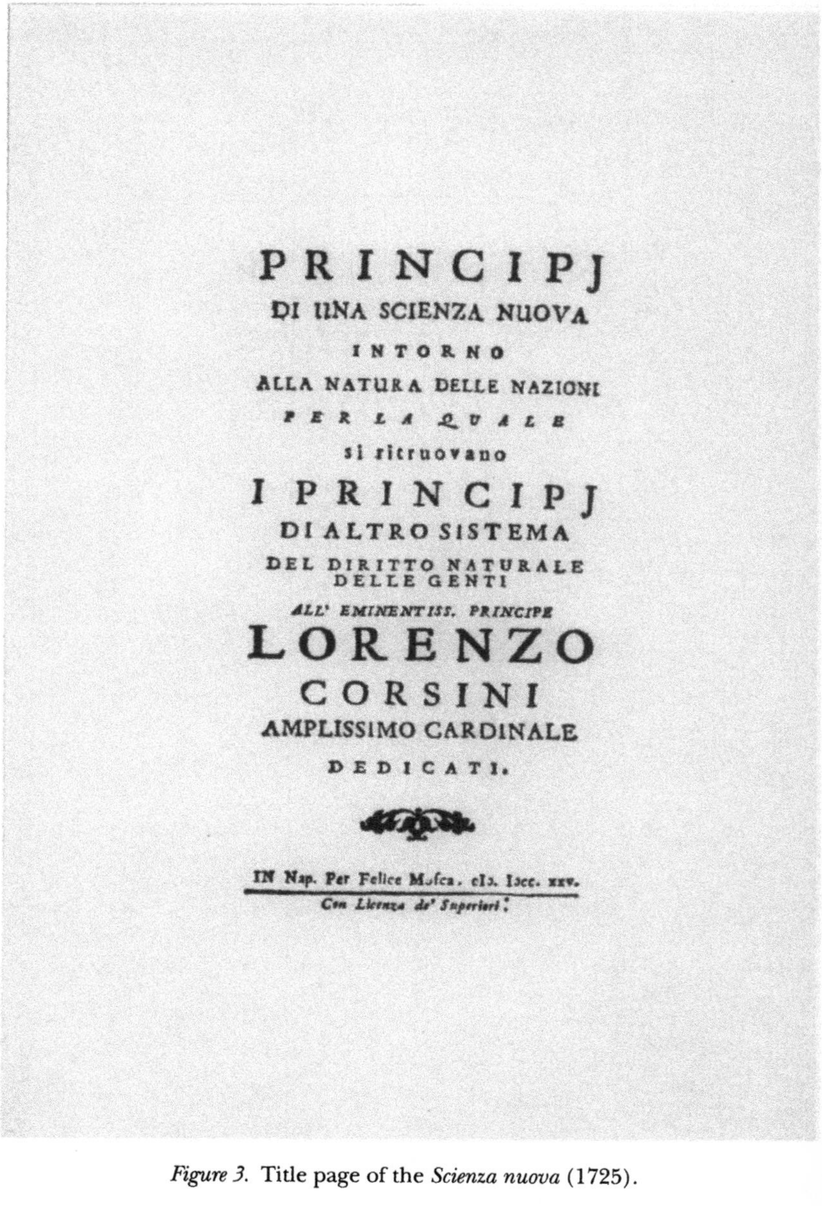

PRINCIPJ

DI UNA SCIENZA NUOVA

INTORNO

ALLA NATURA DELLE NAZIONI

PER LA QUALE

si ritruovano

I PRINCIPJ

DI ALTRO SISTEMA

DEL DIRITTO NATURALE
DELLE GENTI

ALL' EMINENTISS. PRINCIPE

LORENZO

CORSINI

AMPLISSIMO CARDINALE

DEDICATI.

IN Nap. Per Felice Mosca, cIɔ. Iɔcc. xxv.

Con Licenza de' Superiori.

Figure 3. Title page of the *Scienza nuova* (1725).

Vico's Reply to the False Book Notice

The *Vici Vindiciae*

Translation and Commentary by
DONALD PHILLIP VERENE

General Reception of the *New Science*

In October 1725 Giambattista Vico published in Naples what he later in his *Autobiography,* called the *First New Science* (*A* 192–94). In August 1729, four years after its publication, there appeared in a bookstore in Naples an issue of the *Leipzig Acta Eruditorum* of August 1727, containing an anonymously written, malevolent notice of Vico's book.[1] In the last half of November 1729 Vico printed a pamphlet with his regular publisher, Felice Mosca, containing his reply, with the title *Notae in "Acta eruditorum lipsiensia,"* which is usually cited by the other title that appears on its title page, *Vici Vindiciae* (Vindication[s] of Vico).[2]

---

1. See Vico's letter to Bernardo Maria Giacco, December 4, 1729. See Giambattista Vico, *Epistole,* ed. Manuela Sanna, vol. 11 of *Opere di Giambattista Vico* (Morano-Napoli: Centro di Studi Vichiani, 1992), 156–57. The copy of the *Acta* Vico saw was in the bookstore of his childhood friend Niccolò Rispolo, in via San Biagio dei Librai, no. 34, the same street on which Vico's father had his bookstore and on which Vico grew up.

2. Giambattista Vico, *Le "Vici Vindiciae"* in *Varia,* ed. Gian Galeazzo Visconti, vol. 12 of *Opere di Giambattista Vico* (Naples: Guida and Centro di Studi Vichiani, 1996), 25–109. This edition gives the Latin text with opposed Italian translation. The text of the *Vindiciae* is edited by Teodosio Armignacco. Armignacco's text and Italian translation of the *Vindiciae* first appeared in *Bollettino del Centro di Studi Vichiani* 12–13 (1982–83): 237–315. See also his "Sulle *Vici Vindiciae,*" in *L'edizione critica di Vico: bilanci e prospettive,* ed. Giuseppe Cacciatore (Naples: Guida, 1997), 167–70. Part of the digression in the *Vindiciae* (pars. 20–29) appeared in the 1968 issue of the *Forum Italicum,* published in honor of the tercentenary of Vico's birth, as "A Factual Digression on Human Genius, Sharp, Witty Remarks, and Laughter,"

Vico's book had not been received by the Italians with the "tedium" claimed in the Leipzig book notice, but by Vico's own assessment it was also not received with applause. Between October and December of 1725, numerous copies of the book were distributed locally, and through Abbé Luigi Esperti, Vico provided for its distribution in Rome and Venice.

Vico is clear in a letter of October 25, 1725, to his Capuchin friend Father Bernardo Maria Giacco that he regards the *New Science* as the crowning achievement of his life, the work toward which all his other works had been leading. Vico sees himself "clothed as a new man," and writes that the work has filled him with a "heroic spirit" such that he does not fear death. This fits with Vico's conception of the thinker as heroic. Heroic action and heroic being can truly occur only in the heroic age. In the age of men, thought can be conducted to a heroic level, a view that Vico makes clear in his later oration "On the Heroic Mind" (1732). But in this letter Vico also complains that his words are like someone crying in the desert and that those to whom he had already sent a copy make no acknowledgement of having received it when by chance he meets them in the city. The lack of reaction is so unpleasant, he says, he even tries to avoid such encounters.[3]

In the first few days of January 1726, Vico wrote to Esperti that his book

has come out in an age whose spirit—in the expression of Tacitus in which he reflects on his times that greatly resemble ours—is "to seduce and to be seduced" [*corrumpere et corrumpi seculum vocatur; Germania* 19], and because the book either disgusts or disturbs the many, it is unable to attain universal applause. Because it treats the idea of providence as the basis for justice in the human race, it refers the nations to a strict standard. But today the world either fluctuates and undulates among the tempests of human customs

---

trans. A. Illiano, J. D. Tedder, and P. Treves, *Forum Italicum* 2 (1968): 310–14. I have incorporated a good portion of the English of these passages into the present translation, but with substantial modification. A French translation based on the Visconti edition has recently appeared; see Giambattista Vico, *Vici Vindiciae*, trans. Davide Luglio and Béatrice Périgot (Paris: Éditions Allia, 2004).

3. Vico, *Epistole*, 113–15.

in accord with the chance of Epicurus or is nailed down and affixed to the necessity of [René] Descartes; and thus it either abandons itself to blind fortune or allows itself to be dragged along by deaf necessity; it cares little or nothing to control the one by the indomitable forces of reasonable choice or to avoid, and where it is not possible, to temper the other. Thus the only books that please are those which, like clothes, are produced in accord with fashion.[4]

In a letter of January 5, 1726 to the French Jesuit Father Edouard de Vitry, who served in Rome as censor for books written by members of his order and who had written Vico to thank him for a copy of the *New Science* of 1725 (which he received through Esperti), Vico gives a further characterization of the times and offers a list of how thought has declined in all principal areas of investigation. Vico's tone is not so much aggressive as it is melancholic. The "barbarism of reflection" of Vico's third age has infected all areas of learning around him in Naples. He foresees that the republic of letters has now "almost reached its end."[5]

In a long letter written three years later on January 12, 1729, to Francesco Saverio Estevan, a lawyer in Naples of Spanish descent who wrote Vico expressing interest in his works, Vico turns from his earlier, more general account of causes for the poor reception of his *New Science*—that it is difficult to read, requires erudition on the part of the reader, is not fashionable in its form of thought, and appeared in an age in which learning in all fields has declined—to a deeper and more systematic statement of the causes.[6] He claims the ill fortune his work has experienced is due to the decline in modern thought of eloquence and the ancient and humanist union of eloquence and wisdom. The art of topics upon which eloquence depends and upon which thought itself depends for the generation of its beginning points has been put aside in favor of the art of criticism formulated in terms of Descartes' pursuit of method.

4. Ibid., 126–29.
5. Ibid., 131–33.
6. Ibid., 142–48.

The sense of the divine and the connection between the human and the divine that classically defines wisdom has been lost. Those truths that can be expressed only in fables are ignored, and it is principally divine and ideal truths to which fables afford us access. The learned cultivate metaphysics divorced from what the orators, historians, and poets provide. Since the *New Science* is built from the insights and approaches of these topical ways of thought and regards them as necessary to the art of criticism itself, the work can have no success. It is in principle excluded from the age. A work which is not *of* Vico's third age of ideal eternal history can expect no real reception in that age. The actual fate of his work in his own time provides Vico with a kind of proof of its truth.

Vico's account of the reception of his *New Science* might be summed up in the way David Hume described the reception of his *Treatise:* "it fell *dead-born from the press,* without reaching such distinction, as even to excite a murmur among the zealots."[7] G. F. Finetti maliciously reports that when he asked one learned Neapolitan what was thought of Vico's *New Science,* he replied that originally Vico was held to be a truly learned man, but by the time of the *New Science* "he had become completely mad."[8]

Vico had hoped for a reception of his book not only among Italian scholars but for significant attention to be paid to it throughout northern Europe. Thus he wrote, at the opening of the *New Science* of 1725, a statement addressed "to the academies of Europe," introducing himself and announcing his discovery of the principles of a new system of science. He sent a copy of the book to Isaac Newton in London and to Jean Le Clerc in Amsterdam. Le Clerc had favorably reviewed the two major parts of his *Universal Law, On the One Principle and One End of Universal Law* and *On the Constancy of the Jurisprudent,* in the *Bibliothèque ancienne et moderne* (1727) but, as Max Harold Fisch points out, Le Clerc's complimentary letter to Vico about these, as well as his review of

---

7. David Hume, "My Own Life," in *An Inquiry Concerning Human Understanding,* ed. Charles W. Hendel (Indianapolis, Ind.: Bobbs-Merrill, 1955), 4.

8. See Donald Phillip Verene, *The New Art of Autobiography: An Essay on the "Life of Giambattista Vico Written by Himself"* (Oxford: Clarendon, 1991), 31.

them, showed "no real understanding of what Vico had done."[9] Le Clerc did not respond to Vico regarding receipt of his new book, and Newton may have received his copy only about a year before his death in 1727. Vico's only positive response from the scholars of northern Europe on any of his work remained Le Clerc's courteous treatment of the *Universal Law*. The other attention he received from northern Europe in his lifetime was the Leipzig book notice.

Identity of the *Ignotus Erro*

The great mystery of the false book notice is, who wrote it and sent it to the *Acta*? Who is the *amicus italus*, "the Italian friend" whom Vico refers to as the *ignotus erro*, the "unknown vagabond"? Vico may have thought it was Pietro Giannone, author of the *Civil History of the Kingdom of Naples*, published in Naples in February 1723 (and translated into English in London in 1729–31, in two volumes). Giannone's book gave the history of southern Italy from Augustus to his own day, showing how the Kingdom of Naples developed as a sovereign political entity. He shows Naples as a remarkable community of original legal scholars and scientific thinkers but at the same time a community economically stagnant due to the power the papacy had exerted over it.

As Harold Stone has pointed out, the message and the effect of Giannone's history was to ask its readers to reconsider the papacy's self-serving claims about divine law and to raise the question of what it meant to be a Neapolitan and what it meant to be a Catholic.[10] The Church and much of the nobility were disturbed by these theses. In April 1733 Giannone fled to Vienna; several days later his printer was excommunicated. On July 1, 1733, his work was placed on the Index. In 1734, when Charles of Bourbon conquered Naples, Giannone attempted unsuccessfully to return to Naples, going first to Venice, then to Milan, and finally taking up residence in Geneva. He was betrayed and turned over to the soldiers of the

---

9. Max Harold Fisch, "Introduction," in *A* 10.

10. Harold Samuel Stone, *Vico's Cultural History: The Production and Transmission of Ideas in Naples, 1685–1750* (Leiden: Brill, 1997), 211.

King of Savoy, which resulted in his imprisonment in Turin, during which he died, in 1748, four years after Vico's death.

Vico and Giannone were very different personalities. As Gustavo Costa puts it, "they cordially disliked each other."[11] They were both opposed to the Counter-Reformation but they employed different approaches. Giannone attacked the old regime directly and stood clearly for the tenets of modern thought. Vico appeared to support the old regime, yet in fact he admired modern science. Vico could never have obtained permission to publish his works unless he seemed to be against what others such as Giannone openly supported. Costa sees Vico as deliberately working within the system in order to sap its roots. As he puts it, "The *New Science* should be viewed as a Trojan horse, full of forbidden ideas having the potential to destroy the Counter-Reformation system, which were unwittingly allowed to enter the citadel of the old regime."[12] Although Vico's *New Science* has proved itself to be indeed such a Trojan horse, this was not its reputation upon publication.

Giannone might well have seen Vico's work as shoring up exactly what his own work was against. This apparently political stand of Vico's *New Science* might be motivation for Giannone to discredit it in the eyes of the scholars of northern Europe, as well as any personal animosity or personal dislike Giannone may have had for Vico. Giannone's life in exile in Vienna fits with Vico's decision to call the author of the book an "unknown vagabond"— *ignotus erro,* or "vagabondo sconosciuto," as he puts it in Italian in his *Autobiography (A* 189–90).

Giannone may have been the source of the book notice to the Leipzig *Acta,* but Fausto Nicolini offers the hypothesis that it originated in Naples at the instigation of Vico's colleague and *gran tormentatore* Nicola Capasso, holder of the "first morning chair of law," which became vacant in 1717 because of his promotion to the first "afternoon" chair, the vacancy for which Vico competed in his aborted concourse of 1723. Nicolini notes that while it cannot be absolutely excluded "that the malevolent informer was the

---

11. Gustavo Costa, review of *Pietro Giannone e il suo tempo,* ed. Raffaele Ajello, *New Vico Studies* 2 (1984): 128.

12. Ibid., 130.

wandering Pietro Giannone, then in exile at Vienna (that would explain the Vichian '*erro*'), it could still be considered a humiliating trick played on Vico by Capasso, a collaborator to the *Acta*, and by other Neapolitan scholars."[13] The perpetrators, Nicolini asserts, may have caused suspicion to converge on Giannone as the author, fanning the flames of Vico's wrath, causing him to give birth to the *Vindiciae* and to think that the ignotus erro did not reside in Naples.

Nicolini's support for this view—in addition to the fact that Capasso promoted the unflattering epithet of Vico as "Mastro Tizzicuzzo," and who, upon reading the *New Science*, ran to a noted physician to have his pulse taken, claiming that he feared he had suffered a stroke that had taken all reason from him—is Vico's letter to Giacco of December 4, 1729, sending him a copy of the *Vindiciae*. Vico writes that

> the volume of the "Acts of Leipzig" of the year 1727, where there is printed in the section on new literature a notice of my *New Science*, arrived here in Naples finally at the first of last year, 1728, and was kept under lock and key by its author, who from here had written to the learned gentlemen of Leipzig, and it was cunningly dissimulated by a few others who were aware of it along with the author.

In a footnote to this sentence regarding the identity of the author, Nicolini writes, "namely, the '*amicus italus*' or '*ignotus erro*,' who from Naples had sent to [Burkhard] Mencken the information on which the learned German sketched out his little note."[14] This is very solid evidence of what Vico actually thought.

Capasso was the author of the secular letter of approval sought by Giannone for the publication of his *Civil History*.[15] Capasso in his own views distinguished the law of nature from the law of reason, taking a view of natural law very different from that of Vico

---

13. Giambattista Vico, *Opere*, ed. Fausto Nicolini (Milan-Naples: Ricciardi, 1953), 82, n. 3. See also Benedetto Croce and Fausto Nicolini, *Bibliografia Vichiana*, 2 vols. (Naples: Ricciardi, 1957), 1:180, 1:200.

14. Vico, *Opere*, 139–40, n. 1.

15. Stone, *Cultural History*, 212.

in the *New Science*.[16] Giannone had chosen not to seek an ecclesiastical letter, being certain he would not obtain one and that even making such a request would cause authorities to block publication of his book.

According to Nicolini, among the few in Naples who would have had access to the copy of the *Acta* when it arrived early in 1728 were Abbè Giovanni Acampora, who in 1701 had edited a collection of Neapolitan poems, including a sonnet by Vico, and Carlo Giannone, a lawyer who was the brother of Pietro Giannone. Pietro wrote to Carlo on June 13, 1728, that Acampora would be "sickened [*stomacato*] on seeing that the compilers of the *Acts of Leipzig* have troubled themselves so much in order to understand the fantastic and imperceptible [unintelligible] ideas of Vico, when, in order to twist one's brain, it is only necessary to sniff his little books."[17]

If we take Vico's characterization of the author of the book notice as intended literally to denote someone who is a wanderer, then Giannone would appear to be the likely person. But if Vico intends the term *ignotus erro* symbolically, then Capasso can be considered. On this view Vico may intend that the author is not literally someone living a wandering life or a life in exile from his country but someone who, because of his lack of civility and character, is a fugitive from society. The unknown vagabond is like one of the feral men in the *New Science* who are unable to respond to the new phenomenon of Jove by founding a family. These feral men, wandering the earth, become *famuli;* they are the first *socii*, who must come to the fathers of the families for protection and who then can become civilized only indirectly, through a servile relation to the fathers of the families. A vagabond is a fugitive; "a vagabond shalt thou be in the earth" (Gen. 4:12).

Vico may be playing on this sense of *erro*, intending it to mean someone whose character is like that of a wanderer or vagabond.

---

16. Ibid., 104.

17. This is quoted in Nicolini's comments on the *Vindiciae* in *La Scienza nuova prima*, ed. Fausto Nicolini (Bari: Laterza, 1931), 343. Harold Stone reports that in a letter of May 1728 Giannone "makes fun of the *Acta* for calling Vico an abbé"; see Stone, *Cultural History*, 274, n. 12.

Error, "a wandering about," in its wider meaning is to be in error, to be mistaken, even to be the source of error, deception. The unknown vagabond is a feral mind and soul, a holdover from a primal state of humanity, not a true member of the Augustinian "great city of the human race." *Ignotus* is, literally, "unknown," but it can have the connotation of "ignoble" and even "ignorant." The pejorative senses that can be associated with these two terms are what Vico intends to attribute to the author of the book notice, whoever he is.

Reviews and book notices that fail properly to represent the major claims of a book or that distort the author's aims abound, from the beginning of academic journals to the present day. Vico even speaks of this general problem (see par. 46 in the translation that follows). Few authors are surprised when statements about their work contain inaccuracies, and most authors are gratified when, even if expressing disagreement, a reviewer rightly presents their claims. The academic world is full of authors who would wish to reply publicly to their mistaken reviewers. But Vico's situation is completely different from this phenomenon of academic distortion and dissatisfaction. It is difficult to imagine how one would feel, having spent decades of one's career developing the principles of a book of great learning and originality, to have it openly and anonymously ridiculed before the scholars of Europe to whom it was explicitly addressed—and, to make things worse, to discover such ridicule only very long after many others would have read it!

Vico had to wonder why Mencken, the director of the *Acta,* would publish such an anonymous note. In the summary of the *Vindiciae* that Vico gives in the 1731 continuation of his autobiography, he includes the text of the letter he drafted to Mencken that he planned to send with the published pamphlet of his defense (*A* 190). Vico says that on reflection he thought that the letter would convict Mencken and the scholars of the *Acta* of a grave breach of duty, so he decided that even though the letter was written with the utmost courtesy, it would be still more courteous not to send it. Perhaps there are other examples of false book notices of this order, but I do not know of any of this level of deliberate malevolence, and apparently neither did Vico. The notice and Vico's reply seem unique.

The Meaning of Vico's Title
and Legal Terminology

The key words of Vico's condensed title, *Vici Vindiciae Notae*, contain the jurisprudential metaphor on which his reply to the false book notice is based. As mentioned above, *Vici Vindiciae* is not part of Vico's manuscript; he added it to the title page in the published copy. It also appears in the conclusion of his work (see par. 50 in the translation that follows). *Vindiciae* is a term of Roman law for a legal claim, made of a thing, either to hold the thing to be the claimant's own property or to restore it to a free condition. It is an issue of civil law taken before the praetor, involving both contending parties; hence, the term—*vindiciae*—is in the plural. *Vindiciae* appears in the *Law of the Twelve Tables* in the context of the adjudication of a false claim of ownership (as opposed to a simple contest of ownership between two persons): "If a person has taken a thing by false claim... [*Si vindiciam falsam tulit...*]," the person (defendant) must pay double damages because of the falsity of the claim (Table XII.3).

Vico's claim to be both author and owner of his work would seem to correspond more to the principle of false claim than to a straightforward dispute concerning ownership, in which both parties equally claim ownership before the praetor or magistrate, based solely on the general principle of what elsewhere in the *Twelve Tables* is called *manum conserere* (Table VI.5a–b). Aulus Gellius in *Attic Nights,* referring to the *Twelve Tables,* explains this principle as "*Manum conserere,* 'to lay on hands.'...For with one's opponent to lay hold of and claim in the prescribed formula anything about which there is a dispute, whether it be a field or something else, is called *vindicia,* or 'a claim'" (XX.10.7–8; see also Varro, VI.64, and Cicero, *pro Murena* 26). In calling the ignotus erro to judgment before the Leipzig *Acta,* in his dedication to Charles of Austria in the *Vindiciae,* Vico uses the expression *manum conserere.* Both parties placing their hands on the object of the disputed claim has its origin in a trial by battle, "to join hands in combat" (see also *NS* 961).

In *On the One Principle and One End of Universal Law,* Vico defines the origin of the legal principle of *vindiciae* as action in which possession was maintained by physical force, with such a dispute, if between equals, settled by a duel.[18] *Vindico* has the meaning not only of laying claim to or placing a thing in a free condition (as related especially to restoring a slave to free status, in Roman law) but, with respect to a wrong perpetrated on someone, to avenge, revenge, punish; to take revenge upon the perpetrator. Vico's appeal under the principle of manum conserere, I suggest, has the further sense of *vindiciam falsam tulit,* for the dispute arises because something has been taken from him (see his comparison of the vagabond's actions to a robbery in par. 44 in the translation that follows).

Because of the interrelatedness of *vindiciae, vindicatio,* and *vindico,* I have translated Vico's title with the English cognate "vindicate." More precisely, Vico's claim is one of revindication(s) (It. *rivendicazione[i]*), in the sense that he is reclaiming or restoring his work to its rightful state, about which false claims have been made by the ignotus erro. The *Digest,* in its definition of the *vindicatio* of property, makes clear, "This particular action *in rem* is used both in regard to all movable things, whether animate or inanimate, and in regard to land" (6.1.1.). Justinian's *Institutes* state, "We call real actions 'vindications' [*vindicationes*]" (4.6.15) and, "Without first identifying the possessor, it is impossible to begin the vindication. Logic and law both require one party to possess and one to claim from that possessor. It is far better to be possessor than to be plaintiff. So there is often, in fact almost always, a hot dispute as to possession itself" (4.15.4). Cicero, in "The Second Speech against Gaius Verres" asks, "Now, how can it affect the praetor which of the two parties *is* in possession? Is not the point to be settled which of the two *ought* to be in possession? You do not, then, eject the man in possession, because he is in possession: would you then refuse the same man possession if he were not?" (*Verr.* II.1.45, sec. 116.)

Vico's act of reclamation is not the attempt to produce reasons to attain the right to something he does not already possess, but the attempt to show that, as author of his own work, he has always been its possessor and that there has been a false claim

18. *UL* bk. 1, chap. 100, pars. 7–8.

made as to its author: that its author conceals his name, is an abbé, that the work is not a system, but a fabrication, and so forth. In accordance with Vico's legal metaphor, the book notice is a false claim made about Vico's work. Vico, as its true possessor, offers his defense before the members of the Republic of Letters and the academies of Europe, who stand in the place of the praetor— most specifically, the learned gentlemen of Leipzig and Burkhard Mencken. Like Cicero against Gaius Verres, Vico is against the unknown vagabond, whom he intends to discredit "before the eyes of the whole world" (*Verr.* I.3, sec. 7).

Vico organizes his claim as a series of notae, taking issue with each point in the book notice, concerning its title, authorship, contents, and intent. These notes have the appearance of *note d'udienza,* the counsel's written remarks on the argument of the other side at a civil court hearing. The book notice is the statement of the other side; the *Notae* are Vico's written record of the objections to them from his side. This manner of vindicating himself has the rhetorical power of bringing the reader into the process of Vico's defense: the other side claims such and such, but the truth is thus and so— point by point. The reader becomes Vico's advocate.

Vico seems to be playing on this form of legal notes more than following the five main parts of a forensic speech as would be presented in open court: prooemium, narrative, proof, refutation, and peroration. As Quintilian notes, there can be, in addition, partition, proposition, and digression; the first two of these are subdivisions of proof (*Inst. orat.* 3.9). One striking feature of Vico's *Notae* in relation to the general parts of forensic speech is his use of digression (see the translation that follows, pars. 20ff). In Vico's *Institutiones Oratoriae,* the textbook on rhetoric from which he taught throughout his career, he speaks very favorably of the use of digression, which he says should flow from the narrative (Quintilian seems more cautionary concerning its use). Both Quintilian and Vico cite Cicero's use of digression in "Against Verres" as a model (Quintilian, *Inst. orat.* 4.3.13; Cicero, *Verr.* 2.2.1f.).

There is a general sense in which Vico's text follows these stages, in that they are natural stages through which expression must pass to state any case. There must be a beginning that passes into the narrative of the issue, followed by a proof, preceded or not by a digression. Any proof has to divide its claims into parts followed by a refutation of their opposites and, finally, conclusions must be drawn. There is an old principle in philosophical thought that what is most important occurs in digression, and Plato, called by Vico the "divine philosopher," is one of its greatest users. In the *Vindiciae* the "Digression" on ingenuity and laughter has long been considered the most interesting part of Vico's remarks. In it he freely takes up the issue of what it means to mock, and its effect on thought and the human spirit. Implied is the difference between the unwise and unphilosophical act of mockery, as embraced by the unknown vagabond, and the use of irony, which Vico, in his doctrine of "poetic logic" in the *New Science,* holds to be the trope distinctive to philosophical discourse.

In addition to having a meaning in relation to a process in civil law, *nota* has a particular historical status in Roman practice, in the sense of *nota censoria.* This refers to the mark affixed by the censors to the name of anyone on the list of citizens whom they censured primarily for immorality or lack of patriotism, which could include avoidance of military service (Livy, *Hist. of Rome,* 39.42.5–6; 29.37.1–3; 24.18.4–9; see also Cicero, *Clu.* 129).

The concept of *infamia* or legal disgrace had its origin in the nota of the censors. The *Digest* states, "The following incur *infamia:* one who has been discharged from the army in disgrace ... one who in criminal proceedings has been judged guilty of vexatious litigation or collusion in anything; one who has been condemned in his own name for theft, robbery with violence, insult, fraud, trickery or compromised in such a case ..." (*D.* 3.2.1). *Infames* are closely connected to *intestabiles:* "When a person is declared by a statue to be *intestabilis,* the effect is that he is not acceptable as a witness and furthermore, in the view of some, that witnesses cannot act for him either" (*D.* 28.1.26). Also, "If someone has been found guilty of writing defamatory verses, it is expressly laid down by *senatus consultum* that he be *intestabilis...*" (*D.* 28.1.18.1). Vico may have these legal principles in mind. He accuses the author of the book notice both of immorality and lack of patriotism to Italy. Furthermore, the author of the notice is intestabilis in that such a person cannot or should not be allowed as a witness to the scholars of Leipzig on the nature of Vico's book.

A further wordplay in Vico's title is that the Latin genitive of his own name, *Vici*, recalls one of the most famous declarations in Roman history: Julius Caesar's "Veni, Vidi, Vici," used in celebration of several of his foreign victories achieved in close succession—including the defeat of Pharnaces, son of Mithridates the Great, in a single battle at Pontus. Suetonius writes that Caesar, "[i]n his Pontic triumph displayed among the show-pieces of the procession an inscription of but three words, 'I came, I saw, I conquered,' not indicating the events of war, as the others did, but the speed with which it was finished" (*Lives of the Caesars* I.37.2). Vico's name is a pun on "I conquered." What Caesar could do with the sword Vico could do with the pen. In his oration to the Academy of Oziosi in 1737, Vico refers to Cicero's successful defense of Quintus Ligarius before Caesar, who had openly condemned Ligarius. Vico quotes Caesar: "Had Cicero not spoken so well today, Ligarius would not flee from our hands." Vico regards the *Pro Ligario* as Cicero's most glorious oration, and writes that Cicero "triumphed with language over him who with arms had triumphed over the whole world."[19]

In the declaration of his title Vico claims to win his case of ownership as decisively as Caesar claims his victories in the banner in his procession. This may seem too clever a pun, but Vico was not required to increase his title of *Notae* (the title he used in its manuscript form) with the addition of *Vici Vindicae* when he published his text as a little book, and even in so doing there was no necessity for him to use this combination of words. The pun on *Vici* seems of a piece with the self-important style that many of his readers find in Vico's *Autobiography*—not the least of whom is Giannone, who claims that Vico's *Autobiography* is "both the most insipid [*sciapita*] and most braggadocian [*trasonica*] thing one could ever read."[20]

19. Giambattista Vico, "The Academies and the Relation between Philosophy and Eloquence," trans. Donald Phillip Verene, in Giambattista Vico, *On the Study Methods of Our Time*, trans. Elio Gianturco (Ithaca, N.Y.: Cornell University Press, 1990), 88–89.

20. See Verene, *The New Art of Autobiography*, 28. Giannone's remark is quoted in Alain Pons's edition of Vico's autobiography, *Vie de Giambattista Vico écrite par lui-même*, trans. Alain Pons (Paris: Grasset, 1981), 45, n. 18.

The most problematic term in the text of the *Vindiciae* is *ingenium* (*ingenio*). I have rendered it consistently as "ingenuity." The English reader will know that where "ingenuity" occurs, *ingenium* occurs in the original. The corresponding term in English in Vico's day was "wit," which is the term used by Anthony Ashley Cooper, the Third Earl of Shaftesbury in his *Characteristics* and can be found in John Locke's *Essay* and Thomas Hobbes's *Leviathan*. *Ingenium* and wit have the sense of a mental ability that can grasp an intellectual meaning in an immediate, explicit way, diverse from the understanding. *Ingenium* also can mean of persons, "a natural temperament or disposition," and of things, "a natural quality."

The author of the book notice uses *ingenium* in a pejorative way against Vico, taking it to be a power through which only figments, fabrications, fictions, and fables are generated, a mentality that simply invents things and connections between things, and of which the primary purpose is to formulate clever, convincing, but false reasonings. Vico, throughout the *Vindiciae*, throws *ingenium* back at the author of the book notice as a positive term. Fisch characterizes *ingenium* as "the faculty of discerning the relations between things, which issues on the one hand in analogy, simile, metaphor, and on the other in scientific hypotheses."[21] The modern Cartesian rationalist and advocate of the *Port-Royal Logic,* whose focus is on method, analysis, and understanding, thinks only critically, at every turn presupposing, but giving no attention to, the power by which the mind finds its starting points.

In his *Autobiography,* Vico states, "The Latins called nature *ingenium* whose principal property is sharpness [*l'acutezza*]" (*A* 148–49; and see pars. 20ff. in the translation that follows). In the *Most Ancient Wisdom of the Italians,* Vico discusses ingenium and ties it to the synthetic powers of thought at the basis of geometry, a view he echoes in his discussion of the role of Euclidean geometry in education in *On the Study Methods of Our Time. Natura* is synonymous with *ingenium,* because it derives from *nascor* deriving from *gigno* (to beget, bring forth), *nascere* (to give birth, be born). In accordance with this etymology, which Vico likely took from Gerhard

21. *A* 216, n. 141.

Johann Voss's *Etymologicon* of the Latin language, the power of the mind to bring forth things and their connections is analogous to the power of nature to do so in the physical world.[22] *Ingenium* is analogous to the divine power of God, and mind is the divine element in man. Ingenium, as a power stemming directly from human nature, allows human beings to see what is unseen in things—the divine structures in nature and in history—and express this unseen in language.[23]

The Rhetorical Principles and Motive of Vico's Defense

Vico's defense is based on four main tactical principles: repetition of the opponent's errors of fact; attribution to the opponent of the same form of thought the opponent has criticized; employment of the same manner of speech in addressing the opponent that the opponent has used; and affirmation of the most sensitive critical claim made by the opponent not as a defect but as a great truth of the case.

In regard to the first, Vico repeatedly cites the factual errors made in the book notice: the misrepresentation of the identity of the book, its author, its printed format, and its subject matter. As Vico insists, its subject matter is not first and foremost a new system of natural law but the common nature of the nations, of which this system is the principal corollary. The insistent repetition of these errors is a tour de force; they are so driven into the reader's memory that they cannot be forgotten. In regard to the second, Vico terms the book notice itself a brief fable or fabrication, turning back on its author his claim that Vico's system is not a system but a figment or fabrication. Vico asks the reader to decide who is the true fabricator.

In regard to the third tactical principle, Vico questions why the author of the book notice attacks him with such rectitude and

---

22. Giambattista Vico, *Opere*, ed. Andrea Battistini, 2 vols. (Milan: Mondadori, 1990), 2:1280, n. 9.

23. For a discussion of "Ingenuity and the *dicta acuta*" see Michael Mooney, *Vico in the Tradition of Rhetoric* (Princeton, N.J.: Princeton University Press, 1985), 135–58.

mocks him and his book. He repeatedly addresses the vagabond with the greatest sense of rectitude and offense. Vico also elaborately mocks him from this rectitudinous position, portraying him as foolish, a traitor to his nation and religion; as criminal, insane, inhuman, and failing to grasp what fame is; and as intellectually incapable of comprehending serious writing. In regard to the fourth, Vico realizes that the heart of the attack in the book notice is the criticism of his support of the papal Church. Vico's response is categorically to embrace the support his system gives to the papal Church as its most important feature. To underscore this he repeatedly asks why anyone who is an Italian and a Catholic would disagree with such a work on these grounds, thus putting his opponent in the absurd position of needing to defend himself.

In pursuing these four strategies Vico develops his case by pointing out all aspects of the issues, calling attention to things both great and small and to things both far-fetched and clearly crucial to his case. He leaves nothing unsaid in his defense if it can possibly be in his favor, for, as in a judicial case, he never can know what point may strike a particular chord with his potential supporter or with the literati of Europe and Leipzig, who stand in the place of the praetor.

Finally, what is Vico's motive in writing the *Vindiciae*? Gustavo Costa suggests that Vico may have been concerned with ecclesiastical censorship of the *New Science*. Costa asks whether the *Vindiciae* is an excessive reaction to the Leipzig book notice, or whether it is a calculated maneuver to neutralize the accusation of ecclesiastical censure.[24] In an earlier article, Costa reported the discovery of a file on Vico, in the Archives of the Congregation for the Doctrine of the Faith, proving that the proposed Venetian edition of the *New Science*, which Vico claims he withdrew from the press because of a disagreement with the printers, was in fact blocked by the Holy Office in 1729.[25] In the more recent article, Costa relates the career of Giovanni Rossi, a Theatine and theologian who

24. Gustavo Costa, "Perchè Vico pubblicò un capolavoro incompiuto? Considerazioni in margine a *La scienza nuova*, 1730," *Italica* 82 (2005): 567.

25. Gustavo Costa, "Vico e l'Inquisizione," *Nouvelles de la Republique des Lettres* 2 (1999): 93–124.

enjoyed the favor of the pontif Benedetto XIII Orsini. Rossi was, by pontifical appointment, recorder of the meeting of the Congregation of the Index held in the Palazzo Apostolico Vaticano on January 15, 1725. He became a bishop and served throughout his career in various locations.

Rossi pronounced an ecclesiastical censure of Vico's *New Science* of 1725 on October 19, 1729, in the convent of S. Maria della Minerva, a place famous for proceedings of the Inquisition. He had an absolutely negative judgment of Vico's book, thinking Vico to be blinded by vanity and wishing to appear to make astounding and ingenious discoveries. As a result, Rossi thought, Vico had lost his senses. He found the book obscure and labyrinthine, its parts incoherent, and its heterodox claims irreconcilable with the Bible. As Costa reports, "According to Rossi, it is above all the systematic contamination of the sacred scriptures with pagan myths that makes the *New Science* an extremely dangerous work."[26] A serious problem of biblical interpretation is Vico's claim in his "Supplement on Antediluvian History" in the final book of the first *New Science* that a race of giants began with Cain, before the universal flood—a view that Vico prudently does not pursue in the second *New Science* (cf. *FNS* bk. 5, chap. 3 with *NS* bk. 2, chap. 2).

Given this background, Vico's response to the false book notice may not simply have been an occasion for him to express his outrage and to seek vindication for wholly academic and intellectual reasons. Costa's remarks on Rossi suggest a basis for why Vico, in the *Vindiciae,* emphasizes so strongly and so repeatedly, to the point that the reader almost cannot bear being told another time, that his book is in agreement with the Catholic religion and the pontifical Church. Although Vico claims that all of the book notice is false, there is one charge in it with which he in effect agrees; he claims that agreement with the Church is not a defect of his *New Science* but its great achievement.

On this hypothesis, the publication of the *Vindiciae* would be Vico's opportunity to contain the effects of Rossi's censure, or at least to counter it so as not to find himself at some point in

26. Costa, "Perchè Vico pubblicò," 568.

Giannone's position of exile. It also might be a reason for Vico publicly to seem to point to Giannone as the author of the book notice while at the same time privately holding that the author or authors of the notice may actually reside in Naples, as he makes clear in the abovementioned letter to Giacco. The date of Rossi's public announcement of censure, October 19, 1729, is very close to the appearance of Vico's pamphlet in the last half of November 1729.[27]

One cannot comprehend Vico's work without the awareness that the Inquisition de facto functioned in Naples throughout Vico's career. His early poem "Affetti di un disperato" expresses Lucretian, not Christian sentiments. Vico, while absent from Naples when serving as a tutor at Vatolla, had sympathy for his friends Giacinto de Cristofaro, Nicola Galizia, and Basilio Giannelli, who were stigmatized by the Inquisition in 1692, the same year that he wrote the poem (which was published in 1693). In a letter of October 12, 1720 to Giacco, Vico wrote that errors of his early years were remembered in Naples and used against him.[28] Vico's befriending of members of the clergy during the mature years of his career was a way to preempt any anticlerical and anticurial accusations. Another way would be his support of the pontifical Church in the *Vindiciae.*

The commentary to Teodosio Armignacco's Italian translation of the *Vindiciae* concludes that Vico "vindicates the integrity and autonomy and profound piety of his thought [*rivendica la coerenza e l'autonomia e la religiosità profonda del suo pensiero*]."[29] The consistency, independence, and devoutness Vico shows in his criticisms of the ignotus erro and his support of Roman Catholicism and the pontifical Church in the *Vindiciae* are what make this work something more, according to the commentary, than "an irascible ineffectual work [*una stizzosa opera inutile*]."[30] This view seems to see Vico as completely sincere in his professions of piety in the

---

27. See the remarks on the publishing of the *Vindiciae* in Vico, *Varia*, 26–27.

28. Vico, *Epistole*, 88–90. See also Donald Phillip Verene, *Knowledge of Things Human and Divine: Vico's New Science and Finnegans Wake* (New Haven, Conn.: Yale University Press, 2003), 50–51.

29. Vico, *Varia*, 266.

30. Ibid.

work and not as formulating strategic overstatements to protect claims in the *New Science* that are at odds with biblical interpretation and orthodox Christian theology.

The resolution of this issue depends on the view one holds regarding Vico's personal religiosity and the compatibility of the principles of his metaphysics with Christian theology. Because Vico uses the term *providence* to refer to the metaphysical ground of his cycles and *providence* is a term of Christian theology, is by no means evidence that Vico's principle, as it appears in the *New Science,* is in accord with a Christian conception of history as a drama of events moving toward the day of judgment. But full consideration of this issue lies beyond the scope of these remarks.[31]

Given the evidence produced by Costa and by Nicolini, the most convincing account, to my mind, of the events that surround the *Vindiciae* is the following. Capasso (who was, as Nicolini reports, a *collaboratore* of the *Acta*) wrote Mencken, informing him of the appearance of this new book in Naples. Capasso and some scholars of his acquaintance saw this as a capital opportunity to torment Vico because of personal animosity and animosity toward what they perceived to be his political and ecclesiastical sentiments. From the information Mencken received he formulated the book notice (as Nicolini also reports) in good faith, believing its details to be correct.

Vico, on finally being shown a copy of this issue of the *Acta,* realized that the details the notice contains might have originated from Naples, but that to accuse Capasso and his circle openly as the perpetrators would require evidence he did not have. (In the aforementioned letter to Giacco on this view he does not give names.) He also cannot completely rule out the authorship or involvement of Giannone. Thus, thinking in jurisprudential terms, Vico considers the authorship of the notice as by "person or persons unknown." To call the author an unknown vagabond implies that the author may be Giannone. To attack Giannone has the advantage of also attacking Capasso, since Capasso was the secular censor of Giannone's *Civil History.*

31. See Verene, *Human and Divine,* 191–203.

In the *Vindiciae*, Vico seems to imply that the vagabond is someone currently in Naples who "might know me all too well" (see par. 9 in the translation that follows). Capasso's personality fits well the portrait of the mocker that Vico draws in the "Digression," but as part of his admonition to the unknown vagabond Vico seems to describe Giannone in exile, "having no place where you can stay, on either side of the Alps" (see par. 49 in the translation that follows; cf. par. 8). Rhetorically, Giannone is an appropriate opponent, as he is on Vico's intellectual level, and, to Vico's advantage, he is a prominent symbol of opposition to the pontifical Church.

Vico did not send a copy of his *Vindiciae* to Mencken, but he did publish it in Naples, which assured local circulation. It was prudent not to attack the scholars of Leipzig too strongly, for later in Jöcher's *Lexicon* (1750–51) there appeared a substantial entry on Vico, but no entry on Giannone.[32] Vico was also prudent to claim so strongly the agreement of his work with the Roman Catholic religion and the pontifical Church, given its censure by Rossi (as Costa reports).

In these matters things are never what they seem. Vico is a clever thinker, and a rhetorical writer of the first order. The equable reader must keep in mind not only the points that Vico makes in the *Vindiciae* but also that his defense does not occur in purely intellectual time and space. The *Vindiciae* is a document with highly complex and interesting problems, only some of which are suggested in the foregoing remarks.

32. Gustavo Costa, "Vico, Johann Burkhard Mencken e Christian Gottlieb Jöcher," *Bollettino del Centro di Studi Vichiani* 4 (1974): 143–48.

VINDICATION OF VICO

NOTES OF
GIAMBATTISTA VICO

ON THE *ACTA ERUDITORUM* OF LEIPZIG

OF THE MONTH OF AUGUST IN THE YEAR

1727

WHERE

AMONG THE NOTICES OF NEW LITERARY

WORKS THERE IS ONE OF HIS

BOOK WHICH IS TITLED

PRINCIPLES OF A NEW SCIENCE

CONCERNING

THE NATURE OF THE NATIONS

TO CHARLES OF AUSTRIA

EMPEROR OF THE ROMANS
AND KING OF SPAIN
PIOUS AND FELICITOUS WHO
AS AUGUST PROTECTOR
OF THE ROMAN CATHOLIC RELIGION
IN ITALY HAS GIVEN RISE
THROUGH PUBLIC INSTRUCTION
TO THE INGENUITY
OF A NEAPOLITAN CITIZEN
SUCH THAT
HE HAS MEDITATED
IN HIS BOOK
CERTAINLY SMALL IN SIZE
BUT GREAT IN ARGUMENT
A NEW SCIENCE
CONCERNING THE NATURE OF THE NATIONS
WHICH DEMONSTRATES
THAT THE SYSTEM
OF THE NATURAL LAW
OF THE GENTES IS TRUE
AND IS WORTHY OF SUCH A POLITY
IN WHICH HE WAS BORN
ON THE OCCASION
OF SUCH A NEW SCIENCE
GIAMBATTISTA VICO
PROFESSOR OF ELOQUENCE
OF THE ROYAL UNIVERSITY OF NAPLES
BOWED IN HOMAGE
PRESENTS AND DEDICATES
THIS GLORIOUS VINDICATION
IN WHICH
WITHIN THE MODEST LIMITS
OF THE BOOK ITSELF
THERE IS VINDICATION
OF THE PIETY
OF THE GREATEST COUNTRY
THE DIGNITY
OF THE ITALIC WISDOM
THE TRUTH
OF THE ROMAN CATHOLIC CHURCH
AND THE MAJESTY
OF YOUR RIGHT OF MONARCHY
AGAINST
A VAGABOND HIDING FROM JUSTICE
CALLED TO JUDGMENT
BEFORE THE *ACTA ERUDITORUM*
OF LEIPZIG

Whose one dread was that they
might seem to comprehend him.

Tacitus, *Annals* I.11

On the Book as Reported and Judged[33]

[1] One of my true friends, in this current month of August of the year 1729, informed me that among your "New Literary Works" of the month of August of the year 1727 I and my book are unfavorably received by you, illustrious gentlemen of letters of Leipzig; he brought me the volume of that year and pointed out the following for me to read:

> [2] Published in the same place (Naples) is a book titled *Principles of a New Science* (a), in octavo (b), and although the author of this book conceals his name from the learned (c), we have made certain from a friend (d), an Italian (e), that he is an abbé (f), a Neapolitan by the name of Vico (g). The author in this small book advances a new system of natural law (h), or rather a figment of such (i), deduced at great length from principles that differ from those the philosophers have heretofore followed (k), and that are more adapted to the ingenuity (l), of the pontifical Church (m). He greatly labors (n) against [Hugo] Grotius and [Samuel von] Pufendorf (o) debating their doctrines and principles (p), however, he indulges more in ingenuity (q), than in truth (r); because of the large shapeless mass of his conjectures he fails at his own endeavor (s), and by the Italians themselves he is received more with tedium (t) than with applause.

Purpose of the Notes

[3] All these pronouncements are false, but one thing is true, that your reproval can in fact be regarded as an act of consideration of

---

33. Vico's title, "*De libro relatio et iudicium,*" employs two terms with legal connotations: *relatio*, a retorting of the accusation upon the accuser, a carrying back, a report; and *iudicium*, a trial, legal investigation, judgment.

109

my work, and because of this I will show in these *Notes* that the pronouncements you have published are the deceptions of a fraud.

Notes

[4] [*Published in the same place (Naples) is a book titled Principles of a New Science* (a)] Of the subject matter of the science itself, which concerns the nature of the nations, the reviewer, however, remains completely silent, which, without a doubt regarding a new work, he should have stated clearly from the beginning.

[5] [*in octavo* (b)] He who has put forth these pronouncements has not even examined the form of the book that is not in octavo but in duodecimo.

[6] [*and although the author of this book conceals his name from the learned* (c)] In the first pages of the book, however, I clearly wrote my name, Giambattista Vico; it occurs for the first time in the letter of dedication to the most eminent Cardinal Corsini and for the second time in my address of the book to all the Academies of Europe.

[7] [*we have made certain from a friend* (d)] Ah truly, gentlemen of Germany, pay close attention to whether or not this friend of yours might be a false friend who with such ignoble pronouncements on literary matters mocks your good faith and whether he plays with it to such an extent that, with manifest and self-serving lies in your *Acta,* he condemns you as clearly culpable of having ineptly taken for true things that are absolutely false.

[8] [*an Italian* (e)] I am not able in any sense to persuade myself that this man is an Italian; on the contrary I would be inclined to believe that he is someone foreign from beyond the Alps, who, because of a jealousy of Italic glory and a hatred of the Roman Catholic religion, has ascribed these things to me and my book. In fact, could this "Italian" really be one of us, who says that a rigorous system of the natural law of the gentes and that conforms to the Roman Catholic religion is received with tedium by the Italians, who are all Roman Catholic? Because this unknown and anonymous gentleman invents another nationality and denies his own, I, in these *Notes,* will call him "unknown vagabond."

[9] [*that he is an abbé* (f)] In truth I took a wife thirty years ago and still live with her in harmony and by her have five children now living. But this unknown vagabond lies on purpose about this point, perhaps because he does not wish to suggest that he might know me all too well. Or, perhaps instead this man does not really know me, for how could a Neapolitan invent that I am an abbé on the grounds that I elaborated a rigorous system of natural law conforming to the Roman Catholic religion? As if the only Neapolitan men of letters who conform their doctrine to their religion are members of the clergy! Can there be a citizen who would act with so much impiety against his own country?

[10] [*a Neapolitan by the name of Vico* (g)] Now, then, to the obscurity of my name, I ask you, setting aside other testimonials, to look in the *Bibliothèque ancienne et moderne* of Jean Le Clerc where in the second part of volume XVIII, article VIII he discussed at length several of my works; and to look in my *Vita* that I wrote after the repeated insistence of the illustrous Count Gian Artico di Porcía, brother of the most eminent Cardinal di Porcía; the *Vita*, against my will, as the publisher openly acknowledged, was published in Venice in the *Raccolta degli Opuscoli degli Eruditi* of the Reverend Father Calogerà, in which, at the end, is added a *Catalog* of my works that have intermittently appeared over thirty years, during which time I have taught and still teach eloquence at the Royal University of Naples.

[11] [*The author in this small book advances a new system of natural law* (h)] The specific thesis of this science is not the natural law of the gentes but the common nature of the nations, from which there arises and is diffused throughout all peoples a constant and universal consciousness of things human and divine; the result is the discovery of a new system of natural law that is the principal corollary of this science.

[12] [*or rather a figment of such* (i)] Look at who dislikes fabrications, rigorous philosopher indeed, one who lies about me, who invents so many fabrications about my name, my status, and my book! But let us put aside the man and come to the issue itself. Does this unknown vagabond hold that the doctrines and the principles that are in accord with those of the pontifical Church,

what he calls "fabrications or figments," are a mass of badly amalgamated incoherent conjectures and thus simply foolish fables? Could it be, I do not say Neapolitan, I do not say Italian, but some kind of Roman Catholic, who has spoken so abusively of his own true religion?

[13] [*deduced at great length from principles that differ from those the philosophers have heretofore followed* (k)] Why does this unknown vagabond say these things? Can it perhaps be because Grotius and Pufendorf, to which [John] Selden can also be added, the three principal exponents of this doctrine of natural law, seem to this vagabond to alone be philosophers, on the grounds that none of them is Roman Catholic? Or is it perhaps because he wishes to claim that I am not a philosopher? If this is what he thinks, then he intends one of the following things: either ignoring the opinion of the learned, he holds, in accord with the vulgar, that I am not a philosopher but a professor of philology, in particular of eloquence, and on this account he believes, in accord with the common view, that eloquence is something separate from philosophy; or he has not in fact read the work, which constantly joins philology, as those things that depend on the freedom of human choice (that is, language, customs, and deeds in times of war and peace), to philosophy (as it rightly is, and has been so held to be up to the present); thus by proceeding from well-noted philosophical principles it recasts philology into the form of science. Or is it perhaps because in this system I defend the legitimacy of monarchy with reasons that until now have not been considered by the philosophers? If this is what this vagabond thinks, his views very evidently incur serious contradictions. He not only abandons but also confutes Grotius, who this vagabond in his own writing considers a philosopher and of whom he proclaims himself to be in favor. In fact Gronovius [Johann Friedrich Gronow], who wrote his *Notes* against Grotius with no other intention than to write in a mode conforming to the taste the Dutch people have for popular liberty, censured him as a supporter of monarchy. Was this deserved? But this is not the place to discuss it. Now then, which of us writes in a manner conforming to the ingenuity of another—characterized in that elegant expression to be found in Tacitus, *per ambitionem* [eager to

win favor][34] and that can be rendered in Italian as *a compiacenza* [desire to please]—I, who write according to the truth that the Catholic Church teaches and that Grotius also recognizes, or this vagabond, who writes to please your citizens of Leipzig, with their love of popular liberty?

[14] I do not understand why this vagabond would accuse me of having abandoned the path the philosophers have always followed; unless the motive is this, that I have always been concerned to found my system on the principle of Divine Providence; something that is not done in any sense by Grotius, who, having openly denied any idea of God omnipotent, still holds that his system is well grounded; Pufendorf has done it, but he is accused by the learned and equally by the religious of having clearly accepted the Epicurean principle of man as thrown into the world without divine intervention or design; and he was forced to defend himself from this accusation with a dissertation published just on this issue. Besides the principle of Divine Providence, and in accordance with it, I advance the principle of the free choice of good and evil on the part of man; without these philosophical principles one could not in any sense speak of justice, of what is right, and of laws. If for all this the vagabond accuses me of having abandoned the path until now followed by the philosophers; thus he, I am certain, with a caprice close to madness, would need to strike from the album of philosophers Plato, the divine philosopher, who placed Divine Providence among his principles and who ascribed to man the free choice of honor or dishonor. If this is how things stand, this vagabond betrays himself to be a Protestant, because certainly no one else would criticize my system for being in conformity with the ingenuity of the pontifical Church. If someone who, as a follower of [Martin] Luther or [John] Calvin, forcibly introduces into Christian philosophy the belief the Stoics have in fate, he would dogmatically enslave the free will of man by maintaining the existence of a blind necessity that submerges and overwhelms everything.

---

34. Tacitus, *Agricola* 40.4; *Annals* 3.12 and 16.17.—Ed. "Ed." indicates that the note appears fully or partially in the edition of Vico's *Varia* (see n. 2, above).

[15] [*and that are more adapted to the ingenuity* (l)] Not by chance at this point is the term "ingenuity" [*ingenium*] used by this vagabond;[35] this term in fact reveals the language with which the Protestants express themselves when speaking of the Roman Catholic Church, as they claim it bases itself on the ingenuity of argumentation and not on the truth of the foundation of Christianity, that is, on the Gospel, and for this reason the vagabond in question accuses me of indulging, in a system that conforms more with the ingenuity of the pontifical Church, than with the ingenuity of truth.

[16] [*of the pontifical Church* (m)] But this, I believe, is greatly to my credit; I am very far from feeling myself in any sense at fault. And why would I not have needed to conform my system to that of the church that presents the truth to whomever professes its religion? Indeed, it is just this Church that has offered me the possibility of formulating this system adapted to all the human race and has taught me its two dogmas, one of Divine Providence, the other of the free will of man. All of the human race is in accord concerning these two dogmas, so much so that even the followers of both Luther and Calvin are prohibited to speak openly against them, which occurred in one instance to Theodorus Beza in Switzerland, where he succeeded Calvin as the head of his religious movement, when he, having delivered a sermon against these dogmas, caused his audience to become disheartened of ever being able perfectly to perform all of the Christian duties. As a result it was forbidden by the magistrates to preach against these doctrines of the Catholic Church in the future.

[17] [*He greatly labors* (n)] Is this unknown vagabond perhaps a diviner who tells this truth about me? Because in fact in the elaborating, establishing, and finishing of this system I, who according to this vagabond have indulged in too much ingenuity, have spent nearly thirty years of my life.

[18] [*against Grotius and Pufendorf* (o)] The vagabond says this in order to provoke you to hate my book because of my criticism

---

35. "Ingenuity" (*ingenium*) has the sense, here, of mentality or intellectual taste. In his summary of the book notice in the *Autobiography* Vico uses "taste." He writes that the notice "observes that the work is suited to the taste [*gusto*] of the Roman Catholic Church" (*A* 187). See my remarks on *ingenium* in this chapter.

in it of Pufendorf, your fellow countryman, and he thought that you would be more indignant because of this criticism than because of the fact that my system conforms to the ingenuity of the pontifical Church. But you are fair and impartial judges in literary matters and certainly would remain so in the assessment of a book, and not be led astray by love of country, not even a nail's breadth.[36]

[19] [*debating their doctrines and principles* (p)] Why does he leave out Selden, the third but chronologically the second exponent of this science whose doctrines and principles I have disputed because he does not establish his Noachian system of natural law on the principle of Providence and does not thus have a ground from which rationally to deduce the order of things human and divine?[37] Ah! now finally I understand. To this vagabond Selden does not seem to be a philosopher because he introduces the concept of Providence drawn from the sacred book of Genesis. Thus for this vagabond not even Cicero is a philosopher, who claims not to be able in any sense to discuss the laws with Atticus if he does not concede this truth, of which by common consent all of the human race is convinced, that all things human are deployed from Divine Providence according to what is appropriate and just.[38] Hence Grotius should consider if by putting aside any cognition of omnipotent God his system could be true! Furthermore, the learned interpreters of the system of Roman law should consider whether it is good and proper to insert Stoic and Epicurean principles into its *Institutes,* in which the natural law of the gentes is defined as law established by Divine Providence![39] This unknown vagabond declares impious war against the principle of Divine Providence, to such a point that for him neither Cicero, who because of the unanimous consent of all nations and of all

36. Cf. Plautus, *Aulularia,* or *The Pot of Gold,* 57: "[S]i hercle tu ex istoc loco digitum transvorsum aut unguem latum excesseris aut si respexis..." [You budge a finger's breadth, a nail's breadth from that spot...].—Ed.

37. Vico writes, "Next came Selden, whose excessive passion for Jewish erudition, in which he was extremely learned, led him to locate the origins of his system in the few precepts that God gave to the sons of Noah" (*FNS* 17).

38. Cf. Cicero, *De legibus* 1.21.—Ed.

39. Justinian, *Institutes* 1.2.11.—Ed.

peoples, desires that Divine Providence be considered as a divine will participating in human events,[40] nor Plato, who rationally demonstrated that there is an intelligent order independent of the order of nature, can be considered philosophers![41]

Digression on Human Ingenuity, Acute and Argute Remarks, and Laughter Arising from the Foregoing

[20] Philosophy, geometry, and philology, as well as any other branch of knowledge, clearly show the great absurdity of the opinion that ingenuity conflicts with truth.

[21] [*however, he indulges more in ingenuity* (q)] Let us begin with philosophy, for philosophers agree with and approve of the popular saying that ingenuity is the divine source of all discoveries. It would be desirable for philosophers to work in accordance with [Francis] Bacon's *Novum Organum* in order to substantiate with experiments the truth of their theories, for this is what Bacon meant to do when he labored to supplement his *Novum Organum* with his *Cogitata et Visa*. Certainly the art, or science, of thinking has been characteristic of the British since antiquity when, as Tacitus wrote in his *Life of Agricola*, the wise Agricola urged them to cultivate a humane education by stating that he preferred the "natural ingenuity of the Britons to the trained abilities of the Gauls."[42] This is why, even today, the British honor experimental philosophy above all other branches of philosophy. In fact, if the philosophers dedicated themselves to physics, not only could one hold, with Socrates, that the cobblers are to be more highly esteemed than the Sophists because the cobblers produce something useful to mankind while the Sophists produce nothing,[43] but one might maintain further that those who apply philosophy to physics become somewhat like God omnipotent, in whom knowing and making are one and the same.

---

40. Cicero, *De divinatione* 1.117.—Ed.
41. Plato, *Laws* 900C–D and 903B–C.—Ed.
42. Tacitus, *Agricola* 21.2.—Ed.
43. Plato, *Apology* 22C–D.—Ed.

[22] Although I have made only a rudimentary study of the elements of geometry, I nevertheless understand that, by using the synthetic method of the ancients, one could rapidly survey the innumerable propositions of Euclid (which are the basic principles of size and quantity) and could select and bring together those propositions that, so long as they were read separately and at random, did not seem to have among them any πρός τι [relation][44] or *rapporto,* as one says in Italian. I also understood that synthetic geometry bases its demonstrations of truth on these same principles with respect both to problems construed with ruler and compass, even though the latter may be purely imaginary, and with respect to the theorems that it regards as true.[45] Surely this can be achieved only by those who have been endowed with extraordinary ingenuity. Hence, the specialist in geometry is like a god in his world of figures just as God omnipotent is somewhat like a geometer in the world of minds and bodies. It is certainly significant that the Italians should call *ingegneri* [engineers]—a very fitting term fraught with scientific significance—those who apply geometry to mechanics in both civil and military projects. The analytic method in no sense upsets what we are saying about synthetic geometry, for it stems from a godlike, hidden power of ingenuity that makes students of algebra feel as if they were divining when they arrive at a demonstration of truth by means of a well-conducted rational process. What the synthetic student often achieves by a very hard process the analytic student achieves by a quick, easy, and clever process. This analytic process can certainly be the result of nothing other than some supreme power of ingenuity.

[23] I have already remarked on physics, the adjunct of which is medicine. As for politics and its related topics of statesmanship, leadership, oratory, and jurisprudence, if we take oratory as an example, we can easily make out that they alone can achieve most who are able to prevail by their ingenuity. Our feeble human ingenuity is overcome only when faced with theology, which is revealed to us by the divine ingenuity of God omnipotent who is the first

44. Aristotle, *Categories* 1^{b}.27.
45. Cf. Cicero, *De fato* 11.—Ed.

truth. Theological truths, because they exceed the possibility of human understanding, must be held to be truer than those based on the demonstrations of geometry; and algebra demonstrates its indubitable truths with a minimal amount of that divine ingenuity that, as we have said, surpasses human understanding.

[24] Finally, we learn from philology that ingenuity in rhetoricians cannot exist without truth. And truly, this acuity focuses on, and binds together within a system of common relationships whose truth is hidden, things that to ordinary people seem utterly diverse and disparate. By formulating a long series of reasonings, these diverse things can be shown to be close and mutually interrelated, held together by a harmonious bond. This is why, according to Aristotle, we so much like acute remarks, because, upon hearing such remarks, our mind, which by its very nature hungers for truth, learns many things in the brief span of a moment.[46]

[25] On the contrary, argute remarks are the product of a feeble and narrow imagination that either compares mere names of things, regarding only their external appearances (and not all of them), or presents some of them absurdly or unsuitably to an unthinking mind that, while expecting appropriate and suitable ones, is deluded and frustrated in its expectation. Therefore, when the brain fibers, focused on an appropriate and suitable object, are disturbed by an unexpected one, they become disordered. Being agitated, they transmit their restless motion to all branches of the nervous system. This shakes the whole body and removes man from his normal state. Animals are deprived of laughter because they have one sense only, which enables them to pay attention to but one object at a time. Hence, any one object is continuously expelled and deleted by the subsequent one. It is thus perfectly obvious that since animals have been denied by nature the ability to laugh, they are also deprived of all reason. At this point, I must mention that those who laugh at a serious thing are secretly impelled to do so, even if they do not realize it. Precisely because laughter is a human prerogative, they feel that by laughing they are experiencing that they are men. But laughter

---

46. Cf. Aristotle, *Poetics* 1457^b 6–32.—Ed.

comes from our feeble human nature, which "deceives us by the semblance of right."[47] And, in fact, from this interpretation of laughter, laughing men [*ridiculi*] are halfway between austere, serious men and the animals.

[26] By "laughing men" [*ridiculi*], I here mean both those who laugh immoderately and without reason, who should be more properly called "cacklers" [*risores*] and those who make others laugh, who should properly be called "mockers" [*derisores*]. Serious people do not laugh because they pay attention to one thing only and are not distracted by other things. Animals also do not laugh, because they too pay attention to but one thing at a time; but, when they are distracted by another object, they immediately turn all their attention to it. Because they attend so lightly to one thing, the cacklers are easily distracted by another. Quite remote from serious men and the nearest to the animals are the mockers, who corrupt the very appearance of truth. Not only do they naturally corrupt truth, but they pervert it. By using a certain force or violence on themselves, on their minds, and on truth, they take "that which is" and contort it into something else. Gnatho, the parasite in Terence's play, speaks of this force when he says: "Whatever they say, I praise it; if they say the opposite, I praise that too."[48] Poets added to this truth with their fables, in which they depicted cacklers as satyrs, as if they were between men and animals.

[27] Deprived of divine truth by their own perverse nature, the mockers are forever precluded from the treasures of truth. And when they delight in mocking true and serious things, the words of divine wisdom truly apply to them: "If you are wise, you are wise for yourself; if you are a mocker, you alone will bear it."[49] From this explanation of the nature of laughter it follows that comic characters delight us especially when they say foolish things seriously, whereas they often leave us without reaction when they try to make the audience laugh by laughing themselves. Humor is never more agreeable than when the mimes imitate serious

47. Horace, *Ars poetica* 25.—Ed.
48. Terence, *The Eunuch* 252–53.—Ed.
49. Proverbs 9:12.—Ed.

and austere men with their facial expressions, walk, and actions; through their imitations they bring such men onto the stage in order to make people laugh at and ridicule them. These observations return us to our original premise that laughter stems from deception perpetrated on human ingenuity that hungers for truth, and consequently erupts the more profusely the greater the simulation of truth.

[28] This simulation of truth is why Cicero says truly and elegantly that "the seat of laughter lies in the unseemly or 'slightly base': not the 'disgraceful or immoderately base.'"[50] By "immoderately base" I mean, in point of fact, that which is shamefully false, contrary to truth or, even worse, self-negating and "contradictory," as one says in scholastic terms—contradictory being something that exerts a painful influence on the mind, which, as a result, is enraged and offended by these shameful untruths. By "slightly base," on the other hand, I mean something such as when an acute remark refers to one thing as appearing different from, but really being the same as, another [that is, truth disguised as falseness]; an argute saying concerns something that appeared identical to, but later is revealed to be different from, another [that is, falseness veiled in some appearance of truth]. If the latter is presented when least expected, it provokes laughter as, for example, when some comic characters suddenly appear on the stage. Divine wisdom teaches that "laughter abounds in the mouths of fools,"[51] who the Latins aptly described as "not resolute of mind," because the brain fibers are always faltering, vacillating, and lapsing. Nature itself teaches us this very truth by means of visible, physical movements when, at the sight of somebody falling or slipping, we can hardly refrain from laughing.

[29] Because this instability of mind is the principal cause of foolishness, philosophy dedicates itself to overcoming this instability above all else and principally aims at reinforcing the wise; from this same fact it can be understood how different is the pleasure that spectators procure from plays in which the characters

---

50. Cf. Cicero, *De oratore* 2.236 and 264; Quintilian 5.3.8.—Ed.
51. Cf. Ecclesiastes 7:6.—Ed.

are morally well delineated than from those that the Latins called Oscan or Atellan and are now by us called *commedie burlesche* [commedia dell'arte].[52] In effect the former produce a delight worthy of the wise, whose minds tend always toward the uniform, suitable, and appropriate; this delight is in intensity the same as that which pervades the spectator at a game, as for example, when he sees the trajectory of a ball finish exactly where the player had directed it and to where the ball should go. Because of the difficulty of properly representing characters, only those who engage in the study of moral philosophy can compose representations in which characters are properly delineated; farcical representations produce instead a type of excessive dissolute pleasure and can reduce even the sane to the insane, in whom by means of laughter all powers of right reasoning are annulled.

[30] Demosthenes, undoubtedly the most acute of all orators, continually used an inimitable manner of speaking in which he distracted his listeners from his theme and directed their attention to other arguments ever more diverse so that they foolishly asked themselves where Demosthenes, wandering from point to point, wished to go to make his case. Yet in these divergent but elegant expressions he always found the way to return to the argument of the subject he was treating,[53] happily developing it according to his thesis. In so doing, his great ability to argue always reached out to insert within his vibrant words brief and efficacious considerations, *enthymemes*,[54] to use the Greek term, which, like a flash of lightning, struck all the more violently the more unexpected they were. Hence he was called *orator enthymematicus*, and by Longinus was compared to lightning.[55] He learned this mode of discussion from Plato to whom for many years he listened.[56] And Plato, making use of Socratic dialectic, while he spoke with various persons of one thing, put forth a question about another thing that seemed

---

52. Cf. Horace, *Ars poetica* 319–20.—Ed.

53. Longinus 22.3–4.—Ed.

54. Juvenal, *Satire* 6.449–50.—Ed.

55. Cf. Ausonius, *Epistles*, "Ausonius to Symmachus" 2; Longinus 12.4 and 34.4; Cicero, *De oratore* 234.—Ed.

56. Cf. Cicero, *De oratore* 15.—Ed.

completely different. Then he showed that what the interlocutor considered as different coincided in reality with the very thing that had initiated the discussion. This mode of proceeding, which the Greeks call *dialectica,* was introduced by the most wise of the philosophers, Socrates, to exercise the distinctive logical capacity of the Greeks, who surpass in ingenuity all the nations of the earth. Demosthenes, who was very adept in ingenuity, was never able to any extent to arouse laughter with his orations, and if at any time he wished to attempt it, he was so very inept at it, as Cicero relates, that the result was to make himself appear ridiculous.[57]

[31] From all I have said let this unknown vagabond show how much ingenuity is contrary to truth, for there is nothing to equal how ingenuity seeks with infinite care to arrive at truth; from the moment that this question arose, I have over and over insisted on showing how this vagabond, along with the opinion of the vulgar, holds as true the doctrine that eloquence is something completely other than philosophy.

[32] [*than in truth* (r)] Oh, indeed, what a masterful lover of truth this fellow is, who manifestly lies about my book being in octavo, who claims I have concealed my name from the learned, and that I am an abbé! And I, every time I consider and reflect further on this matter, am more than a little amazed that a bad habit can not only corrupt but pervert upright human nature. This unknown vagabond must have been born, nurtured, and raised among falsities and lies. These having taken root in him, he who, in the preceding, made up lies—that my system is a "figment" or "fabrication"—now makes up lies about my book, holding that I do not indulge in truth. And so this miserable man, in accord with an example of how miserable one can be, shows himself to be one of those men who, as the divine Plato says, pass all of life in a cave with their backs to the entrance, seeing only the shadows they themselves project on the wall of the cave, and who, if by chance, turn toward the entrance of the cave, erroneously hold that the bodies existing outside the cave are shadows.[58]

57. Cf. Cicero, *De oratore* 90; Longinus 34.3; Dionysius of Halicarnassus, "Demosthenes" 54; Quintilian 6.3.2 and 10.1.107.—Ed.

58. Plato, *Republic* 514A–D.—Ed.

[33] [*because of the large shapeless mass of his conjectures he fails at his own endeavor* (s)] But look! In my science concerning the common nature of the nations, which extends to all peoples and that embraces all ages, this strict and authoritative critic of philosophical systems laments the lack of coherence; he who in this brief fable that he fabricates of me contradicts himself at every step!

[34] First, what are the incoherencies among these affirmations? The author, a Neapolitan, of a new system conforming to the ingenuity, the mentality, of the Roman Catholic religion, conceals his name among Roman Catholics! And a Roman Catholic system is received with tedium by all of the Italian nation that is Roman Catholic! Has perhaps the author concealed his name just for this reason—that is, in order not to be crushed by this tedium of the Italians? But there are only two things that will crush authors of new doctrines: when such authors with their doctrines undermine the basis either of religion or of the government of their state.

[35] Second, how credible are his other affirmations? A very small book in duodecimo has annoyed to the point of tedium the whole Italian nation! And supposedly the author, who has annoyed to this extent all his fellow countrymen, has been able to conceal from them his first name, status, and social class!

[36] Finally, how are these affirmations at odds with themselves? Is it because this book has driven to tedium the whole Italian nation? Is it perhaps because the author has labored to debate the doctrines and principles of Grotius and Pufendorf? But it derives just from the nature of nations that he who enters into a forceful polemic with the most illustrious and learned of other nations procures, because of his emulation of the glory of his own nation, the greatest pleasure for his people and wins the favor of them all. Or perhaps it is because the argument of the book is already amply treated by the learned transalpine thinkers, which indeed comprise a rich group of writers: Grotius, Selden, Pufendorf, the principal exponents of this doctrine; various Grotian thinkers such as [Wilhelm] van der Muelen, [Jean] Barbeyrac, [Johann Heinrich] Boeckler, [Gaspar] Ziegler; refiners of the work of Grotius, Gronow [Gronovius], [Philippe Reinhald] Glaser; and also [Johann Franz] Budde, [Johann Joachim] Zentraw,

[Ulrich] Hüber, [Christian] Thomas,[59] and beyond these most famous thinkers, a great many others of minor fame! This is just the way things stand. But if someone by the name of Vico, after having confuted the principles of the natural law of the gentes of these transalpine thinkers, had elaborated a new method, would this cause so much tedium throughout Italy? In these times in which everyone wishes to comprehend things easily, it is alone sufficient for the titles of books to announce a new method to render them acceptable and of interest. This fellow has explicitly reported that this book of Vico is an absolutely new system. It is the things that are repeated, customary, and old that generate satiety, distaste, and tedium, but "all new things are pleasurable," as a well-known proverb says. My book, the unknown vagabond says, more than a system is truly a "figment" or "fabrication." I know that there is nothing more pleasing than a fabrication that is appropriate, graceful, and harmonious in all of its aspects. With this point this unknown vagabond thought he already had me in his fist because he thought that in this fabrication, because of its mass of conjectures, I would fall into contradictions. He just says these things. In the brief little fable he fabricates about me and my book, does he not at every step contradict himself, as we have seen?

[37] In considering his lies I cannot but remain amazed by seeing how this unknown vagabond entangles himself abortively in his own contradictions and by seeing how shameless he is! He wishes his fable to be believed and he thinks it can be believed even though what he demonstrates as true is in fact the contrary; he cannot fabricate this fable about me and my book without at the same time claiming to demonstrate as true what he claims cannot be demonstrated as true, yet what he demonstrates as not true is exactly in opposition to reality [he creates a fable (that in reality is untrue) to demonstrate that something is not true because it is a fable]. In fact he is so preoccupied that he withholds his name from you, concealing himself behind these words "an Italian" as if an Italian would disapprove of a system conforming to the ingenuity of the pontifical Church? This is how this

---

59. For information on each of these, see Vico, *Varia*, 262–63.

delicate person comports himself. Does he wish to make credible
that I have concealed my name for reasons opposite to those for
which he has concealed his name? Why does he wander unknown
through all of Italy concealing himself behind this generic name
of "an Italian"? Is it not perhaps because of the fear that the place
in Italy from which he originates will be discovered, is he in reality
bitten by a bad conscience, and in danger of being hated by all
the Italian nation, because he claimed that a system conforming
to the ingenuity of the pontifical Church was received with tedium by all the Italian nation? Why does he comport himself with
such rectitude toward me? Does he wish it believed that I annoy
the Italians for the same reason that he is hated by the Italians?
He laments the lack of coherence in an almost infinite system
that is meditated with very great diligence, and laments this in a
very brief fable that is so incoherent, so incongruent, and so in
contradiction with itself!

[38] [*and by the Italians themselves he is received more with tedium* (t)
than with applause] Although in the preceding note all the causes
of the tedium of the Italians are exposited and confuted, it is still
necessary to consider one more time that there subsists a reason
for this unknown vagabond to make these claims; what is it? He
declares it, but he declares it without realizing it. In fact I will
extract it precisely from his review: It is because he did not understand the book. Why, then, has he remained silent about this
reason? Is it not because he is ashamed to put it in his review, in
which he has not hesitated to invent many jokes about me and to
create so many falsities about my book? Why, then, has this great
shame not been mastered by him who is himself so clever that he
in effect puts in writing that he cannot comprehend this book?
And is it not even more shameful that he has told these impudent
lies about me and my book? I will explain it for him: Because the
principles of the nations being treated in this book, with nothing
being proposed in it at any point that is at odds with the common
sense [*sensus communis,* viz communal sense] of all human beings,
he himself, if he had adduced the personal motivation of his tedium, would have put in writing his failure to have such humane
common sense. I will attempt to look into the heart, mind, and
animus of this unknown vagabond and show you his character.

[39] He, with a mind obscured by the accumulation of lies of which I have spoken, with an animus swollen with arrogance, opened by chance this book and, reading what he could understand, now on this and now on that page, was unable to comprehend the meaning of the book—in fact, how has he been able to comprehend even one thing with such a mentality? He immediately despised the book and was annoyed by it. Just as there are persons who are wont to be bored and bothered by the smallest amount of contrariety and who arrogantly attribute to others their own faults, so he attributes as my incomprehensibility his own incapacity to understand; and as in general it is the habit of human beings, that from the state of their own mind judge the state of mind of everyone else, he has attributed to all Italians his own tedium. But perhaps with a point that is so evident, to attempt to prove or make conjectures about it is unnecessary. From the moment that this book was published it was received in Italy by men of very great fame and doctrine with very much favor, as containing, in a very small book, an argument respectful of religion that is profound and important. In a year or a little more the book has become difficult to find, and if found, it is sold throughout the bookstores in the same city in which the author was born at the price of two gold coins. The most illustrious men of nobility and doctrine in Venice, Count Giovanni Artico di Porcía, whose great importance I have mentioned above, the Reverend Father Carlo Lodoli, official censor of the Most Serene Republic of Venice, and the most eminent Abbé Antonio Conti, member of the most important order of senators, well known among the English, Dutch, you gentlemen of Germany, and of France, who, thanks to the results of his personal studies, has won the esteem of the most famous men of letters of our age, insistently exhorted me with their letters to send my book to Venice with my annotations or comments so that it could be reprinted in an elegant format in Claudian or royal paper. Initially I obediently heeded their exhortations. But because of the success of this book, I believe, a good many booksellers and printers in Venice requested, through the bookseller Bernardino Gessari and the printer Felice Mosca, both of Naples, to have sent to them all the books that, as I said above, are listed in the catalog added to my *Vita*, in order to

reprint them in one corpus in elegant format. But on reflection, having thanked these gentlemen of Venice for their courtesy, I refused to do it, and I responded negatively to Gessari and to Mosca, because I wish, if humanly possible, that of all the books written by me, this one alone, the book I now discuss with you, to be my only work to remain.

Conclusion of the Notes

[40] To summarize what has been said and to bring it to completion, I strongly suspect, and, because all these considerations point to the same conclusion, I firmly make the following conjecture: that this unknown vagabond will through his own experience find out if whether or not I have failed is due to "the large shapeless mass of my conjectures."

[41] This reporter has passed over in silence the specific argument of the *New Science;* he has lied, saying that the form of the book is in octavo and that I have concealed my name from the learned; further, he has lied about my status, said nothing of my profession, and also in his contact with you he withheld my first name; he declared that the principal argument of the *Science* is the natural law of the gentes, but he passed over in this declaration that I also criticize Selden, who although holding a somewhat different doctrine from Grotius and Pufendorf is one of the principal exponents of natural law; he has declared that my system is a figment or fabrication and has falsely said that it is not derived from the true doctrine of the Roman Catholic Church but conforms to the ingenuity of the pontifical Church, and he has absurdly held that in this system I indulge more in ingenuity than in the truth; finally, and in this alone he is consistent: by lying he both began and continued his report, and by lying he concluded it, saying that this book is received with tedium by all the Italian nation. There are one after another, all these falsities, as I said above, about me and my book in your *Acta Eruditorum.* This reporter, I repeat, has related all these falsities because he wished in one malicious contrivance to gain five objectives: first, to injure my dignity; second, to assure that you would not make a careful investigation of the book; third, to render it difficult

to find a copy of it in case you would make a diligent search for it; fourth, to make you believe that if you did find the book that it was a completely different book by a completely different author; fifth, to conceal himself from you in the obscurity of his dark night of lies and continue to be considered by you as a faithful friend. Of these five objectives, the first aims at making my name obscure to you, the next three aim at diminishing the esteem for you throughout all of Europe by those into whose hands this book may come, the last aims to protect the obscurity of his name, in which he places all of his hope for impunity.

[42] Let me first of all treat the three points in regard to you, because the first regards me, and the last regards him. In case you were to ask a book dealer for a book in octavo, titled *Principles of a New Science of the Natural Law of the Gentes* by an anonymous author certainly he would respond that he had no knowledge of such a book by an anonymous author, with this title and in such a format. Thereupon you would say that although the author of this book conceals his name from the learned, nevertheless you are informed by an Italian friend that he is a Neapolitan abbé named Vico. If you were to search for this book in Naples where everyone knows that I am neither celibate nor without children the dealer would tell you that he was not acquainted with such a Neapolitan author of such a book. But he would tell you of knowing a Neapolitan by the name Giambattista Vico, who is married with children and who is the author of a book in duodecimo, not in octavo, titled *Principles of a New Science concerning the Nature of the Nations*. Finally, you should investigate all the books on the same topic that are more important than mine by more celebrated authors and then ask of the same book dealer, and if not him then another, if by a lucky chance he happens to have my book in his bookstore.[60] If he has it, he would have to sell it to you for a very high price because in this short time it has become very rare, as I have said above. Reading the book you will see that the specific argument of this science is the common nature of the nations, which is derived from the fact that all peoples have an equal consciousness of the

---

60. Terence, *The Eunuch* 134.—Ed.

origin of things human and divine. You would see that from this discovery there arises a new system of the natural law of the gentes that confutes not only those systems of Grotius and Pufendorf but also that of Selden, another principal exponent of this doctrine. You would also become aware of the fact that this system is based on principles common to all the human race and also to the pontifical Church and, as I am convinced, that this system is supported by a solid and coherent demonstration. Furthermore, having paid a very high price for this book in relation to its small size and in relation to so many other recent publications, and because elevated prices are the best demonstration of the best and most sought-after products, you would understand why this book is much requested by the Italians. For all these reasons, certainly you would conclude, by Hercules, that this book has nothing to do with that of which this unknown vagabond has spoken, and, having recognized that I am this same Giambattista Vico whom he lies about and whom the most honorable Monsieur Le Clerc spoke about with the greatest dignity and respect in regard to my other book, which, as I recalled earlier, treats the same argument, even if only in outline, you would present it more truly and judge it more equably and speak of me more respectfully.

[43] Thus, erudite gentlemen of Leipzig, in these *Notes* I have discussed your responsibility; now it remains for me to treat the rest of my case, which is to speak in a manner for his own good to the unknown vagabond who has lied by claiming one thing to be another and who, about other things, has spoken wrongly.

Admonition to the Unknown Vagabond

[44] Tell me, my good man, if you were a member of the lowest social class of your city, one of the foul plebs engaged in economic activity admiring only vile money and you were to rob money from your master, do you not know that you would be condemned for fraud and be subjected to a shameful punishment? And if you deserve a punishment this severe for being guilty of the criminal pursuit of vile money, would you not deserve an even greater punishment if you with all your might committed an offense against the dignity and the reputation of an honorable

Neapolitan who never has done anything against you? He who in fact has conducted his life in a respectful manner toward everyone, helping many, not harming anyone, and having experienced misfortune himself and just because of such experience, in order to find consolation, took comfort in the study of wisdom, who with great effort and dedication sought simply within the limits of his modest means to increase the fame not only of the Neapolitan people, but of all Italians, and the glory of the Roman Catholic Church, and this most important branch of studies on the natural law of the gentes, in which the men of letters beyond the Alps who above all are the most illustrious and dedicated, was he not absolutely the first among the Italians to render most solid the basis of the natural law of the gentes in accord with the principles of the Roman Catholic religion? To have committed such villainy, if you are Catholic, is it not grave, and if also Italian, yet even more grave, and if in addition, Neapolitan, the most grave? I wish only to put aside, unknown vagabond, your villainous statements and acts done against me, as you will soon realize that they do not remain as things said and done against me.

[45] Why do you say these things to the illustrious literati of the community of scholars of Leipzig, who make every effort to be useful to the Republic of Letters, giving their attention to reviewing literary works; who proclaim to be tied to you by a sacred bond of friendship, calling you "our Italian friend," who entrust their dignity and their good name to your scrupulousness and your rectitude, who have such great trust in your good faith that they have sworn on your words, accepting for true the shameless lies that you recount to them, not hesitating to publish them in their name and divulge this as the truth to all of learned Europe; and you trick them, you deceive them, you betray them to such an extent that they are induced to write a notice of a work and of an author absolutely contradictory, as if it was a completely different work and a completely different person, which is certainly a monstrosity, and who have no way to understand that you are responsible for their errors, because in their German good faith why should they believe that you would inform them of a different book and a different author? In doing what you have done, in the name of immortal God, have you not canceled friendship

from human relations and from civil life, and even more serious, overturned the foundations of human society?

[46] Perhaps you would say that the carelessness in the investigation of my book, the difficulty in procuring a copy of it, the error concerning another book and another author, are things which you, Oh Vico, say that I have wished to induce the literati of Leipzig to believe, but they are, in fact, three types of errors that are commonly encountered by the men of letters of Europe, and thus the particular dignity of those of Leipzig is safe. But if this were your argument you would clearly demonstrate the unjust rage with which you obscured your mind, you who do not realize that the wrong you believe you have done to me has in reality no substance; in fact this defense that you might be inclined to adduce as your proof of innocence resolves itself to my advantage and that of the literati of Leipzig; because the book, the genuine offspring of my mind, is already noted in all of Italy, beyond the Alps, and across the ocean, with which literati of Europe have you hurt my dignity? Or do you think perhaps that the fame of someone's name consists in this: that those among whom the fame of an illustrious man is spread are preoccupied to know his countenance, shape, complexion, stature, and bearing? Oh illustrious men, you who are now dead or who are alive in distant places, you who have acquired the fame of your name with virtue, doctrine, and wisdom, according to this fellow are empty shadows because your bodily features never can be known by posterity or by foreigners!

[47] Because, therefore, you were not successful in injuring my dignity with all of those who in error have been led to believe that the book is not mine and that another is the author of it, you had certainly wished to injure my dignity among those who clearly know that this hypothetical book and the hypothetical author do not in reality exist. And who are these if not the community of learned gentlemen of Naples? Therefore, Oh vagabond, your personal hatred of me, which you vomit and spew out to all of the learned Neapolitans, who according to the chatter that you spread to all peoples—namely, that they are annoyed with my book because it demonstrates the validity of the true religion and that of the monarchical regime by which they are ruled—do you

think that they would instead aspire to the popular liberty of the citizens of Leipzig? And then, consider the incredible perversity of your soul, you who have done all this only because you remain to the end frustrated in that which you desire, which makes you burn much more forcefully with the jealousy that consumes you. And in fact by wishing to spread the view that a nonexistent man is summarily judged by the literati of Leipzig, together with the false information that the Italians have met with tedium the book that also does not exist, you have offered me a splendid possibility of glory; for from what you have said my personal case accords well with the love of my homeland, the glory of Italy, and the sanctity of the Roman Catholic religion, and my personal defense is united with the defense of my homeland, of Italy, and of the Roman Catholic religion! Whether what I say about you is either true or false is not the issue, but did you not think, as anyone might, of the consequences if someone from Naples were to notify the literati of Leipzig that this book and this Neapolitan author did not exist and never did exist, did you not think what a deep reaction they would have, how penitent they would feel having put their trust in you with their excessive good faith, how strongly they would have lamented the fact that you betrayed their friendship? Perhaps you could respond, a response that is always base, and one habitually used by those who would excuse their acts by pleading ignorance[61]: "I did not intend to injure them, only to injure you." And is it not sufficient from what I say to you for you above all to understand that, by denigrating me, you were necessarily harming the authority of all the academies of letters, that the just review of this book is the one all those academies will make, not yours, that of the unknown vagabond, that in fact it is those of posterity, immune from any form of complaisance, who are ultimately entrusted with its just evaluation, and that, most seriously, have you understood that your attempt at inflicting a grievous wound on me, your envy of Italian glory, and your hatred of the Roman Catholic religion are wrong enough to make you

---

61. Cf. Seneca, *Epistles* 76.35. See also Vico, *On Humanistic Education (Six Inaugural Orations 1699–1707)*, trans. Giorgio A. Pinton and Arthur W. Shippee (Ithaca, N.Y.: Cornell University Press, 1993), 70 (Second Oration, par. 14).—Ed.

an enemy? Furthermore, in raising your hostile sword against me how many of your friends and how many literati have you also been obliged to wound?

[48] See to what a precipitous place you have come, so extreme that you implore us to excuse you for your grave criminal acts, adducing as your proof of innocence greater and more grave criminal acts! What you have done should not in fact be called cruel, but inhuman. If a soldier who is upright in his love for his countrymen would save one of them by killing an enemy he would deserve to be decorated with a medal, but if it emerges that he did this by running his sword through another of his countrymen in order also to pierce this enemy, it would not be cruel but inhuman. Is this not what you have done, not in battle but in the tranquil leisure of letters—have you not committed exactly the same monstrous act against duty, loyalty, and friendship? Or do you perhaps believe that it is a crime to wound a body, but it is no more than a joke and a prank to wound the mind and soul, thanks to which we alone are human beings. But the jealous rage that agitates you turns back against you and it torments you with blind fury, you who through your ferocious hate, in attempting to strike me perforated and pierced through the shield that protected you. You struck out at me just as I was out of range, you who gave notice of another book and another author, and because this other book and other author do not in reality exist, you certainly are a crazy person who strikes out at shadows, and the enemy you strike is one who in reality you have invented.

[49] This is who you are, an empty shadow, closed in the thick darkness of your name. Because you are hurtful to friends and enemies alike, not having the courage to confront in public the looks of men; because you flee from your own homeland without anyone persecuting you, having no place where you can stay on either side of the Alps; and because doctrine and erudition make men of good character better, but they make wicked men perverse in the extreme, for all these forceful reasons, I exhort you and invite you to renounce and remove from yourself as rapidly as possible your claim to be a learned man; it is better to be uncultivated but have integrity than to wander unknown and guilty, banished from the human race, even if greatly learned.

[50] Finally, gentlemen of letters of Leipzig, in order to repair your negligence in not reading my book, brought about by using this fellow as your source for it, I have, with these *Notes*, made it necessary for you to read it; I do not wish you to remain any longer in the erroneous view of my book this vagabond has caused, but I no longer possess a copy of it and am waiting for it to be reprinted in Venice so that a copy may be sent to you. Please know in the meantime what I affirm in these *Notes*, that I am the true author of the true book and that I rightly claim to be the true Vico, the identity this vagabond took from me, hence at the beginning of this book is inscribed *Vici Vindiciae*.

Appeal to the Equable Reader

[51] You then, equable reader, know that I composed this little work while I was ill with a gangrenous ulcer of the throat, not only a deadly illness with a rapid course, but one with a dangerous treatment that can cause apoplexy in older persons. For a good twenty years I have consulted all works possible with my weak powers to make a contribution to the doctrine of the natural law of the gentes; working tirelessly, I entombed myself completely in the silence of a great library rich in all the various works of human thought, where I meditated on the most ancient authors of all nations from whom after more than a thousand years modern writers take their beginnings. Thomas Hobbes proceeded in this way and among his literary friends and contemporaries he prided himself in being the initiator of the doctrine of natural law and of having enriched philosophy with it, but he was instead mistaken in this self-praise because he did not consider Divine Providence. Such a consideration would have illuminated for him the route he was seeking that would lead back to a knowledge of the obscure origins of humanity, lost in the nighttime of antiquity. Instead he remained with the blind chance of Epicurus, whose doctrine and principles I have criticized and for which I received the most ample praise from Monsieur Le Clerc in his *Bibliothèque*. I forgot to say this in the note marked with the letter *k* above. In his remarks the vagabond maliciously remained silent concerning what the principles are by which the philosophers,

according to him, deduce their systems of the natural law of the gentes; among these philosophers is Pufendorf, but he must be set aside because of the suspicion that he adhered to Epicureanism, also Grotius because of the influence of Socinianism on his thought that teaches that Providence is common to all religions and identical in each of them and that thus does not acknowledge the possibility of attributing any originality to the truth of the Christian religion. Grotius wrote an early book on just this subject [*De Veritate Religionis Christianae*]. In his *De Iure Belli et Pacis* [*On the Law of War and Peace*] he did not even consider Providence in the sense that it conforms to the truth of the Christian religion, something, if I do not err for love of my own work, I have demonstrated in my system.

[52] For these reasons and the preceding example of the serious lapse of memory I have offered,[62] if I have left something incompletely treated and not fully polished in its expression,[63] kindly consider it equably.[64]

---

62. Tacitus, *Annals* 3.68.—Ed.
63. Horace, *Satires* 1.5.35; *Ars poetica* 294.
64. Quintilian 1.6.32.

PART 3

Additions to the
Second New Science
(1730/1744)

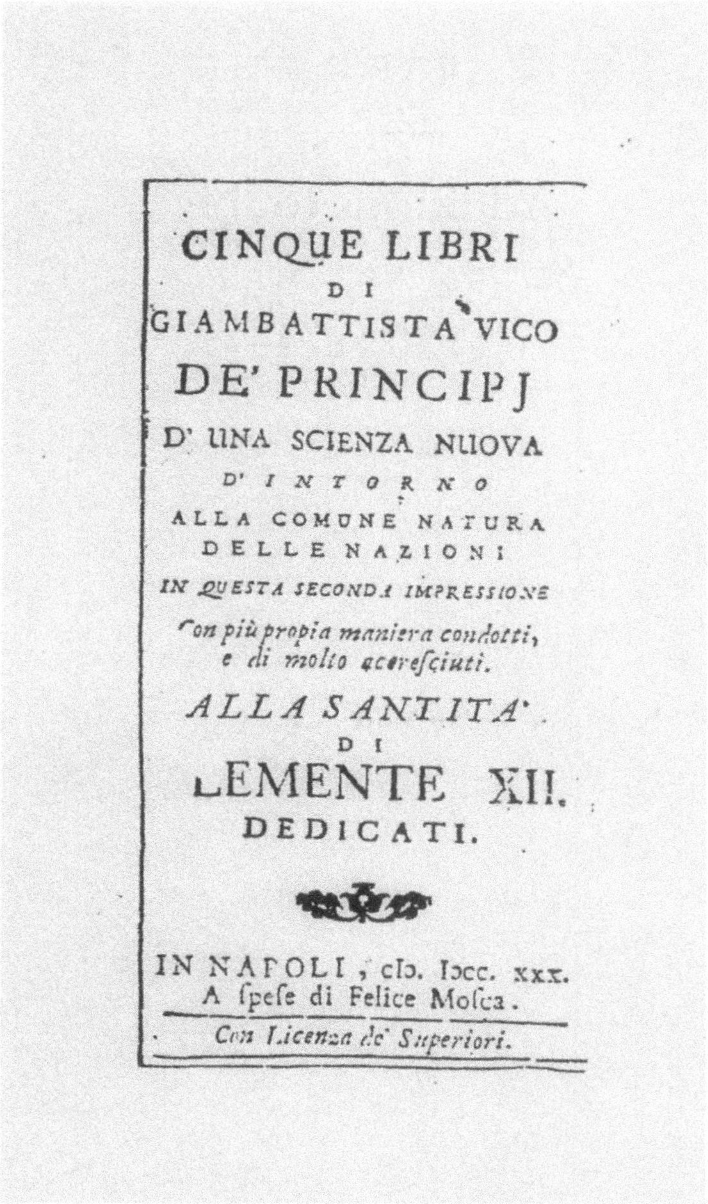

CINQUE LIBRI
D I
GIAMBATTISTA VICO
DE' PRINCIPJ
D' UNA SCIENZA NUOVA
D' I N T O R N O
ALLA COMUNE NATURA
DELLE NAZIONI
IN QUESTA SECONDA IMPRESSIONE
con più propia maniera condotti,
e di molto accresciuti.

ALLA SANTITA'
D I
CLEMENTE XII.
DEDICATI.

IN NAPOLI, cɔ. Iɔcc. xxx.
A spese di Felice Mosca.
Con Licenza de' Superiori.

Figure 4. Title page of the *Scienza nuova* (1730).

Figure 5. Dipintura or frontispiece of the 1730 edition of the *Scienza nuova*.

Figure 6. Portrait of Vico with couplet by Domenico Ludovico (1744).

Figure 7. Dipintura or frontispiece of the 1744 edition of the *Scienza nuova*.

PRINCIPJ

DI

SCIENZA NUOVA

DI

GIAMBATTISTA VICO

D'INTORNO ALLA COMUNE NATURA
DELLE NAZIONI

IN QUESTA TERZA IMPRESSIONE

Dal medefimo Autore in un gran numero di luoghi
Corretta, Schiarita, e notabilmente Accrefciuta.

TOMO I.

IN NAPOLI MDCCXLIV.

NELLA STAMPERIA MUZIANA

A fpefe di Gaetano, e Steffano Elia.

CON LICENZA DE' SUPERIORI.

Figure 8. *Impresa* of the title page of the 1744 edition of the *Scienza nuova.*

Vico's "IGNOTA LATEBAT"

On the Impresa and the Dipintura

DONALD PHILLIP VERENE

Vico's Three Editions of the *New Science*

The Edition of 1725

Giambattista Vico published the first edition of his *New Science* in October 1725. It has come to be known as the *First New Science* (*Scienza nuova prima*), the term that Vico himself applied to it in his *Autobiography* (A 192–94). The *frontespizio,* or what is commonly known in contemporary English-language books as the "title page," contains (1) the title in full, *Principj di una scienza nuova intorno alla natura delle nazioni per la quale si ritrouvano i principj di altro sistema del diritto naturale delle genti* (Principles of a new science concerning the nature of nations by which are found the principles of another system of the natural law of the gentes); (2) a dedication of the work to Cardinal Lorenzo Corsini; and (3) publishing information (Naples, Felice Mosca, 1725). Vico's name does not appear on this page. This frontespizio of the 1725 edition has been variously reproduced,[1] and

---

1. For example, reproductions of the title page of the 1725 edition are to be found in the UTET edition of Vico's works edited by Nicola Abbagnano (Turin, 1952) and in the introductory discussion material of Paolo Rossi's edition of *La Scienza nuova* (Milan: Biblioteca Universale Rizzoli, 1977). But the standard Laterza edition edited by Fausto Nicolini (Bari: Laterza, 1931) does not reproduce the 1725 title page in facsimile; neither does the earlier Ferrari edition (Naples: Stamperia de' Classici Latini)—at least, not in the printing dated 1859).

the edition itself has been reproduced in a facsimile printing by Tullio Gregory.[2]

The Edition of 1730

Vico published a completely rewritten version of the *New Science* in December 1730. In his *Autobiography* Vico calls this the *Second New Science* (*Scienza nuova seconda*) and describes how he withdrew the manuscript he had sent to printers in Venice for this second edition and how he totally rewrote the work in a new version for publication under his own direct supervision in Naples. Vico regarded this second edition as completely replacing the first edition except for three passages that he thought the reader should still consider from book 3 of the first edition (*FNS* chaps. 30, 38, and 43), which concern the discovery of origins of family coats of arms as a kind of language, the discovery of the true causes of the Latin language, and the idea of a common mental language of all nations.[3] This second, definitive version of his work, Vico notes, was begun on Christmas morning 1729 and completed at nine o'clock on Easter Sunday evening, April 6, 1730. Not only was this a completely rewritten rather than revised text of Vico's original work, but the front matter of this second edition, when published, contained a dramatic change.

Vico claims in his *Autobiography* that he had suffered an affront by the person in charge of the printing of the second edition in Venice (A 192). The underlying reason may more likely have been ecclesiastical opposition to the edition (see the discussion of this in the commentary on the *Vici Vindiciae*). Vico demanded that the material he had originally sent be returned to him, a process that took six months. This involved a lengthy correspondence with Father Carlo Lodoli, who had originally requested and arranged for a second edition to be printed in Venice. Vico planned that the

---

2. Giambattista Vico, *Principj di una scienza nuova intorno alla natura delle nazioni* ("Ristampa anastatica dell'edizione Napoli 1725, seguita da concordanze e indici di frequenza"), ed. Tullio Gregory (Rome: Edizioni dell'Ateneo e Bizzarri, 1979).

3. The ideas of these three chapters of the *First New Science* are integrated into Vico's discussion of corollaries on the origins of languages and letters in this theory of poetic logic in the *Second New Science* (*NS* 428–55, esp. 445 and 452).

second edition, now being typeset in Naples, would begin with a *novella letteraria* that would publish the exchange of letters with Father Lodoli and a commentary especially presenting Vico's side of the affair. But after more than half of the second edition had been printed in Naples, Vico received a communication from Venice that caused him to suppress the novella, leaving a gap of eighty-six pages of the typeset text. To replace the material from this unhappy dispute, Vico commissioned the now well-known allegorical engraving, or *dipintura*, designed under Vico's supervision by Domenico Antonio Vaccaro and engraved by Antonio Baldi. Vico then wrote an explanation of the "idea of the work" by explaining the meaning of each of the items in the engraving with the specific title, "Explanation of the Picture [dipintura] placed as Frontispiece to Serve as Introduction to the Work." This was of the correct length to fill the pages left empty by the suppression of the novella.

The frontespizio proper, or title page, as opposed to Vico's additional frontispiece of the dipintura of the 1730 edition, is not commonly reproduced. The title page of the 1730 edition contains: (1) the title in full, stated more succinctly than that of the first edition and containing Vico's name: *Cinque libri di Giambattista Vico de' Principj d'una scienza nuova d'intorno alla commune natura delle nazioni, in questa seconda impressione* (Five books of Giambattista Vico on the principles of a new science concerning the common nature of nations, in this second edition); (2) a dedication, again to Lorenzo Corsini, who had in the interim become Pope Clement XII; and (3) publishing information (Naples, Felice Mosca, 1730).

The Edition of 1744

In the months preceding his death in late January 1744, Vico was revising and seeing through the press a third edition of the *New Science*. He had begun to correct printer's proofs, prepared the dedication for this edition to Cardinal Troiano d'Acquaviva, and had written instructions for the engraving of himself that appears at the front of this edition. Below this portrait of Vico is a couplet by his admirer, the Jesuit father Domenico Lodovico: "Vicus hic est: potuit vultum depingere Pictor, / O si quis mores posset, et ingenium" (This is Vico: the artist has been able to depict the expression of the face, / Oh, if someone were able to depict his character and genius). On receiving a copy of the 1730 edition of the *New Science* Lodovico wrote Vico, suggesting that a dwarf should be added beside the alphabet, in the dipintura, like Dante's mountaineer who is struck dumb with astonishment when he enters the city,[4] and that beneath the dwarf should be written "Lodo-Vico" ("I praise Vico").

Even as Vico was publishing the second (1730) edition of the *New Science* he was writing sets of annotations to be incorporated into the work when it would be printed for a third time ("quando si ristampi la terza volta"), as he reports in his *Autobiography* (*A* 197). There were four sets of these annotations and corrections made by Vico in the first three or four years following the publication of the 1730 edition. The fourth, comprehensive, set was done in 1733 or 1734; it became the basis for the revision of the text done in 1735 or 1736, which was to become the basis of the third edition of the *New Science* in 1744. Because the 1744 edition was a revision of the 1730 text and not a rewriting, Fausto Nicolini extended the term *Scienza nuova seconda* in the standard Laterza edition of Vico's works to cover the 1730/1744 editions. The Thomas Goddard Bergin and Max Harold Fisch English translation was made from the Laterza edition of Nicolini.

The front matter of the third edition of 1744 reprints the allegorical engraving or dipintura of the second edition of 1730 and adds the portrait of Vico and the new dedication mentioned above. This edition was published not by Felice Mosca but by Stamperia Muziana. Because the page size was enlarged from that of the 1730 edition the engraving had to be enlarged; this was done by Francesco Sesone. It is his enlargement of the dipintura rather than the earlier engraving by Baldi that is reproduced throughout the various editions of the *New Science*, including the Bergin and Fisch translation.[5] In addition to these items the 1744

---

4. Dante, *Divine Comedy, Purg.* 26.67–70.

5. The prominent exception to the practice of using the Sesone engraving of the *dipintura* is Ferrari's mid-nineteenth-century edition of Vico's work. In this edition the engraver, Gataneo, has created his own, greatly inferior version of

edition carries a very different title page. In addition to the title and publishing information, the lower half of this page is taken up by an *impresa,* or emblematic device, depicting a robed female figure with winged temples, seated on a globe while resting her right forearm on the surface of a large, adjoining plinth. She is holding a triangle in her right hand, and in her lowered left hand is a round mirror, into which she is gazing. On the side of the plinth is inscribed "IGNOTA LATEBAT."

In the two originals of the 1744 edition that I have seen, one in the Vatican Library and one in the Beinecke Rare Book and Manuscript Library at Yale University, Vico's portrait appears on the first verso page; across from it, on the recto, is the dipintura. As the reader turns past the dipintura the back of its page its verso, is blank, and on the opposite recto stands the title page with the impresa. Thus the reader encounters first Vico, vis-à-vis the dipintura, and then, turning the page, a second, smaller dipintura— the impresa, upon which Vico does not comment. Perhaps Vico would have left some comment on this impresa in an annotation to the text or in a letter, had he lived to see the publication of the 1744 edition—or perhaps not. It is reasonable to think that the impresa may be included at Vico's direction, on the grounds that before his death he was issuing instructions to the printer for the volume and preparing the front matter. This is circumstantial.

Vaccaro's design. Although one can recognize this as something like Vico's dipintura, the figures of both Homer and metaphysic are rendered very differently. The crack at the base of the statue of Homer has been eliminated, as have the signs of Virgo and Leo from the band around the globe, all the hieroglyphs of the civil world have been positioned slightly differently. This may have been undertaken to make the dipintura have a more "contemporary" or nineteenth-century look, as it has the visual sense and atmosphere of a romantic piece of that period. The result, however, is a truly "barbaric" presentation of Vico's original conception of these images.

Sesone's engraving of the dipintura is uninspired. Vaccaro, whom Vico commissioned to do the original design, was an eminent artist in the Naples of his day. Modern editions of the *Scienza nuova* simply reproduce the 1744 engraving of Sesone rather than the original 1730 engraving of Baldi. These editions apparently take the Sesone engraving as definitive because it is attached to the definitive version of the text, but a more definitive edition would combine the 1730 dipintura, done by Baldi under Vico's and Vaccaro's direction, with the 1744 text.

I know of no direct evidence that Vico commissioned the impresa in the way that it is known that he commissioned the design and engraving of the dipintura, and there is no artist's signature on the impresa. Whether it is deliberate on Vico's part or whether it may have entered the book through the printer, let us consider what it may signify as an existing part of the text. The reader may wish to compare the above remarks and those that follow with the reproductions herein.

"IGNOTA LATEBAT"

In the understanding of a text certainly no aspect of it can be ignored, as though it obviously had nothing to do with either its meaning or even the author's intentions. This is especially true of works in the Renaissance and modern periods, in which there is a great interest in devices and emblematic meanings. In connection with Vico's second *New Science* one has only to think of the emblematic character of the frontispiece of Thomas Hobbes's *Leviathan,* or of Jean-Jacques Rousseau's (later) use and comments on the emblematic scenes that adorn his two *Discourses.* Fisch suggests that Vico's use and explanation of the dipintura may have been influenced by Anthony Ashley Cooper, the Third Earl of Shaftesbury's procedure in the *Second Characters,* a point also made by Nicolini in his *Commento storico alla seconda Scienza nuova.*[6] Vico himself, in the first sentence of the *New Science,* compares the dipintura to the Tablet of Cebes; part of Shaftesbury's plan of the unfinished *Second Characters* was a commentary on this tablet, which in form would have been much like Vico's commentary on his engraving of the dipintura.

I think that the impresa of the title page of the third or 1744 edition of the *New Science* must be interpreted in connection

---

6. Fausto Nicolini, *Commento storico alla seconda Scienza nuova,* 2 vols. (Rome: Edizioni di Storia e Letteratura, 1949–50), 1:21. Shaftesbury spent the last fifteen months of his life (1711–13) in Naples. Nicolini also notes the possibility that Vico intends the female figure of metaphysic in the dipintura as a kind of counter to the materialist figure of the omnipotent power of the state in Hobbes's frontispiece.

with the dipintura. The principal element they have in common is the female figure with winged temples; she is seated on the globe in the impresa but is standing upon the globe in the dipintura. I think the analysis of the impresa itself must begin with the meaning of the inscription on the plinth: "IGNOTA LATEBAT." This is the written text of the emblem, so to speak, and it must be the key to how we are to give the emblem a literary meaning. The dipintura, unlike the impresa, contains no inscription. The literary meanings it signifies are contained in Vico's extended introductory commentary to the *Second New Science* (1730/1744). In the case of the impresa we are given not a commentary but a single statement, declared from within the scene of the device. How are we to understand this sentence, *Ignota latebat?* A fair rendering of the Latin is, "She, unknown, was lying hidden." The Latin is certainly clear enough, but a consideration of its basics may be useful as groundwork for understanding the meaning of the other elements in the impresa.

1. *Latebat.* The infinitive is *latere* (connected with the Greek *lanthanein*), "to escape notice"; *latebat* is the third person singular imperfect active indicative; thus, "was lying hidden." *Latere* in its literal meaning is "to lie hid," "to be concealed"; among its transferred meanings it can have the senses of "to live in obscurity" or "to be unknown." It is helpful to consider this in relation to the English *latent,* which derives from the present participle of *latere* (*latent:* "existing in hidden, dormant, or repressed form but usually capable of being evoked, expressed, or brought to light"). *Latent* is synonymous with potential, quiescent; the opposite of *patent.* It can also have the meaning of concealed, disguised. The Italian *latente* is similar in meaning, indicating something that does not manifest itself outwardly, something that is *riposto* ("hidden or secret"). A synonym is *nascosto* ("that which is not seen, hidden, concealed, or secret").

2. *Ignota.* The subject of the sentence is feminine, *ignota* being the feminine singular perfect passive participle of *ignosco, ignoscere,* having the sense of to take no cognizance of, to overlook; hence, "She, unknown..." or, "She, having been overlooked, not recognized...." The opposite of *ignoscere* is *cognoscere,* which is "to become

acquainted with, to get to know, to learn" (and, in the perfect tenses, "to know"). *Ignoto* ("unknown") in Italian has the synonym of *incognito*, "obscure"; as a substantive it can mean an unknown person. The feminine subject of the sentence surely refers to the female figure in the impresa. What does this *femina* or *donna* represent? She would appear to represent *filosofia* or, specifically, *la metafisica*, because of her similarity with the figure in the dipintura.

In the second paragraph of the second *New Science*, Vico calls the female figure or donna in the dipintura "la metafisica." This figure represents the new science itself, since Vico goes on in various places to identify his "scienza nuova" with "la metafisica"; for example, in his explanation of the "idea of the work" he writes, "*cosi questa Nuova Scienza, o sia la metafisica...*" (Thus, this New Science, or metaphysic..., *NS* 31). What has been overlooked and lying hidden is metaphysic as redefined and found in Vico's "new science." Because of the passive sense of the expression, *metaphysic* here has more the sense of something that has gone unrecognized than of something that has been actively or deliberately concealed. The sense of metaphysic that Vico wishes to endorse or being to light in his work is that of something that has been there in the background of human thought all along but has not been "found" or "discovered." It has gone unnoticed because we have not had the right perspective; no one has concealed it from us except ourselves.

The Impresa and the Dipintura

Those who know Vico's second *New Science* from only the English-language edition of Bergin and Fisch will not have been aware of the existence of the impresa. Only the dipintura is reproduced in it; Vico's original title page of the 1744 edition with the impresa is not reproduced. The Bergin and Fisch translation is made from the 1928 (third) edition of the standard Laterza edition of the *Scienza nuova*, edited by Nicolini. This edition, which is part of the major *Scrittori d'Italia* series, does not reproduce the impresa, only the dipintura. Later editions by Laterza, for example, in the *Biblioteca filosofica* (1974) and the *Universale Laterza* (1978) series, however, do include reproductions of the original 1744 title page. Among other Italian editions, some reproduce the impresa and others do not. For example, the UTET edition of the *Scienza nuova* and selected works edited by Nicola Abbagnano (1952/1976), the Rizzoli edition of the *Scienza nuova* edited by Paolo Rossi (1977), the volume on Vico in the *Grandi libri* series of Garzanti edited by Pasquale Soccio (1983), and the two-volume *Opere* edited by Andrea Battistini (1990, rpt. 2000) do, but the frequently used Sansoni edition of Vico's *Opere filosofiche* edited by Nicola Badaloni (1971) does not. Having been omitted from the original standard Laterza edition of the *Scienza nuova*, the impresa has made its way into only various recent editions. Nicolini does not comment on the impresa in his *Commento storico;* his commentary begins with Vico's own first paragraph on the dipintura.

Until recently no real attention was given to the emblematic character of the second *New Science*, including analysis of the dipintura. In the abridged version of the English edition of it, which circulated for some years in paperback but which is no longer available, Bergin and Fisch eliminated the dipintura and that part of Vico's introduction that refers to it.[7] Such an editorial decision was quite in accord with the usual philosophical approach to the work, which focuses on its conceptual and systematic parts, regarding its employment of images as inessential embellishments, and holding the true beginning of the work to be Vico's presentation of his axioms. In his *Le sterminate antichità* (1969), Paolo Rossi noted that the female figure of the dipintura may have its origins in the 1611 Padua edition of Cesare Ripa's *Iconologia*.[8] Franco Lanza's *Saggi di poetica vichiana* (1961) has also called attention to

7. This revised and abridged version was first published as a Doubleday Anchor paperback in 1961, and reissued as a Cornell University Press paperback in 1970. This was replaced by a Cornell Paperbacks edition, unabridged, including "Practic of the New Science," in 1984. This is now the standard English edition, yet it, like the earlier hardbound unabridged editions of the Bergin and Fisch translation (1948, 1961, 1968), unfortunately does not reproduce the original title page with the impresa.

8. Paolo Rossi, *Le sterminate antichità: Studi vichiani* (Pisa: Nistri-Lischi, 1969), 184–85; 2nd ed. (Florence: La Nuova Italia, 1999).

the iconographic and emblematic character of Vico's text.[9] In this connection, Enzo Paci's earlier *Ingens sylva* (1949) should also be mentioned.[10]

The one work that has attempted systematically to explore Vico's images and to develop a comprehensive theory of them as keys to Vico's thought is Mario Papini's two-volume *Diptychum vicianum: Il geroglifico della storia* and *Arbor humanae linguae* (1984).[11] In these volumes Papini presents a discussion of the impresa in relation to the dipintura. Attention is beginning to be given to the meaning of the dipintura and its connections to the emblematic character of Renaissance texts; two very useful essays have appeared: one by Margherita Frankel,[12] and one by Angus Fletcher.[13] Neither of these essays mention the impresa. The only independent work to date on the significance of the impresa is an article by Papini in the *Bollettino del Centro di Studi Vichiani* titled "'IGNOTA LATEBAT': L'impresa negletta della *Scienza Nuova*."[14]

This article is a fuller treatment of the meaning of the impresa than Papini gives in his *Diptychum vicianum* and is essentially an expansion of it to the end of explaining how the impresa fits with his total reading of Vico's work. Papini sees the impresa as the difficult expression of a clash between the eternity of the hieroglyph and the temporality of the written word. Working from the Renaissance background he interprets the interplay of forms within the impresa—the triangle formed between the head and

9. F. Lanza, *Saggi di poetica vichiana* (Varese: Magenta, 1961).

10. Enzo Paci, *Ingens sylva: Saggio sulla filosofia di G. B. Vico* (Verona: Mondadori, 1949; rpt. Milan: Bompiani, 1994).

11. Mario Papini, *Diptychum vicianum* I. *Il geroglifico della storia. Significato e funzione della dipintura nella Scienza nuova di G. B. Vico;* and II. *Arbor humanae linguae. L'etimologico di G. B. Vico come chiave ermeneutica della storia del mondo* (Bologna: Cappelli, 1984).

12. Margherita Frankel, "The 'Dipintura' and the Structure of Vico's *New Science* as a Mirror of the World," in *Vico: Past and Present,* ed. Giorgio Tagliacozzo (Atlantic Highlands, N.J.: Humanities Press, 1981), 43–51.

13. Angus Fletcher, "On the Syncretic Allegory of the *New Science,*" *New Vico Studies* 4 (1986): 25–43.

14. Mario Papini, "'IGNOTA LATEBAT': L'impresa negletta della *Scienza Nuova,*" *Bollettino del Centro di Studi Vichiani* 14–15 (1984–85): 179–214. See also Andrea Battistini, "Teoria delle imprese e linguaggio iconico vichiano," *Bollettino del Centro di Studi Vichiani* 14–15 (1984–85): 149–77.

hands of the seated figure, the square of the plinth upon which she is leaning, and the sphere upon which the figure is seated—as representing the interplay in Renaissance thought between *mens, animus,* and *anima.*[15] Thus, Papini approaches the impresa both in semiotical terms of the image versus the word and in terms of the transformation of Renaissance concepts that he sees in Vico's metaphysics.

My purpose here is not to summarize Papini's complicated and learned discussion; his interpretation is very rich and set in terms of a total reading of Vico's work. What I wish to do is call attention to some of the possible meanings of the impresa as part of Vico's text that may be of interest especially to English-language readers of Vico who do not follow the developing Italian scholarship on his images. What I am suggesting is not derived from any comprehensive theory of the relation of Vico's images to the text other than my own interest in Vico's conception of "imaginative universals" and the view I certainly share with Papini and others that Vico intends the reader to take his use of iconic images as very important to the understanding of his work.

I also agree that the background of Vico's dipintura and impresa is the Renaissance, but my approach is not to interpret the meanings of the impresa in terms of Renaissance concepts, except that I believe its context to be Neoplatonic. Papini remarks that Vico's motto in the impresa is in "stile baconiano" (Baconian style).[16] Francis Bacon writes that "emblem reduces intellectual conceptions to sensible images; for an object of sense always strikes the memory more forcibly and is more easily impressed upon it than an object of intellect."[17]

The Meaning of the Impresa

I believe that the impresa and the dipintura are "before and after" depictions of Vico's "new science of metaphysic." In the

---

15. Papini has this in diagrammatic form; see *Il geroglifico,* 75, and his "IGNOTA LATEBAT," 187.

16. Papini, *Il geroglifico,* 76.

17. Francis Bacon, *Works,* vol. 4; new ed., ed. James Spedding, Robert Leslie Ellis, and Douglas Denon Heath (New York: Garrett, 1968; 1870), 436–37.

1744 edition Vico adds a depiction of what metaphysic was before the creation of the new science. In the two original 1744 editions I have seen, the title page with the impresa comes after the dipintura in the order of the front matter (although when it is reprinted in various modern Italian editions it is usually placed before the dipintura; an exception is the edition of Battistini, mentioned earlier). But in the order of the 1744 edition as it was originally printed, the "before" of the impresa comes after the dipintura, as a type of visual footnote on the meaning of the dipintura. The impresa has the character of an extra remark Vico is making on the dipintura in its own imagistic language, similar to the annotations he continually made on the text for preparation of the third edition.

The female figures in both the dipintura and the impresa symbolically represent two different stages of metaphysic. In the impresa the figure is seated upon the globe and is leaning on the plinth. In the dipintura this figure has been raised to a standing position atop the globe, which has come to symbolize nature and is banded by the signs of Virgo and Leo. The plinth of the impresa has become the altar of the dipintura and the globe of the impresa has been raised to balance upon the edge of the altar. The right-angled triangle held in the right hand of the seated figure in the impresa has been merged with the circular shape of the mirror held in her left hand and has become an equilateral triangle framing the eye of God in the dipintura. The mirror itself has been transformed into the convex jewel that is placed on the breast of the female figure of metaphysic in the dipintura and now reflects the triangle of the eye of God onto the statue of Homer.

Perhaps the best way to compare the dipintura and the impresa is side by side, with the dipintura on the viewer's left and the impresa beside it on the right (as it appears in Battistini's edition). It can then be seen that the impresa is a depiction of metaphysic pure and simple, so to speak; we see just the symbols of metaphysic itself. In the impresa the divine eye of God is absent and the things of the civil world are missing, including Homer. The elements of the impresa are all moved upward and turned inward to the right into the scene, to form the figure and position of metaphysic in the dipintura. The triangle and the mirror no longer portray an internal relationship within metaphysic (between the two hands) but are formed upward into the divine eye, and an aspect of the mirror, its reflective power, is retained by metaphysic in the convex jewel. The globe is brought up onto the plinth, which has now become an altar supporting the globe of nature upon which metaphysic is standing. In the impresa metaphysic appears as a self-contained process based upon nature. In commenting on the globe in the dipintura, Vico says that until now the philosophers have contemplated providence through only the natural order (*NS* 2). In the dipintura metaphysic becomes a mediator between the divine eye and the world of civil things. Through metaphysic the divine order is reflected into the world of civil things.

The impresa may be related to one of the additions that Vico drafted for the second *New Science* regarding the error of modern metaphysics, which appears in the *"Brani delle redazioni"* at the end of the Laterza edition (not part of the Bergin and Fisch translation). This has the title "Riprensione delle metafisiche di Renato delle Carte, di Benedetto Spinosa e di Giovanni Locke," and was intended as a draft of a final chapter of the section on "poetic metaphysics" of book 2.[18] Vico's "reprehension" of René Descartes, Benedict Spinoza, and John Locke, who represent the various perspectives of modern metaphysics, is that they all fail to base metaphysics on the knowledge of the divine that is present in ancient poetic wisdom (see the translation of the "Reprehension" and commentary in this volume).

It is presumed in modern metaphysics that metaphysical reasoning can proceed directly from nature and logic. But the fundamental error of metaphysics, Vico states in the "Reprehension," is not to begin with the poetic apprehension of the divine. He writes,

For the metaphysics of the philosophers must agree with the metaphysic of the poets, on this most important point, that from the

18. Giambattista Vico, *La scienza nuova*, vol. 4, pt. 2, in *Opere di G. B. Vico*, 8 vols. in 11, ed. Fausto Nicolini (Bari: Laterza, 1911–41), pars. 1212–17. See also the translation in this volume.

idea of a divinity have come all the sciences that have enriched the world with all the arts of humanity: just as this vulgar [poetic] metaphysic taught men lost in the bestial state to form the first human thought from that of Jove, so the learned must not admit any truth in metaphysic that does not begin from true *Being*, which is God.[19]

In the "before" depiction of the impresa, metaphysic is shown gazing into itself.

Also missing from the impresa are the things of the civil world, *cose civili*. As Vico makes clear in his introduction and in his discussion of method, philosophy can avoid the abstraction of past metaphysics only if it connects the general truths formulated by the philosophers with those of philology, which he defines as all that depends upon human choice, such as, "all histories of the languages, customs, and deeds of peoples in war and peace" (*NS* 7). Philosophy must undertake to examine philology. Thus, in the dipintura Vico includes objects symbolizing the civil world of nations. No suggestion of this civil element is present in the impresa, with the exception of the plinth bearing the inscription. If the plinth corresponds to the altar in the dipintura then it is what points downward to the civil world, as the mirror and triangle become the basis in the dipintura for the upper world of the divine eye. The impresa shows metaphysic as self-sufficient and thus the producer of abstractions. The dipintura shows metaphysic as the mediator of the divine and the civil and thus is a portrait of Vico's new metaphysic or redefinition of metaphysic as "fatto istorico della provvedenza" (what God has wrought in history; *NS* 342).

To this point my observation has been that the impresa depicts metaphysic as self-involved. Its potential to become the agency for showing what God has wrought in history has not been discovered. In the dipintura the elements of the impresa are transformed so that metaphysic becomes a mediator between the divine and civil orders. I wish to make three further observations regarding (1) the

19. Vico, *La Scienza nuova*, par. 1212.

Platonic or Neoplatonic elements; (2) the role of Homer; and
(3) the allusion to Hermes.

(1) The figure of metaphysic in the impresa holding the mirror
in one hand and the triangle in the other suggests a mediation
between the first stage of Plato's divided line, the stage of images
or *eikasia,* and the third stage of the mathematicals. Metaphysic
appears to be about to turn from gazing at the triangle in the mirror to regard the triangle itself, which may symbolize geometry or
that form of reasoning that is suppositional in form. Metaphysic
then would pass from the appearances of things to reasoning
about things in a hypothetical manner. But in the impresa the
fourth stage of thinking beyond assumptions is not depicted. The
figure of metaphysic then, in the impresa, becomes a symbol for
the state of modern metaphysics, which moves only from appearances to a suppositional method of reasoning, which Vico criticizes in his "Reprehension." But it is also a portrayal of Platonic
metaphysics because Plato, in Vico's view, turns his back on the
poetic knowledge of the divine in his quarrel with the poets in
the tenth book of the *Republic* and elsewhere. Thus, the dialectical
thought of the fourth stage of the divided line will end in an abstract knowledge of the forms if it is built from a transformation of
the suppositional method of mathematical thinking rather than
being a transformation of the apprehension of the divine that is
originally apprehended in myth or poetry.

As Vico clearly states in the passage quoted above from the "Reprehension," the "metaphysics of the philosophers must agree with
the metaphysic of the poets." Thus, as the motto of the impresa
states, metaphysics "unknown was lying hidden." The basis for Vico's metaphysic is there in classical and modern metaphysics, but
metaphysic requires a positive connection with the poets, with the
power of *fantasia* (imagination), to bring forth its truth. Metaphysic
can make its truths or intelligibilities only if it makes them through
a transformation of the original form in which they are made by
the poets in their practice of *sapienza poetica* (poetic wisdom).

No convertibility of the true and the made is possible by a
method of doubt or rational reasoning through supposition. All that
can be made in this way is an intellectual certain of consciousness,

but a certain that is not connected with a true.[20] Metaphysics, when it passes by a turning of its attention (turning of the head of the figure in the *impresa*) from perception to rational judgment, has no subject matter. This is because what is reflected in the mirror is just what is already presupposed by the rational or suppositional judgment. The philologies of the civil world are not present. The certains that the civil world presents and have been made by the original poetic founders of the civil world are not apprehended by metaphysics as connected to the general trues or intelligibilities that philosophy can produce in its reasonings.

(2) The Platonic quarrel with the poets takes a negative approach to the thought of Homer. Homer's wisdom is seen as a form of false philosophy that is presented in images for which no consistent sense can be made. It, then, is a form of eikasia (the first division of Plato's divided line) masquerading as the form of the highest wisdom—the bottom of the divided line pretending to be the top. Vico's resolution to this ancient quarrel is to take a positive approach to poetry and to deny that it is philosophy.

Thus, Vico can assign to poetry its own form of wisdom, or *sapienza poetica*, and once this is done Vico can see philosophy as emerging from poetry. Poetry or myth is then seen as the original and true apprehension of the divine as revealed, and as the original relationship out of which the civil world is founded. The power of the first fathers and founders of families is based on their knowledge of the ways of the divine through augury. To reconceive the relationship between philosophy and poetry Vico must show that poetry has a positive content. The crucial step in this is Vico's "discovery of the true Homer." Vico shows that Homer is not to be regarded as an early philosopher thinking in confused images, but that he is the Greek people themselves (*NS* 873). The actual texts of Homer then become summations of that poetic wisdom by which the ancient Greek peoples organized

---

20. This is the essence of Vico's criticism of Descartes' first truth, "Cogito ergo sum." See Giambattista Vico *On the Most Ancient Wisdom of the Italians Unearthed from the Origins of the Latin Language,* trans. Lucia M. Palmer (Ithaca, N.Y.: Cornell University Press, 1988), 53–56.

their world and founded their society based on their original apprehension of the divine.

Within this wisdom there is a poetic metaphysics that becomes the basis of the later rational or Platonic metaphysics. The negative side to the appearance of philosophy following Homer's age is that once rational philosophy appears, the original poetic apprehension of the divine of religion has been lost. The original creative and formative power of fantasia begins to fade in the philosophical pursuit of intellectual forms.

There is an analogy with the inscription of "ignota latebat" in the impresa and what Vico says of Homer in his explanation of the dipintura. Vico explains that the cracked base of the statue of Homer in the dipintura symbolizes that in the *First New Science* he sensed but did not understand the significance of the discovery of the true Homer. He writes of Homer that "il quale, non saputosi finora, ci ha tenuto nascoste le cose vere del tempo favoloso delle nazioni..." (unknown until now, he has held hidden from us the true institutions of the fabulous time among the nations...; *NS* 6). Vico's motto that "she or metaphysic unknown was lying hidden," presumably until now, suggests that until metaphysic could discover its basis in the apprehension of the divine in poetic wisdom it could not become true metaphysics.

Thus, the two figures of metaphysic in the impresa and the dipintura are a before-and-after sequence that is parallel to the before-and-after of Vico's first inadequate understanding of the significance of Homer (symbolized by the cracked base) and the discovery of the true Homer (the statue itself, in the dipintura). Further, it would imply that until metaphysic had made the proper connection with poetry through the discovery of the true Homer, metaphysic would remain in the self-involved state of the impresa. This parallel might imply a comment by Vico that in the *First New Science* the full sense of metaphysic was not realized and thus that the *First New Science* had not fully accomplished its liberation from the standpoint of the modern systems of metaphysics that he attacks in the "Reprehension."

(3) Finally, a comment must be made on the status of the winged cap of Hermes, which is pictured among the hieroglyphs of the civil world in the dipintura. It is interesting that in his commentary

159

on the hieroglyphics of the civil world that are aligned along the bottom of the dipintura Vico enumerates and comments on each from right to left, but stops short of mentioning the winged cap. His enumeration ends with his explanation of the caduceus of Hermes or Mercury. He writes that the caduceus is "l'ultimo de' geroglifici" (the last of the hieroglyphs; *NS* 30). Perhaps he means simply to include the winged cap as part of the hieroglyph of Mercury, but Vico so carefully comments on each other thing in the scene that it is curious that he says nothing of the cap. The figures of metaphysic in both the dipintura and the impresa have winged temples similar to the cap. In his commentary on the dipintura Vico introduces his remarks on the figure through reference to the winged temples ("La donna con le tempie alate..."), but he does not explain their significance. Although perhaps the winged temples simply fit with an iconic tradition for such female figures, could Vico intend the winged temples to signify a connection between metaphysic and the role of Hermes in the founding of civil society?

At one point in the work, independent of his explanation of the dipintura, Vico does comment on the cap of Mercury. In the section on poetic politics Vico discusses Mercury as the carrier of the first agrarian law to the mutinous *famuli*. He says that the rod of Mercury, or caduceus, with its two serpents signified the rights of ownership given to the famuli and those retained by the heroes. He states, "There are two wings at the top of the rod (signifying the eminent domain of the [heroic] orders), and the cap worn by Mercury is also winged (to confirm their high and free sovereign constitution, as the cap remained a hieroglyph of [lordly] liberty)" (*NS* 604). At the point when the heroic order of society is threatened with dissolution by the mutiny of the famuli, Mercury is the bringer of a new balanced order that allows the heroic order to continue for a time in a new way.

Metaphysic is in an analogous position with Mercury in that, like Mercury, it brings the message of the divine, the divine eye reflected from the breast of metaphysic into the civil world. But further, does Vico's metaphysic allow metaphysics to remain a little longer as a heroic enterprise, by uncovering what is lying hidden in metaphysics present in the third age that is dominated by "la barbarie della riflessione" (the barbarism of reflection; *NS* 1106)? Of his three ages, the middle age or that of the heroic is most to Vico's liking. It is clear that Vico himself lives in the third age of intellectual barbarism in which fantasia and poetry, the power of the myth and religion, have ceased to dominate social institutions. In "On the Heroic Mind," his oration of 1732, Vico writes of heroic education and heroic modes of thought. Although the ethos of the heroic is lost as a basis of social action, it need not be lost as an activity of thought that attempts heroically to recover the sense of the divine and the poetic wisdom that modern metaphysics has lost. In this sense Vico's new art of metaphysic—like Mercury, the bringer of the new agrarian law—allows for metaphysics to refound intellectual order in a new way that will allow the project of metaphysics to survive a little longer.

Presumably this new metaphysics will not itself prevent the age of barbarism from ultimately disintegrating, as the new agrarian law does not ultimately prevent the demise of the heroic age and its supersession by the age of humans. Since for Vico forms of thought are interlocked with forms of social order, the winged cap of Mercury may suggest a parallel—Mercury can actually visit the heroic age as a social force and in the modern age of humans Mercury can visit only as a form of metaphysic; the divine can appear only as a form of oratory and literature. Yet metaphysic, like Mercury, is a messenger of the divine wisdom into the civil order. There is much more that can be said concerning the symbolism of Mercury as an element in Vico's thought, both in relation to his conception of history and his refutation of Descartes, but such commentary goes beyond the purposes of this analysis.[21]

The Impresa and Vico's Four Authors

Could the motto of the impresa itself (ignota latebat) be a quotation or perhaps a gloss on an assertion found in a classical

---

21. Cf. Vico's use of Mercury in Plautus's *Amphitryon* as the vehicle of his refutation of Descartes' "first truth" in his *Ancient Wisdom*. See also Vico's comment on Mercury in his discourse on the Law of the Twelve Tables in the appendix to the Laterza edition of *La scienza nuova*, vol. 4, pt. 2, par. 1447.

or Renaissance text? If we consider Bacon's aforementioned definition—that an emblem (unlike an extemporaneously formed image) transports or reduces a concept to the level of sensibility— then the impresa is a depiction of the thought expressed in its inscription.

As Bacon claims, an object of sense is always more easily impressed upon the memory than is an object of the intellect. The impresa is designed to affect the memory, as is the dipintura (Vico explicitly claims this of the dipintura; *NS* 1). The motto of the impresa may be intended as a kind of circular play on words, perhaps between *nota* (a mark, note, sign) and *ignota* (the unknown, unrecognized female figure) or between the two words of the motto—that is, the redundancy of the "unknown" and the "lying hidden." What is hidden is unknown; what is unknown is often in principle or in fact knowable, and thus is in some sense "hidden." There is a self-referential character to the two terms of the motto, perhaps parallel to the "self-referential" image of the triangle reflected in the mirror and the suggestion that the gaze of the figure holding them could move back and forth between them, regarding first the triangle reflected, then the triangle directly perceived, then the triangle re-perceived, in its reflection.

Could "ignota latebat" refer to the phrase in Tacitus's *Agicola*— "omne ignotum pro magnifico" (the unknown is always magnified)—that Vico quotes in his explanation of his first axiom (*NS* 121)? Certainly the topic of the motto is "the unknown": what is unknown and hidden from us. The unknown and its effects on human knowledge is the topic of Vico's first axiom of the *New Science*. It states, "Because of the indefinite nature of the human mind, whenever it is thrown [*si rovesci*] into ignorance, man makes himself the measure of all things [*regola dell'universo*]" (*NS* 120). Vico's verb for the mind being thrown into ignorance is *rovesciearsi*, which has the sense of being overturned or throwing oneself down. The adjective, *rovescio*, means to be "turned upside down, inverted." It is, for example, the term in Italian for translating G. W. F. Hegel's conception of the "inverted or topsy-turvy world" (*die verkehrte Welt/il mondo alla rovescia*).

Vico's statement of this axiom would seem to imply that ignorance is a state in which the mind turns itself inside out, a state the mind brings upon itself in a certain manner. The form of thought through which the mind maintains itself in this inverted state is *fama*, or rumor, which grows when it is not in the presence of the thing it is about and deflates when the thing in question is brought before the mind. In his elaboration on the meaning of this axiom Vico says that fama has been the perennial source of all the exaggerated opinions held concerning remote antiquities unknown (*sconosciute*) to us.

When something is unknown human beings do not simply admit this; instead they turn the powers of the mind inside out and elaborate this state of ignorance into a state of false opinions that are exaggerated by the power of fama. This magnification of the unknown is drawn forth from the way human beings experience the world; they thus prevent themselves from confronting the unknown as having an origin truly other than themselves.

In his *Autobiography* Vico names four thinkers as being the most influential on the development of his thought—Plato, Tacitus, Francis Bacon, and Hugo Grotius (*A* 138–39; 155). They are Vico's famous "four authors." Vico's axiom that "man is the measure of all things" parallels Bacon's "idols of the tribe." The idols of the tribe arise when the human senses are taken to be the standard of things. Our senses, Bacon asserts, are "uneven mirrors" that distort the properties of objects; we apprehend the world as having more measure, more regularity that it actually has.[22] How might what is depicted in the impresa involve Tacitus's principle of the unknown and Bacon's formulation of the ancient maxim that "man is the measure of all things"?

As discussed above, the impresa depicts the figure of metaphysic as self-involved, seated on the globe. The source or origin of metaphysic is unknown. When the figure is transferred to the dipintura and raised upright atop the globe, the source of metaphysics becomes the divine eye, which transmits to the civil world through Vico's reconception of the meaning of Homer. As Vico states in his "Reprehension," the metaphysics of the philosophers must find its true origin in the metaphysic of the poets,

---

22. On Bacon's idols see Bacon, *Works*, vol. 4, 53–64.

which derives from an apprehension of the divine. This sense of metaphysics as grounded in poetic metaphysic or a "poetic wisdom" is what is "lying hidden" in the picture of metaphysics in the impresa.

The impresa shows us the Platonic metaphysics having been the victor in the ancient quarrel with the poets Homer and Hesiod. From this partial sense of the Platonic conception (omitting, among other elements, Plato's own use of myth) modern systems of metaphysics have proceeded to generate their versions of the world directly out of the human. The prime example of this is Descartes, who purports to generate his metaphysics directly out of the human self, the *cogito*. With no theory of their own origin (in violation of Vico's axiom, "Doctrines must take their beginning from that of the matters of which they treat"; *NS* 314), modern systems of metaphysics have made rumor into a method, the method of suppositional reasoning and doubt, in the belief that they can produce the truth simply through the mind's measure and magnification of itself. Vico, in his new science of metaphysic, would return to Plato as one of his four authors, but with a reconception of the relation of philosophy to the poetic.

The motto of the impresa is a statement about the unknown. Vico's first axiom of his science is a statement of how the mind reacts to the unknown. The impresa depicts how modern non-Vichian metaphysics is a process of the human making itself the measure, its own origin in the poetic appropriation of the divine remaining unknown and outside the frame of the scene.

Seen in this way, three of Vico's four authors have a significant connection with the construction of the impresa: Plato with the depiction (mirror and triangle—*eikasia* and *dianoia*), Tacitus with the motto concerning the unknown (*ignota latebat*), and Bacon with the principle Vico employs to explain the mind's relation to the unknown (*Homo fiat Norma*). Could an element for Vico's fourth author, Hugo Grotius, reasonably be said to be present?

The title page of the 1646 definitive edition of Grotius's *De Jure Belli ac Pacis* (*The Law of War and Peace*, "wherein are set forth the law of nature and of nations") bears an impresa. Like Vico's impresa this encloses a written motto. This work of Grotius was first published in 1625, exactly one hundred years before the *First New*

Science. The last and definitive edition of Grotius's work (published the year after his death), like Vico's third edition of the *New Science* of 1744, is an enlarged edition, undertaken by the author at the end of his career. The impresa on Grotius's work depicts two figures: an angel of death stands on the left with hourglass and scythe; a bearded Hercules stands on the right with his club. Between them is suspended an armillary sphere. Below is the motto *indefessus agendo,* which can be understood in the abstract to mean "untiringly active." I find this phrase to occur in Ovid's description of the death of Hercules in the *Metamorphoses:* "defessa iubendo est saeva Iovis coniunx: ego sum indefessus agendo" (the cruel wife of Jove is weary of imposing toils; but I am not yet weary of performing them; *Meta.* 9.198–99). The context of the motto explains the presence of the figures of Death and of Hercules in Grotius's impresa. The armillary sphere, being an ancient astronomical instrument, may symbolize that on his death Hercules was made a god by his father, Jove, who "set him amid the glittering stars."

This emblem may simply have been included by Grotius's publisher, Johan Blaeu.[23] The *De Jure Belli ac Pacis* went through many editions and translations and was widely circulated. Assuming Vico was familiar with the title page of Grotius's 1646 edition, it may have led him to include, in the definitive edition of the *New Science,* an impresa constructed in the manner of seventeenth-century heroic emblems, and in his own case to use it as a form of visual annotation on the main theme of his work. Vico certainly knew Grotius's *De Jure Belli ac Pacis* well; he once accepted a commission to write notes for a new edition of the work, but did not complete them (*A* 155).

Of Hugo Grotius, John Selden, and Samuel von Pufendorf, Vico writes that they should have begun their doctrines of natural law from an interpretation of the forms of writing and thought of the first nations, their hieroglyphs and fables, and then proceeded "to ascertain their customs by a metaphysical criticism of

---

23. An edition of Grotius's theological writings, *Opera Omnia Theologica* (1679), published a number of years after his death by the same publisher, employs the same emblem.

the founders of the nations" (*NS* 493). The modern natural-law theorists Grotius, Selden, and Pufendorf, like the modern metaphysicians Descartes, Spinoza, and Locke, leave the origin of their subject matter unknown and thus make man the measure of all things. The impresa depicts the state of thought about nations and about reality that Vico inherited from the seventeenth century, before the founding of his new science.

My purpose herein has been to call attention to the significance of an overlooked element in the definitive edition of Vico's *New Science*—the impresa. Ironically, like the motto it bears, the impresa has been lying "hidden unknown," yet has been right before Vico's readers' eyes all the time, for almost two and one-half centuries. Papini considers the impresa to have been selected by Vico, but he does not give direct evidence for this.[24] I have called attention to some circumstantial evidence for Vico having designed or issued instructions for the impresa. Whatever its source, the impresa seems to suggest a before-and-after sequence of metaphysics, before Vico's new science and after it. The impresa does not so much cause us to read the text of Vico's work differently as it causes us to read the dipintura differently. Since Vico says that the purpose of the dipintura is to give the reader an impression of the work before reading it and to allow a basis for recalling it to memory after it is read, the impresa has an important bearing on the text. The impresa seems to be a visual annotation or comment on the dipintura and Vico's conception of metaphysic depicted in it that is analogous to his various annotations on the written text itself.

---

24. In *Il geroglifico* Papini speaks of the *impresa* as "introdotta dal Vico sul frontespizio dell'edizione del 1744" (74); in his "IGNOTA LATEBAT" he puts it, "*L'impresa prescelta dal Vico...*" (180).

Vico's Addition to the Tree of the Poetic Sciences and His Use of the Muses

Translation and Commentary by
DONALD PHILLIP VERENE

HOW ALL THE OTHER SCIENCES MUST TAKE THEIR PRINCIPLES FROM THIS [SCIENCE OF DIVINATION]

[1199] These are the general aspects from which this science can be regarded. Indeed, from this first principle [religion, Jove] of all things divine and human of the gentiles, that which we have found within this metaphysics of the human race, this sublime science alone will give us the principles of all the other subaltern sciences [*NS* 367, 391], those which metaphysics must assure of the truth of all their particular subject matters. They are the primary thread with which the fabric of this book is woven and the first lines with which the design of our history of ideas begins to be conveyed.

I

[1200] Logic takes its primary ideas from this metaphysics, in which all divine ideas are found, as well as the first words in which all mental language is found expressed by means of mute acts [*NS* 401].

II

[1201] Morals takes its primary principle from this metaphysics—that is, conatus [*NS* 340, 504]—which is properly connected to free will, the subject matter of which is the virtues and vices.

167

III

[1202] Economy takes the fear of divinity from this metaphysics; its primary principle is matrimony, which is the origination of the family.

IV

[1203] Politics takes its subject matter from the fact that there are two species of men that make up commonwealths; and it begins from the most noble of those who command, who find themselves to be those *pauci quos aequus amavit Iupiter* [*NS* 389; "few whom just Jupiter loved," *Aenead* A.6.129f], from which it follows that such is the one the others obey. Thus, politics is not other than the science of commanding and obeying in cities.

[1204] And here the branch of the active sciences [*NS* 391] is complete that issues from the trunk of this poetic metaphysics. The other branch, that which we call the speculative sciences, commences from the same trunk with this series [cf. *NS* 1405, "Practic"].

V

[1205] Physics takes its imaginative principles of the divine from this metaphysics, and it begins from that principle that the first pious giants bring forth: *Iovis omnia plena* [All things are full of Jove]; which later in Plato results in a divine physics, that he exposits in the *Parmenides,* where he establishes the eternal idea as the principle of all things in time [*NS* 379].

VI

[1206] And the particular physics of man takes its principles from those giants of vast bodies and bestial souls, from which there begins to evolve as matter, accompanied by fear of the divinity, the form of our just corporature and our human soul [cf. *NS* 692].

VII

[1207] Cosmography thus begins from the primordial sky, which was for the first people as high up as the mountains [cf. *NS* 712], and from the first world, which was their proclivity; this most ancient idea being preserved by the Latins in their expressions *in mundo est* and *in proclivi est*, in order to signify "it is easy" [*NS* 725].

VIII

[1208] Astronomy begins from the ruler of the planets, who is Jove, when the heavens reigned on earth [*NS* 64] and he was of such great benefit to the human race that he had the admirable title from all the gentile nations of "the highest" [*NS* 379].

IX

[1209] Chronology, also from Jove, gave beginning to the age of gods, which is the basis of our Chronological Table; and Jove was the first of the twelve minute epochs of the other major divinities, which serve to determine that the first age of the world lasted nine hundred years [cf. *NS* 69, 734, 736].

X

[1210] And finally geography, which from the regions and measures of the sky ascertained those of the earth, and hence from these regions of the sky come those places designated for the augurs to take the auspices of Jove, what the Latins called *templa caeli* [open places in the sky] [*NS* 391, 478, 711]; the first men in the world attest that Jove was the first thing to contemplate and the first act of contemplation.

[1211] So the nine sciences must be the nine Muses, those that the poets sang of as all being the daughters of Jove [*NS* 508]; and now through all these things is restored to Jove the proper historical significance of the motto *A Iove principium Musae* [*NS* 391; "From Jove the Muse began," Vergil, *Ecologue* 3.60].

COMMENTARY

Vico's Conception of the Muses

Vico wrote these paragraphs between April and August of 1731 as part of what, in the Laterza edition of Vico's works edited by Fausto Nicolini, was designated the third set of corrections, meliorations, and additions to the *Second New Science,* published in December 1730.[1]

Vico drafted a first set of such notes as the *New Science* was in press and a second set in the month after it appeared in January 1731. In his *Autobiography* Vico writes that he drafted these notes as he discussed the book with his friends, and that they can be incorporated in the places indicated when a third edition of the *New Science* is issued (*A* 197).

Vico died during the preparation of the third edition of 1744 and the notes remained unincorporated. They do not appear in the Thomas Goddard Bergin and Max Harold Fisch translation, with the exception of the "Practic" that was added as an appendix in 1984 and appears in later printings. These paragraphs on the poetic sciences are a schematic overview, to be added to Vico's "Exposition and Division of Poetic Wisdom" at the beginning of book 2.

The remarkable feature of these paragraphs is Vico's final statement—that the poetic sciences must be the nine Muses of which the poets sang. Nowhere in the *First* or the *Second New Science* does Vico make this identification.

In the *Second New Science* (1730/1744), Vico speaks of the Muses in three ways: (1) as associated with Apollo and as being the arts of humanity (*NS* 79, 508, 534, 537), dwelling on Mount Parnassus; (2) as the daughters of Mnemosyne, or Memory (*NS* 699, 819); and (3) as the science of divination or first wisdom, the "knowledge of good and evil" of Homer (*NS* 365, 381, 391). From this third sense of the Muses, Vico concludes that "the first Muse must have been Urania, who contemplated the heavens to take the

1. Giambattista Vico, *Opere di G. B. Vico,* edited by Fausto Nicolini, 2nd ed., 8 vols. in 11 (Bari: Laterza, 1928), vol. 4, pt. 2: 195–98. Paragraph enumerations in the translation refer to those of Nicolini's edition.

auguries. Later she came to stand for astronomy" (*NS* 391; see also 508). He asserts that Urania and the other Muses "sing" in the sense in which the Latin verbs *canere* and *cantare* mean 'foretell'" (*NS* 508, 534). This divinatory power is originally attributed to the Muses in the early lines of the *Theogony*, where Hesiod says they have the power to sing of what was, is, and is to come (*Th.* 36f.).

Vico adopts this power of the Muses as the key for proving the new science: "he who meditates this science narrates to himself this ideal eternal history so far as he himself makes it for himself by that proof 'it had, has, and will have to be'" (*dovette, deve, dovr; NS* 349). Vico places these three words in quotation marks, calling attention to their connection to the Muses. He transforms the Muses' power simply to connect events in time into the power to connect things *per causas,* to grasp things in the life of nations so as to see in them a necessary causal order. As the founders of the gentile nations take the auspices of the movements of Jove in the heavens, the founders of the new science (Vico and his readers) take the auspices of the movements of providence in history. The means for the founders of humanity is the language of religion; the means for the founders of the new science of history is the language of reason. Reason is the power to meditate and make a narration of the causal interconnections that make up the whole.

In *The Most Ancient Wisdom of the Italians,* Vico characterizes the Muses as "forms of imagination [*quae phantasiae virtutes sunt*]."[2] He writes that the faculty that stores sense perceptions is called by the Latins *memoria,* and that which recalls them once stored is called *reminiscentia;* further, what the Greeks call *phantasia,* the Italians call *immaginativa* (in the *New Science* Vico will alter this to *fantasia*), and the verb *immaginare* in ordinary Italian is the same as *memorare* for the Latins. Vico is echoing Aristotle's short treatise *On Memory,* in which Aristotle claims that both memory and imagination originate in sense perception and that memory and imagination are one. Aristotle writes, "If asked, of which among

---

2. Giambattista Vico, *On the Most Ancient Wisdom of the Italians Unearthed from the Origins of the Latin Language, Including the Disputation with the Giornale de' letterati d'Italia,* trans. Lucia M. Palmer (Ithaca, N.Y.: Cornell University Press, 1988), 96.

the parts of the soul memory is a function, we reply, manifestly of that part to which imagination [*phantasia*] also pertains; and all objects of which there is imagination are in themselves objects of memory" (*Mem.* 450a 21–23).

The Muses as the daughters of Memory are imagination, that power to imitate and alter in form what is called to mind in the act of recollection. The poets in their songs inspired by the Muses—the power of imagination—can imitate objects originally stored in the memory through sense perception or they can alter what is stored into objects not as such acquired in sense perception by combining sense perceptions in new ways, as in hippogryphs or centaurs. Horace warns against joining such perceptions in idle ways such that they portray monstrosities (*Ars Poet.* 1–23). The arts of humanity depend on the union between memory and imagination.

In the *Ancient Wisdom,* the chapter on the interconnection of memory and imagination is followed by a chapter on *ingenium,* connecting *ingenium* to *natura.* Ingenium is responsible for the sense of proportion needed to connect what is made in the mind to what is in things. Such correspondence is required by knowledge. Geometry and arithmetic teach the sense of proportion. Those who apply these sciences are called *ingegneri.* In the *Second New Science* Vico incorporates *ingenium* (*ingegno*) into memory. He writes, *la memoria è la stessa che la fantasia* and that *'fantasia' altresì prendesi per l'ingegno* (*NS* 819). He says that in the times of the returned barbarism, *uomo fantastico* was used to signify a *uomo d'ingegno* (*NS* 819). Vico then advances a threefold doctrine of memory: "Memory thus has three different aspects [*differenze*]: it is memory [*memoria*] when it remembers things; imagination [*fantasia*] when it alters and imitates them; ingenuity [*ingegno*] when it surrounds them and puts them in proper order and arrangement. For these reasons the theological poets called Memory the 'mother of the Muses'" (*NS* 819; see also 699). (In Vico's *Second Response* in the *Giornale de' letterati d'Italia* he finds evidence in Terence's *Lady of Andros* of the interconnections of this threefold sense of memory.)[3]

3. Ibid., 161.

The Muses as the daughters of Memory not only inherit the power of fantasia to make what is remembered into ideal forms but also have the power to place what is formed into an order that is a whole. When the Muses sing of what was, is, and is to come, they do it so that one thing passes into another. What is remembered and imagined is arranged in time. When such recollection is accomplished in accordance with the principles of the new science the order is necessary and yields a knowledge through causes.

Clio is the other Muse that Vico comments on by name in the *Second New Science.* He says that the greater gentes "must have conceived the second of the Muses, Clio, the narrator of heroic history" (*NS* 533; see also 555). He says the first history must have been the genealogies of the heroes as in sacred history it is the genealogies of the descendents of the patriarchs. He notes that Apollo, to whom the Muses are dear, begins this gentile history by pursuing Daphne. In the myth, Daphne escapes from Apollo by disappearing into the earth with the aid of Gaea. In her place springs up a laurel tree. Vico regards this as the basis of why the gentiles call genealogies "trees."

In the *Universal Law* Vico also puts forth his doctrine of Urania as the first Muse. It is the basis of his account of how astronomy began among the Greeks after Homer.[4] Vico repeats this view of Urania as the first Muse in the *First New Science* (1725). He then calls Melpomene the "next Muse" and Clio the third Muse (*FNS* 290; on Urania, see also 30; on Clio, see 339). He mentions Melpomene only once in the *First New Science,* and does not mention her in his discussions in the *Second New Science.*

The Meaning of Melpomene

Melpomene, Urania, and Clio are the only Muses that Vico mentions by name in the sequence of his systematic works: the *Ancient Wisdom* (in which the Muses are mentioned only collectively), the *Universal Law* (Muses and Urania), the *First New Science* (Muses, Urania, Melpomene, Clio), and the *Second New Science* (Muses, Urania, Clio). Vico's interpretations of Urania and Clio

4. Giambattista Vico, "Dissertations," in *UL* bk. 3, chap. 13, par. 35.

are based on the functions assigned to them by the various late authors of antiquity. According to these authors, Urania is astronomy, Clio is history, and Melpomene is the Muse of tragedy.

Vico, in his mention of her in the *First New Science,* writes, "Melpomene, serba le memorie de' maggiori con le sepolture" (Melpomene preserves the memory of ancestors through their tombs; *FNS* 290). In a footnote to this sentence, in his recent translation of the *First New Science,* Leon Pompa comments, "This appears to be a mistake since Melpomene was the Muse of tragedy" (*FNS* p. 171, n. 52). Andrea Battistini, in his edition of Vico's *Opere,* does not call this a mistake, but rightly points out in his note that "Melpomene characteristically is the Muse of tragedy, without direct connection to the memory of the ancestors."[5] It is strange to consider this a mistake. Even when Vico's philological interpretations of myth are associative and speculative they are always precise. There is no Muse who represents the memory of ancestors. So Vico has not mistaken one Muse for another. If we presume it may be deliberate, what might Vico mean? Certainly Vico's characterization of Melpomene is so brief as to be unnecessarily obscure for the reader. He should have added a sentence or two, because the connection he intends between Melpomene and the ancestors is not obvious, as is the connection he intends between the traditional view of Urania and divination and that between Clio and heroic history.

Melpomene (Μελπομένη) is the Songstress, from μέλπω, "to sing" which is associated with "to sing to the harp or lyre," as found in the *Odyssey,* "μετὰ δέ σφιν ἐμέλπετο θεῖος ἀοιδὸς φορμίζων" (*Ody.* 4.17; cf. 13.27). I think Vico is playing on Melpomene not as the Muse of tragedy, as assigned by later authors, but on the name originally assigned her by Hesiod, connecting her to singing and to the accompaniment of the lyre (*Th.* 77). In a portrayal of the Muses on a Greek sarcophagus in the Louvre, Melpomene is shown playing a lyre.[6] In Vico's doctrine of the founding and governing of society, the lyre has a particular significance. In the

---

5. Giambattista Vico, *Opere di G. B. Vico,* 2 vols., ed. Andrea Battistini (Milan: Mondadori), 2:1844.

6. *Larousse Encyclopedia of Mythology* (New York: Prometheus, 1960), 128.

"Synopsis of Universal Law" Vico writes that the clients who fled their masters against the law "were mancipated with sinew—that is, tied, rope not being in use; this sinew also was called *fides* [the binding of the body is like the incorporeal bond or cord of fidelity], which later remained to signify the string of the lyre."[7] He says this was "the first word of dominion." Vico repeats this point of the connection of binding and the lyre in the *Universal Law*,[8] noting that the lyre was invented by Mercury and given to Apollo, and that with its sound the Muses sing.[9] In the *Second New Science* Vico writes that the cord was called *chorda* in Greek and *fides* in Latin, as in the phrase *fides deorum* (force of the gods; *NS* 523). He says it persists in phrases such as *recipere in fidem* (to receive in trust or protection).

Vico also identifies the lyre with the invention of law. It was the union of the cords or forces of the fathers who created civil power, putting an end to private force and violence: "Hence the law was defined with full propriety by the poets as *lyra regnorum,* 'the lyre of kingdoms' " (*NS* 615). As the cord of the lyre binds the classes together and establishes civil power, so it binds the heroes together with the ancestors. Vico writes, "Achilles sings to his lyre the praises of the heroes who have gone before [*Iliad.* 9.186ff]" (*NS* 908). Achilles with the lyre calls up the memory of those who had gone before, as Orpheus tamed the beasts of Greece to humanity, and Amphion with the lyre made the stones move and raised the walls of Thebes (*NS* 523; see also 79). Vico writes, "These were the stones that Deucalion and Pyrrha, standing before the temple of Themis (that is, in the fear of divine justice) with veiled heads (the modesty of marriage), found lying before their feet" (*NS* 523).

All of Vico's three principles of humanity are connected to the cord of the lyre. The cord signifies the force of the gods and divine justice (religion) and also signifies the bonds inherent in the basic institutions of society (marriage and family). The power of the lyre through song ties us to the ancestors (burial). If genealogy

7. See the "Synopsis of Universal Law," in this volume.
8. *UL* bk. 1, chap. 183.
9. *UL* bk. 2, pt. 2, chap. 22, par. 3.

is born of Clio, Clio is accompanied by Melpomene as the Songstress, through which we are tied to those who have gone before.

Vico's mention of Melpomene as the third Muse in the *First New Science* is enthymematic. His claim that Melpomene (as Songstress) preserves the memory of the ancestors implies that the lyre is the middle term joining the major premise: "The lyre preserves the memory of the ancestors" and the minor premise that "Melpomene (as Songstress) preserves the lyre," making a syllogism of AAA first figure. This formulation does not include the idea of the memory of the ancestors as occurring through tombs. A possible tie between the lyre and the ancestors are Vico's comments in the second book of the *Universal Law,* where he remarks on the significance of the *cippus* (small pillar) used by the Romans in their houses to support the busts of their ancestors—which also became a gravestone. Vico claims that these sepulchral pillars were the physical basis of the custom of creating genealogical lines.[10]

The Muses and the Poetic Tree of Knowledge

What does Vico intend in the identification of the nine Muses with the nine sciences of his poetic tree of knowledge that he makes in his concluding paragraph (1211)? There does not seem to be a one-to-one correspondence between the characteristics or functions of Vico's nine sciences and the identities assigned to the Muses by the authors of late antiquity beyond Vico's interpretations of Urania (astronomy) and Clio (history). In the standard list the others are Melpomene (tragedy, as discussed), Thalia (comedy), Calliope (epic poetry), Polyhymnia (hymns to the gods, and later pantomime), Terpsichore (dance accompanied by song), Erato (lyre playing and lyric poetry accompanied by it), and Euterpe (flute playing and lyric poetry accompanied by it).

Vico's aim, in the passages translated herein, is to claim how each of his sciences originate from the science of divination, the object of which is the knowledge of Jove's actions. Jove is the father of these sciences and the father of the Muses, having conceived each on nine nights in union with their mother, Memory.

10. *UL* bk. 2, pt. 2, chap. 20, par. 61.

The ancient poet is both a singer of songs and a teller of the future through his ability to recall the past, which is the basis of what is to come in the future. The ancestors look down on the world and see all of time. As with Melpomene in her original role as Songstress, the mediator of the past is the poet and what the poet can make. The science of divination is thus part of the poet's art of memory.

In Vico's world of the third age, typified by the barbarism of reflection—the total rationalizing of thought and society—we are divorced from the original power of the poet to sing and foretell. We have no direct access to the Muses. This is true of Vico's new scientist as well as of those at large in the third age. The new scientist does have access to the original poetic sciences, but only barely. The new scientist cannot truly think *on* the level of the poetic sciences themselves, but can think *about* them. Thought about them allows one to realize how the poetic or mythic is at the basis of human knowledge and how each of these sciences is a way in which the human is based in the divine. As Cicero writes, "wisdom is the knowledge of things divine and human and acquaintance with the cause of each of them" (*Tusc.* 4.26.57).

Poetry is the original form of this wisdom (*la sapienza poetica*). Each of these nine sciences is connected in their original being with Jove. We know this because each of them is a transformation of the original science, which is *scienza in divinità*. The explanation of this for each of the nine sciences is Vico's aim in these paragraphs, a point he has not made so systematically in the second book of the *Second New Science* proper. Hence he made it an addition as he began revision of the work.

Although there is no correspondence of individual Muses to particular sciences, Vico's addition allows us to know why there are nine sciences in number on his poetic tree of sciences. The significance of nine is not evident from the *Second New Science* as published. As the Muses provided guidance to the theological poets and are invoked by all later ancient poets, the poetic sciences provide the necessary guidance to the new scientist in his grasp of history. From a knowledge of them the whole world of nations can be resurrected in Vico's theater of memory. In this resurrection, I think, Vico's strange claim about Melpomene may be the key.

Like Melpomene's art of the song, Vico's new science must open the tombs of the ancestors, and from them encompass the total arc of time. Of the three principles of humanity, religion, marriage, and burial, it is on burial that Vico comments the least. The principle of burial is the principle of history. What is on the tombs, what is known of the ancestors, is the key to the past, to historical knowledge. The ancestors are not only keys to the historical details of the past, being beyond time, they also symbolize the transcendence of the temporal itself. Looking down on the world from their position beyond it, they see all of time at once. The new scientist grasps history through an act of palingenesis or resurrection, of bringing back to life what once was, the revivifying of the origin. Burial is a form of memory, the attempt not to forget but in some way to preserve the sense of the ancestors and what they were. The preservation is humanizing (as Vico writes, "humanity had its origin in *humane,* to bury" (*NS* 537). Following Vico's thought out, in this small way, places his project in a new light and perhaps demonstrates what treasures continue to lie within his new science, always awaiting exploration.

Vico's Reprehension of the Metaphysics of René Descartes, Benedict Spinoza, and John Locke

Translation and Commentary by

DONALD PHILLIP VERENE

THE REPREHENSION OF THE
METAPHYSICS OF RENÉ DESCARTES,
BENEDICT SPINOZA, AND
JOHN LOCKE[1]

[1212] Therefore, if one does not begin from—"a god who to all men is Jove,"[2]—one cannot have any idea either of science or of virtue. Thus is easily dismissed the supposition of Polybius, who says that if there were philosophers in the world, there would be no need of religions![3] For the metaphysics of the philosophers

1. Giambattista Vico, "Riprensione delle metafisiche di Renato delle Carte, di Benedetto Spinosa e di Giovanni Locke," in *Opere di G. B. Vico*, ed. Fausto Nicolini, 2nd ed., 8 vols. in 11 (Bari: Laterza, 1928), vol. 4, pt. 2: 198–99. This passage is part of the section titled "Brani delle redazioni del 1730, 1731 e 1733 circa soppressi o sostanzialmente mutati nelle redazione definitiva" that is printed following the text of *La scienza nuova* in the Laterza edition but is not included in the standard Bergin and Fisch English translation. Paragraph enumerations in the translation refer to Nicolini's edition.

2. The text states, "un dio ch'a tutti è Giove." Nicolini points out in his comment on this paragraph that this is a Tassian paraphrase of the Vergilian "Iupiter omnibus idem." See Fausto Nicolini, *Commento storico alla seconda Scienza nuova*, 2 vols. (Rome, 1949–50), 2:162. The line in Tasso's *Gerusalemme liberata* is "Testimone è quel Dio ch'a tutti è Giove" (4.42). In Vergil's *Aeneid* it is "rex Iuppiter omnibus idem" (10.112). Cf. Vico's *La scienza nuova:* "che Giove era a tutti equale. Ch'è la storia civile di quel motto *Iupiter omnibus aequus*" [that Jove was equal [just] to all. This is the civil history of the expression *Iupiter omnibus aequus*]; see *NS* 415.

3. Vico makes this claim of Polybius the subject of axiom 32 in the *New Science:* "From this point begins the refutation of the false dictum of Polybius that if there

must agree with the metaphysic of the poets, on this most important point, that from the idea of a divinity have come all the sciences that have enriched the world with all the arts of humanity: just as this vulgar [poetic] metaphysic taught men lost in the bestial state to form the first human thought from that of Jove, so the learned must not admit any truth in metaphysic that does not begin from true *Being*,[4] which is God.

[1213] And René Descartes certainly would have recognized this, if he had noticed it in the very dubitation that he makes of his own being. Because, if I doubt whether I am nor not, I doubt of my true being, of which it is impossible that I go in search if there is no true Being, because it is impossible to search for something of which one does not have any idea. Now, if I doubt of my being while not doubting of true Being, true Being is in reality distinct from my being. My being is limited by body and time, that make necessities for me: therefore true *Being* is free from body, and therefore above body, and hence above time, which is the measure of body according to "before" and "after" or (to put it better) is measured by the motion of body. And, in

---

were philosophers in the world there would be no need of religions [*se fussero al mondo filosofi, non sarebber uopo religioni*]. For without religions no commonwealths can be born, and if there were no commonwealths in the world there would be no philosophers in it" (*NS* 179). Vico repeats this point in three subsequent places, the last of which is part of the conclusion to the work as a whole (*NS* 334, 1043, 1110). Vico also concludes the *First New Science* with reference to this dictum (*FNS* 476). Compare his statement, "Atque huc referendum quod Polybius scribt, quem locum impii in suam partem detorquent: quod, 'si homines omnes essent sapientes, istis religonibus et legibus non esset opus'" (*UL* bk. 2, pt. 1, chap. 4, par. 6). In *The Histories* (6.56) Polybius expresses the view that the cohesion of the Roman state was due to its institution of religious superstition in public and private life. This was necessary to control the passions of the common people, Polybius believes, but such activity might not have been necessary if it were possible to form a state composed of wise men.

4. Vico's term is *l'Ente*, as in *l'Ente supremo* (Supreme *Being*, God). Where Vico uses *l'Ente*, it is rendered throughout the translation as *Being*. Vico also uses *l'Essere*, which is rendered as "Being." Although these two terms are normally interchangeable in Italian, Vico uses *l'Ente* quite consistently in the above paragraphs to refer to the doctrine of *Being* he is advocating—that deriving originally from the metaphysic of the poets. He uses *l'Essere* as the term for "Being" in the doctrines he is attacking—as in his criticism of Descartes (par. 1213). He omits capitalization when referring to finite human being, as in *il mio essere* ("my being").

consequence of all this, true *Being* is *eternal, infinite, free.* Thus, he, René, should have, as befitting a good philosopher, begun from a very simple idea, that has no mixed composition, as is that of *Being;* therefore Plato with weight of words called metaphysics *Ontologia,*[5] "science of being." But he fails to recognize *Being* and begins to know things from substance, which is an idea composed of two things: of one that stands under and sustains, of another that stands above it and rests thereon.

[1214] Such manner of philosophizing brought about the scandal of Benedict Spinoza, a man without public religion and, in consequence, rejected by all commonwealths, and for hatred of them all he declared an open war against all religions. And, not giving other than substance, and this being either mind or body, and body not determining mind nor mind body, out of all this he established a God of infinite mind in infinite body, therefore operating by necessity.

[1215] John Locke placed himself on the opposing side, against Spinoza, and, in the same scandalous way as Descartes, he embellishes the metaphysic of Epicurus, and holds that all ideas are in us by supposition and are projections of body,[6] and he is compelled to offer a God all body operating by chance. But Locke should consider whether the idea of true Being exists by supposition, an

5. As Nicolini points out, in no place does Plato call metaphysics *ontologia* (*Commento,* 1213). *Ontologia* is a term coined by scholastic writers of the seventeenth century. It is perhaps first used by Rudolf Goclenius in 1636, nearly a century before Vico's use of it here. Vico gives the term in Greek letters, giving it a Platonic air, but it is a Latin coinage sometimes used interchangeably by seventeenth-century writers with *metaphysic.* It is finally "canonized" as a philosophical term in the works of Christian Wolff and Alexander Baumgarten. See Alasdair MacIntyre, "Ontology," *The Encyclopedia of Philosophy,* ed. Paul Edwards, vol. 5 (New York: Macmillan Free Press, 1967), 542.

6. Compare Vico's assertion in the *Autobiography* that Descartes and Epicurus have a common conception of corporeal substance:

> But in respect of the unity of its parts the philosophy of Descartes is not at all a consistent system: for his physics calls for a metaphysics that should set up a single kind of substance, the corporeal operating, as we have said, by necessity, just as that of Epicurus calls for a single kind of substance, corporeal, operating by chance. For Descartes and Epicurus agree in this, that all the infinitely various forms of bodies are modifications of corporeal substance, and have themselves no substantial being. (*A* 130)

idea that I find myself to have before the idea of my being, which is as much as to say before my having supposed; an idea that, because it is an idea of true *Being* (being an idea of the true good), leads me to search for my being in its Being: so that it [the idea of true Being] has not come to me from my body, of which I am still in doubt in the dubitation of my own being. From body is born time; and from body and from time, which is measured with the motion of body (provided that it is not mind that regulates the motion of body), comes chance.

[1216] With such reasonings, if we are not mistaken, we have manifestly discovered the paralogisms of those metaphysics that follow a completely different path from the Platonic. Because that of Aristotle is not other than the metaphysic of Plato transported from dialogue into didactical method, which we will call "pedagogic"; just as Proclus, great mathematician and Platonic philosopher, in a golden book, carried the physical principles of Aristotle (that are almost the same as the metaphysical principles of Plato) into geometrical method.[7]

[1217] Now let us begin to reason separately of the subaltern poetic sciences [that is, those that are based in poetic metaphysics— poetic logic, morals, economics, and politics—and poetic physics, cosmography, astronomy, chronology, and geography].

COMMENTARY

The "Reprehension"

This *riprensione* is Vico's most concise statement of his objections to all forms of modern metaphysics. Vico wrote these paragraphs between April and August of 1731. They became part of what is designated in the standard Laterza edition by Fausto

---

7. Vico's reference is to Proclus's *Elements of Physics* and its companion work *Elements of Theology*. Both of these works were translated from Greek into Latin in the Middle Ages and were, as Nicolini points out (*Commento,* 1216), known to Vico in the translation of Francesco Patrizzi (Ferrara, 1585), which Vico cites in a letter to Muzio de Gaeta (*Opere,* 5:256) by the title *De principiis physicae Aristotelis geometrice demonstratis.*

Nicolini as "*Correzioni, miglioramenti e aggiunte terze*" (third corrections, meliorations, and additions). These were part of a series of
reflections Vico had immediately upon publishing the second version of the *New Science* (*La scienza nuova seconda*) in December 1730.
Vico drafted a first set of such notes as the work was appearing and
a second set the month after it appeared, in January 1731.

Vico describes these reflections in his continuation of his *Autobiography*, written in April or May of 1731 (the original text of his
autobiography appeared in Venice in 1728): "These first and second annotations, along with some other (few but important)
notes [which became the "Third corrections, meliorations, and
additions"] written from time to time as the author discussed the
book with his friends, can be incorporated in the places indicated
when a third edition [of the *New Science*] is printed."[8]

Among these "few but important notes" that Vico wrote as he
discussed the *Second New Science* with his friends—and which grew
into his third set of "corrections, meliorations, and additions"—
was not only the foregoing criticism of the views of Descartes, Spinoza, and Locke, but also his fragment on "Pratica della scienza
nuova" (his "Practic of the New Science," translated by Thomas
Goddard Bergin and Max Harold Fisch in 1976 and now printed
as an appendix to the 1984 Cornell University Press paperback
edition of the *New Science*).

The "Practic" takes up the question of the application of the
new science. The "Reprehension" takes up the question of the
validity of the metaphysics that underlies this science. The "Practic" was to be a second chapter added to the "Conclusion" of the
whole work and the "Reprehension" was to be a final chapter
added to his section on "poetic metaphysics" (*metafisica poetica*),
which is the foundation of the theory of "poetic wisdom" (*sapienza
poetica*), which is the subject of the largest book of the *New Science*
and the theory upon which the work itself rests.

---

8. These annotations were prompted by Francesco Spinelli, who had been at
one time a pupil of Vico and who read the *Scienza nuova seconda* immediately on
its publication, calling Vico's attention to three errors in the text, for which Vico was
most grateful; see *A* 197. There was also a fourth set of corrections; see Nicolini's
"nota" in *Opere*, vol. 4, pt. 2: 378f.

My purpose in these comments is to attempt to understand what Vico may have intended in drafting this addition to the *New Science*—what it may imply for understanding the conception of metaphysics that Vico claims to lie at the base of his new science and the extent to which he sees this as involving a critique of modern metaphysics. Vico's work is a kind of palimpsest in which he always writes his thoughts on top of the work of other authors and traditions, often only indirectly indicating these underlying strata or not indicating them at all. My remarks only partially go in the direction of discovering these sources and illuminating what Vico had in mind.

The "Reprehension," which as stated above is conceived by Vico as a separate chapter, is in a sense unique in the *New Science*. Throughout the *New Science* Vico periodically takes opportunity to condemn the views of another thinker, usually pointing to the error in some specific claim an ancient or modern author has made. He will also point to a position that is wrong in general terms, often listing several thinkers who hold it. A favorite in this regard is his list of the seventeenth-century natural-law theorists— Hugo Grotius, Samuel von Pufendorf, and John Selden.[9] To take on a complex of major views with several full arguments as he does in the "Reprehension" is not typical. His approach in these paragraphs likely goes back to that of his original version of the *New Science,* which he describes in his *Autobiography* as written in "forma negativa" but which he abandoned and rewrote in a shorter, positive form because of printing costs.[10] This "scienza nuova in forma negativa," the text of which does not survive, was apparently done in a manner wherein Vico showed the truth of his own views by showing the fundamental errors of other views, a technique that must have been very like that followed in the paragraphs under discussion here.

9. This becomes practically a refrain in the *New Science;* see, e.g., *NS* 310, 313, 318, 329, 394–97, 493, 972, 974, 1109.

10. The "Scienza nuova in forma negativa" was completed in 1724, the year before the publication of the *First New Science.* For details of this see *A* 166; *Opere,* 5:48–49, and Croce and Nicolini's comments on this version, *Opere,* 5:119–20.

Epicurean Chance and Stoic Necessity

Vico's criticism of the metaphysics of Descartes, Spinoza, and Locke presupposes a major distinction between types of philosophy that he makes in other writings—that between the Stoic and the Epicurean—as well as his refutation of Cartesianism that has its most explicit statement his 1710 *De antiquissima Italorum sapientia* (*On the Most Ancient Wisdom of the Italians*).[11] In his letter to Abbé Giuseppe Luigi Esperti in Rome, written early in 1726, a few months after the publication of the *First New Science* (October 1725), commenting on the lack of reception of the work, Vico speaks of the *caso* (chance) of Epicurus and the *necessità* (necessity) of Descartes (which he also generally associates with the Stoics). He sees philosophical culture as having either abandoned itself to *cieca fortuna* (blind chance) or of allowing itself to be dragged along by *sorda necessità* (deaf necessity). In opposition to both of these, Vico claims that his work has as its central theme the "idea of providence."[12]

Stoic and Epicurean become categories in Vico's thought whereby he divides all modern metaphysics into two positions. Vico associates Descartes and Spinoza with his category of Stoics and Locke and Pierre Gassendi with the metaphysics of Epicurus. Vico does not make the third ancient tradition, Skepticism, into a category. He does not mention Pyrrho directly in the *Second New Science*;[13] he mentions Pyrrhonism once in the *First New Science*, where he criticizes it in a sentence, along with Epicureanism and Stoicism, for not having a principle of natural law that offers a

---

11. Giambattista Vico, *On the Most Ancient Wisdom of the Italians Unearthed from the Origins of the Latin Language, Including the Disputation with the Giornale de' letterati d'Italia*, trans. Lucia M. Palmer (Ithaca, N.Y.: Cornell University Press, 1988).

12. Giambattista Vico, "All'Abate Esperti in Roma" (Naples, 1726), in *Opere*, 5:201–3. Vico makes a similar claim in his letter to Monsignor Filippo Maria Monti (Naples, 18 Nov. 1724) in *Opere*, 5:181. In fact this is a common theme that runs through a number of Vico's letters.

13. There is an incidental reference to Pyrrho in the *Second New Science* by way of reference to Diogenes Laertius's life of Pyrrho (*NS* 780). But in one of his additional short chapters, titled "Dimostrazione di fatto istorico contro lo scetticismo," Vico writes of the "Academy of Socrates" degenerating into a final version, the "'pirronismo' da Pirrone" (*Opere*, vol. 4, pt. 2, par. 1364).

single justice.[14] In the first and second books of his *Universal Law* (*Il diritto universale*), written in the early 1720s, Vico mentions a list of "skeptics" (Epicurus, Niccolò Machiavelli, Thomas Hobbes, Spinoza, Pierre Bayle, and others) who claim man's social nature to arise through utility.[15] Vico's only concern with Bayle in both versions of the *New Science* is with the claim that there could be a society without God, a claim that Vico asserts is more radical than that of Polybius concerning the possibility of a society based solely on reason.[16]

Vico regards the Stoics and Epicureans as having inadequate moral philosophies, and he regards their metaphysical positions as unable to produce a viable concept of justice and basis for the state. In his *Autobiography* Vico writes, "For they are each a moral philosophy of solitaries; the Epicurean, of idlers enclosed in their own little gardens; the Stoic, of contemplatives who endeavor to feel no emotion" (*A* 122). In contrast to a moral philosophy of solitaries, Vico regards the human individual as deriving moral reality from the life of the commonwealth, which is also the seat of the individual's conception of law and justice. Vico claims to derive this view from Plato and from the concept of providence that he finds implicit in Platonic metaphysics. He claims that "neither the Epicureans, who attribute to God body alone, and chance together with body, nor the Stoics, who (in this respect the Spinozists of their day) make God an infinite mind, subject to fate, in an infinite body, could reason of commonwealths or laws; and Benedict Spinoza speaks of the commonwealth as if it were a society of hucksters [*mercadanti*]" (*NS* 335).

One way to put Vico's argument is thus: Justice, no matter how it may be understood in specific cases of its manifestation, must be based in a sense of the natural order or natural law of a

---

14. *FNS* 71.

15. In *UL,* see bk. 1, chap. 46, par. 1; bk. 2, pt. 2, chap. 3, par. 16.

16. Vico ends the *First New Science* with this point (*FNS* 476) and he repeats this in the third-to-last paragraph of the *Second New Science* (*NS* 1110; cf. 334). Vico's reference is to Bayle's *Pensées diverses* (1683), secs. 161, 172. On the importance of Bayle for Vico's *New Science* see John Robertson, *The Case for the Enlightenment: Scotland and Naples 1680–1760* (Cambridge: Cambridge University Press, 2005), chap. 5.

commonwealth and this must be grounded in a metaphysics that can show such social order to be part of the real order of things. Neither blind chance nor fateful necessity as ultimate concepts of the real can yield such a nonrelative and yet flexible concept of justice and law. Neither can this be derived from an ethic of solitaries that is itself based upon a denial of the social whole.

Vico's strongest and clearest statement on his alternatives of Stoicism and Epicureanism and where his science stands in relation to them is in his elaboration of his fifth axiom. He wishes to dismiss "from the school of our Science the Stoics, who seek to mortify the senses, and the Epicureans who make them the criterion. For both deny providence, the former chaining themselves to fate, the latter abandoning themselves to chance. The latter, moreover, affirm that the human soul dies with the body. Both should be called monastic, or solitary, philosophers" (*NS* 130). Vico then claims that he wishes to admit "to our school the political philosophers, and first of all the Platonists, who agree with all the lawgivers on these three main points: that there is divine providence, that human passions should be moderated and made into human virtues, and that human souls are immortal. Thus from this axiom are derived the three principles of this science" (*NS* 130). The three principles to which Vico is referring are religion, marriage, and burial, which are the minimum practices that must be present, in his view, to denote a society as human (*NS* 333; 360). The "political philosophers" to whom Vico refers are certainly not Grotius, Pufendorf, and Selden, or any holders of seventeenth-century natural-law theory.

Vico's criticism of Descartes in the foregoing passage is set against his specific attack on Descartes' proof for God's existence, which Vico gives in the *Ancient Wisdom*.[17] Vico's line of argument

17. Vico's own early connections with Cartesianism have been discussed by most commentators on the genesis of Vico's thought, including Fisch in his introduction to the translation of the *Autobiography* and Nicolini in his *La giovinezza di Giambattista Vico,* 2nd rev. ed. (Bari: Laterza, 1932). Much can be learned from Yvon Belaval, "Vico and Anti-Cartesianism," in *Giambattista Vico: An International Symposium,* ed. Giorgio Tagliacozzo and Hayden V. White (Baltimore: Johns Hopkins Press, 1969), 77–91, and from Eugenio Garin, "Cartesio e l'Italia," *Giornale critico della filosofia italiana* 4 (1950): 385–405. Beyond his attack on Descartes in

there is that Descartes' dubitation of his own being can produce his own existence as a certain (*certum*), but not a true (*verum*). For something to be true, it must not simply be indubitable and therefore something of which the knower can be certain. For something to be true for a knower, the knower must possess the principle of that thing's being so that he can produce it. The knower must possess its cause so that he can make it (*factum*). To be able to convert the true and the made (*verum et factum convertuntur*) is to be able to begin from the made and discover what is transcendentally true of it—the intelligibility upon which it rests. Science (*scientia*) requires the conversion of true and made. It requires a power of making, which requires the faculty of *ingenium*. A method of doubt can produce certainty, which depends on *conscientia*, a kind of proper witnessing or complete consciousness by the knower of what is known. In his "Cogito ergo sum," Descartes does not have a true first principle. He has something certain but not something true (intelligible) such that he could be the cause of his own being; that is, Descartes can have no "science" of himself in Vico's sense.[18]

Descartes claims that he is not the maker of his own being because he has within himself as thinking being the idea of God's being. From the presence of this idea of ultimate being in his fifth *Meditation* Descartes presents his version of the ontological

---

the *Ancient Wisdom*, Vico says little about Descartes. He attacks the *Discourse* as a false form of autobiography in his own autobiography, and this is most important for understanding his *Autobiography* (*A* 113). In the *Universal Law* he mentions Descartes only twice in passing (see *UL* bk. 2, pt. 1, chap. 5, par. 2 and pt. 2, chap. 1, par. 24); see also *FNS* 98 and *NS* 706. In the "Correzioni, miglioramenti e aggiunte" to the *Scienza nuova seconda*, see *Opere*, vol. 4, pt. 2, pars. 1213, 1215, 1289, 1301.

18. Vico claims that the same "proof" of one's own existence is uttered by Sosia in Plautus's *Amphitryo* (441–47); see *Ancient Wisdom*, 54. I have discussed this elsewhere; see Donald Phillip Verene, "Imaginative Universals and Narrative Truth," *New Vico Studies* 6 (1988): 1–19. I agree with Fisch's view that *verum* is best rendered as "true," not "truth," and that it is best understood as "intelligible"— what is intelligible to its maker. Fisch points out that in this sense *vera* means the trues or intelligibles: "the things, other than sentences or propositions, that are true in the transcendental sense of intelligible." See Max H. Fisch, "Vico and Pragmatism," in Tagliacozzo and White, eds., *Giambattista Vico: An International Symposium*, 408.

argument to establish that God exists independently of his own existence, or at least to remove any doubt that the cosmological proofs for God's existence (in the third *Meditation*) make his certainty of God's existence to be dependent upon his certainty of his own existence. Vico's criticism in the "Reprehension" enters at this point. His claim is that Descartes in his dubitation of his own being has not noticed that in beginning his metaphysic in this way he has not begun with being and therefore he will not be able to obtain God as Being at the end of his reasonings. Descartes, through his method of doubt, can obtain certainty of himself as substance and thus he will be able only to obtain a comprehension of God as substance.

The New Science of Being

Being, or "is," the "isness" of things, is just itself and not another thing. Being, if it is true Being, cannot be "is" in one way and "is" in another. As Vico claims, Being cannot be something composite. It cannot be generated from substance—that is, we cannot reach the idea of true Being as some further sense of substance, moving from our own being as finite substance to God as infinite substance. What we will obtain in this fashion is a further sense of our own being, but we will not obtain Being as a simple idea. The error lies with the method of metaphysical thinking employed, the method of doubt that is a form of suppositional thinking. Through such a manner of metaphysics I can arrive at certainties, but I cannot obtain *ontologia*—that is, I cannot have a "science of Being." The method of doubt presumes that metaphysics can obtain its own starting points by a progression of suppositions about being until a point is found about which nothing more can be supposed and which is thus a certain. From such a certain other certains may be discovered, but the knower cannot convert the certain into something true. The knower is its discoverer but not its maker.

The error in this, in Vico's view, is that metaphysics has presumed that it possessed or could possess its own starting points, its own *archai*. Metaphysics has presumed that through a method of doubt first premises could be obtained from which, so to speak, a series of sound arguments or syllogisms could be framed that would express the real. It is here that the truly radical sense of Vico's claim enters. He claims that metaphysics cannot supply its own starting point—namely, that the idea of true Being that is required for metaphysics to be a science of Being is not available to metaphysics within the sphere of its own activity. The starting point of metaphysics is never present in its own process of reasoning. This starting point can only be taken over by metaphysics from *myth*, or what Vico calls the "metaphysic of the poets" (what he terms *la sapienza poetica* in the *New Science*).

In the *New Science* Vico claims that "doctrines must take their beginning from that of the matters of which they treat" (*NS* 314). It is in the myth that the idea of the divine, or Being, is first formed in human mentality. The metaphysic of the philosophers, in Vico's view, must always be a transference of this original truth of the metaphysic of the poets. The idea of Being does not exist originally outside the mythical form of the poets. The *poeta*, with his power to make and to make poems, presents this idea of Being to the mind. The task of metaphysics of the philosophers is to produce as something discursively intelligible what is originally formed in the myth or the metaphysic of the poets. This allows for a science of Being because the metaphysician converts what is made by the poets. Metaphysics becomes a narration in discursive and intelligible terms of what is already narrated in the myth. In taking this stand Vico shifts the project of metaphysics away from the process of proof and argument and toward the process of speculation in the sense of producing a language in which the nature of Being can be expressed.[19]

Vico's attack on Spinoza is ad hominem. The views of Spinoza were certainly under discussion among the intellectual circles in Naples that Vico was a part of, along with those of other founding

19. Stephen Gaukroger, "Vico and the Maker's Knowledge Principle," *History of Philosophy Quarterly* 3 (1986): 29–44, has criticized the conception of "the true is the made" as an adequate principle for grounding human knowledge. I think Gaukroger's criticisms have some force against the way this principle is commonly and widely discussed in Vico literature and perhaps even as Vico himself formulates the principle in the *Ancient Wisdom*. But once this principle is connected to Vico's conception of fantasia in the new science and to the ancient activity of the poeta, as I suggest herein, Gaukroger's criticisms must be reconsidered.

figures of modern metaphysics and the modern science of nature. Vico does little more than mention Spinoza in a few places in his published works.[20] The passage herein from the *New Science* criticizing his conception of society as a group of *mercadanti* is perhaps his fullest. Vico saw Spinoza as a modern Stoic, as someone who in his metaphysics applied Descartes' method of critical doubt to history and religion, and in this regard shared an approach with Bayle's "skeptical Pyrrhonism." His ad hominem attack in the "Reprehension" is Vico's strongest language against Spinoza. It is likely that it does not so much grow out of a lack of real intellectual respect for Spinoza as it is an opportunity for Vico to declare himself a friend of religion by declaring himself as against as an enemy.[21]

Fisch points out that Vico's works cannot be understood apart from the fact that the Inquisition was present as an active force in Naples throughout Vico's career. Vico himself probably underwent a crisis of irreligion in his early years, and three of his friends were condemned and later imprisoned for such beliefs.[22]

20. Vico does not mention Spinoza in the *First New Science*. In addition to his remark on Spinoza in the *Second New Science* (*NS* 335) there is only an incidental mention of him, as part of a list of figures (*NS* 1109). In a letter to Monsignor Muzio Gaeta of 1 or 2 October 1737, Vico writes of Spinoza as having falsely used the geometrical method in metaphysics (*Opere*, 5:256), which leaves no doubt that Vico's curious sense of "axioms" in the *Second New Science* does not derive from Spinoza. Vico likely sees it as deriving from Proclus, as his comment in the "Reprehension," par. 1216, would suggest.

21. The comparison between Vico's and Spinoza's systems has not been greatly explored, but some work exists; see E. Giancotti Boscherini, "Nota sulla diffusione della filosofia di Spinoza in Italia," *Giornale critico della filosofia italiana* 42 (1963): 339–62 (on Vico, see 349–52); and James C. Morrison, "Vico and Spinoza," *Journal of the History of Ideas* 41 (1980): 49–68, which concerns the Spinozistic elements in Vico's thought, based on a comparison of the *New Science* and Spinoza's "historization of religion" in the *Theological-Political Treatise*. On this connection, see Ernst Cassirer, "Descartes, Vico, and Leibniz" in *Symbol, Myth, and Culture: Essays and Lectures of Ernst Cassirer 1935–1945*, ed. Donald Phillip Verene (New Haven, Conn.: Yale University Press, 1979), 95–107, in which Cassirer makes a similar connection with Spinoza. See also the very informative article by J. Samuel Preuss, "Spinoza, Vico, and the Imagination of Religion," *Journal of the History of Ideas* 50 (1989): 71–93.

22. The critical year for Vico was 1692, during his nine-year period at Vatolla. In this year he wrote and published his first work, his poem "Affetti di un disperato,"

Throughout his works Vico always takes opportunity to assure the reader that what he has just claimed is for the glory of the Christian religion. He was mocked by Nicola Capasso, his grand *tormentatore,* and by others for the many friendships he had among the clergy and for the clerics who were constant visitors at his home. A good deal has been written on Vico's youthful religious crisis and on assessing the extent to which he really intended his metaphysics to be an endorsement of the Christian faith.[23] Vico, like Hobbes, was very careful around those in power and in changing situations. Whatever his true motives, Vico got away with it. Vico certainly brought the Christian together with the pagan as no one had since St. Augustine (whom he called "my particular protector"),[24] but it is certainly not clear in Vico's case that the Christian doctrine of history did not become paganized in the process. My point is that Vico sincerely objects to the "Stoic" metaphysical position of Spinoza, but this passage is a chief example of how he employs Spinoza as a necessary rhetorical device.

Vico's View of Locke

Vico's argument against Locke in the "Reprehension" may at first seem curious. It does not seem to fit with the way Locke's *Essay Concerning Human Understanding* is read today. Although Locke does not support the view that God is an innate idea, neither does he hold that God is all body, as Vico claims. Vico would not have read Locke in English; there is no evidence that Vico knew any English. He would have had access to the Latin translation of the *Essay* of 1701 and also would have been familiar with

---

which is Lucretian in mood and, as Fisch notes, could not have been written by a devout Christian (see Fisch's introduction, *A* 36). In this same year, Vico's friends Giacinto de Cristofaro, Nicola Galizia, and Basilio Gianelli were stigmatized by the Inquisition and a year later imprisoned. Translations of Vico's poem are listed in the appendix, "Vico's Writings in English Translation."

23. The best account of this crisis is perhaps Nicolini's essays; see *La religiosità di Giambattista Vico: Quattro saggi* (Bari, Laterza, 1949).

24. Vico signed the "Correzioni, miglioramenti e aggiunte terze" in this way: "Terminato la vigilia de Santo Agostino (27 *agosto*), mio particolare protettore, l'anno 1731," *Opere,* 5:377.

Locke from the discussions with his circle in Naples.[25] There was a flow of views and ideas from England to Naples; Vico would have been aware of the general views and criticisms that were circulating in discussion and in reviews of Locke's position in the early eighteenth century.[26] The strongest influence on Vico's views of Locke would have been Paolo Mattia Doria, who published a work in 1732 against Locke and other modern systems of metaphysics.[27] Vico writes in his *Autobiography* that Doria was the only person with whom he could discuss metaphysics (*A* 138).

Vico's typing of Locke as Epicurean derives from his association of Locke's views with Gassendi's attempt to found the results of the new sciences upon a Christianized formulation of Epicurus. In the *Autobiography*, where Vico is describing his reading program and self-education at Vatolla, he writes that "at the time he left Naples [to serve for nine years as a tutor to the Rocca family at their castle at Vatolla] the philosophy of Epicurus had begun to be cultivated in Pierre Gassendi's version; and two years later news that the young men had become its devotees made him wish to study it in Lucretius." Farther down the page Vico adds, "And though Epicurus had no knowledge even of geometry, yet, by a well-ordered deduction, he built on his mechanical physics a metaphysics entirely sensualistic just like that of John Locke" (*A* 126). Vico makes no mention of Locke in the *Second New Science*, nor in the *Universal Law*, and he makes one mention of Locke's views of society in the *First New Science* (*FNS* 45). Thus his specific objection to Locke's metaphysics is to be found only in the "Reprehension," in connection with another remark he makes in his third "corrections, meliorations, and additions," setting Locke off against Spinoza.[28]

---

25. John Locke, *De Intellectu humano*, trans. Ezekiel Burridge (London, 1701), reviewed in the *Acta eruditorum* in 1702 and reprinted in Leipzig in 1709 and in Amsterdam in 1729.

26. Little analysis exists on Vico and Locke. Most helpful is the very thorough article by Gustavo Costa, "Vico e Locke," *Giornale critico della filosofia italiana* 3 (1970): 344–61.

27. Doria's work is titled *Difesa delle metafisica degli antichi filosofi contro Giovanni Locke ed alcuni altri moderni autori* (1732).

28. See Vico, "Correzioni," par. 1122.

The most puzzling part of Vico's charge against Locke is his claim that Locke "is compelled to offer a God all body operating by chance." Vico may simply have typed Locke as "Epicurean" and thus concluded that God must be all body. But the solution more likely lies in what John Yolton has pointed out in his researches into Locke and the reception of Locke's ideas. Yolton points out that Locke came more and more under attack from theologians charging that his conception of substance undermined religion. One of the most vehement attacks, which appeared after Locke's death in the first decade of the 1700s, was by William Carroll. As Yolton points out: "In a series of tracts Carroll strove to show that Locke's doctrine of substance was an expansion of Spinoza's pantheism, or the doctrine that there is only one substance in the world and that this is material."[29]

As is well known, Locke in the *Essay* thought that he had made God an exception to the general unknowableness of substance, and he believed he had established God as immaterial and not in disagreement with religion. Carroll, playing on Locke's claim (bk. 2, ch. 13, sec. 18) that people use the confused notion of substance to apply to God, finite beings, and material objects, argues that Locke, like Spinoza, has a singular notion of substance with these three applications of it differing only as modifications. In Carroll's view, as Yolton writes, "With the real essence of substance unknowable, Locke is committed to the doctrine that so far as man can know with certainty, material and immaterial substance may be the same substantially, differing only accidentally. The charge of materialism against Locke was commonly made by his contemporaries on the ground of his suggestion that God might be able to add to matter a power of thinking. Carroll arrived at the same conclusion in a different way, by an analysis of the doctrine of substance."[30]

---

29. John W. Yolton, *John Locke and the Way of Ideas* (Oxford: Oxford University Press, 1953), 144.

30. Ibid., 145–46. Interesting to consider in this connection is the material discussed in Jean S. Yolton and John W. Yolton, "Locke's Suggestion of Thinking Matter and Some Eighteenth-Century Portuguese Reactions," *Journal of the History of Ideas* 45 (1984): 303–7, but not as an influence on Vico, as it is much later.

Vico may or may not have been aware of Carroll's arguments, but he would have been aware of the general charge of materialism against Locke. It is the doctrine of substance that concerns Vico, and his argument seems to be that if all ideas come to us through the body, then what we know of God will be based upon the kind of supposition we can make from the body. Our idea of God will thus have to be either material in some sense or, since it is not innate for Locke, what God is will have to remain unknowable (in the way that the real essence of substance is unknowable) and from this there can come no positive doctrine of being as immaterial.

Supposition as the Basis of Modern Metaphysics

The key term for Vico's reprehension of modern metaphysics is *supposition* (*supposizione*), which he applies to Locke but could also apply in a similar sense to Descartes. Vico writes, "Locke should consider whether the idea of true Being exists by supposition" (see par. 1215). Whether supposition is extrapolation from the senses or whether it is a process of rational dubitation and hypothesis, the idea of true Being cannot be produced. Vico's aforementioned axiom in the *New Science*, that "Doctrines must take their beginning from that of the matters of which they treat," when seen in relation to his conception of the convertibility of the true and the made means that there can be no more in a doctrine that is in its origin. Thus, substance can emerge as a kind of ultimate supposition about the world, even one that we are necessarily committed to have as a certain. True Being is not substance in the sense of an idea we are driven to have by beginning either with our senses or with our logical powers of thought. True Being has to be a true given and not simply the product of an inescapable supposition. In rejecting Locke, Vico does not then also hold to the opposite doctrine of innate ideas. By starting with the poets, Vico has a way to go between the horns of this dilemma, because he begins from God as an idea in human culture itself and one that is actual for the human in this sense.

Vico's claim seems to be that what modern metaphysics, which begins either from body or from finite thought, can give is nothing more than an ultimate version of each, and true Being must be something that is neither of these. The starting point for metaphysics for Vico can be grounded in neither the senses nor in argument. It is grounded in what in contemporary terms might be called "feeling" or, in his terms, more specifically, *fantasia*. This is the power of the *poeta* to make an ultimate intelligible as a fable or a metaphor, as Vico claims every metaphor is a fable in brief (*NS* 404). All human cultures, Vico holds, begin with an insight into true Being, or Jove, and he holds that every nation has its Jove (*NS* 380). Since from this original insight a culture, or what Vico calls a nation, is developed, metaphysics must be a reflection on such a "true" that is originally mythic in form. Metaphysics must be an attempt to unfold what is already present in human fantasia from which culture itself is first made. Metaphysics cannot proceed independently of this because to base it on our powers of sensing or reasoning is to try to generate the nature of Being from faculties that are themselves dependent upon the more fundamental power of formation of experience present in the human powers of fantasia.[31]

Vico's remark about the "supposition" of Polybius (par. 1212), that Polybius is wrong that there could be a society of philosophers, is another way of saying what he says about Descartes, Spinoza, and Locke as leading representatives of modern culture and metaphysics. In like manner, Vico's rather curious ending of the "Reprehension" (par. 1216), in which he merges Plato and Aristotle's metaphysics together—the latter being, he writes, just the extension of the former—is another way of saying that there is an ancient way of doing metaphysics that has been lost in the modern way of suppositional thinking. The project of ancient metaphysics for Vico is always set against myth or the knowledge of the poets. The problem of ancient metaphysics is how to come

---

31. I have attempted to work out the logic of this original mentality, which functions in terms of what Vico calls "imaginative universals" (*universale fantastici*). See Donald Phillip Verene, *Vico's Science of Imagination* (Ithaca, N.Y.: Cornell University Press, 1981), chap. 3. I find support for my account of the logic of imaginative universals in Mary B. Hesse, "Vico's Heroic Metaphor," in *Metaphysics and Philosophy of Science in the Seventeenth and Eighteenth Centuries*, ed. R. S. Woolhouse (Dordrecht: Kluwer, 1988), 185–212.

to grips with the making of the poets and to make their truths in a new way. Plato's dialogue is a struggle with the poets, and once accomplished its results can be made "pedagogic" by Aristotle and even geometrically formed by Proclus. Vico saw geometry as an instance of synthetical thinking based on fantasia—that is, guided by the mind's power of the image.[32]

Jove's union with Mnemosyne on nine nights produces the nine Muses, who are the arts of humanity. In the line that immediately precedes paragraph 1212, Vico writes, "So that these nine sciences must be the nine Muses that the poets also sing of as being all daughters of Jove; and through all of them the motto 'From Jove the muse began' is now restored to its proper historical significance" (par. 1211).[33] Vico's tree of knowledge of the poetic arts and sciences—of which metaphysics is the trunk and the branches are logic, morals, economy, politics, physics, cosmography, astronomy, chronology, and geography—is in some way, which Vico does not specify, derived from the nine Muses.[34] Thus, Jove is the source of both science and virtue. In Vico's view this is a way of saying that metaphysics must be a metaphysics of historical experience. The problem of modern metaphysics, of that of Descartes, Spinoza, and Locke, is the failure to confront the reality of Being in the reality of history. Metaphysics then strives to be a self-sufficient enterprise and is no longer the trunk of the tree

32. In his *Autobiography* Vico quotes with pride the remark of Jean Le Clerc in his review of Vico's work on *Universal Law*—that it is constructed by a "mathematical method" (*A* 164). In Giambattista Vico, *On the Study Methods of Our Time*, trans. Elio Gianturco (Ithaca, N.Y.: Cornell University Press, 1990), his criticism of the geometric method is only of analytic geometry as a way of thinking that is not to be taught too early to the young and is not a basis for metaphysics. From that early work on Vico held that classical or Euclidean geometry required fantasia and was suitable as a model for synthetic thinking. Certainly this is the sense in which he intends the axiomatic formulation he gives of his doctrine in the *Second New Science*, which in this sense is to derive directly from the form of such thinking among the ancients, not to represent the new metaphysics of Descartes or Spinoza.

33. In his section "Method" in the *New Science*, Vico describes the proof of his science, that which "regna in questa scienza," in terms of a quotation of the traditional power of the Muses as found in Hesiod's *Theogony* (see *NS* 348–49). Vico cites the claim "A Iove principium musae" in *NS* 391, 508.

34. See "Vico's Tree of the Poetic Sciences and His Use of the Muses" in this volume.

of knowledge; it attempts to operate without its connections with cultural life.

These last comments may seem a little extreme. They are intended to point to the fact that this little set of paragraphs from Vico's annotations is more than some criticisms he has considered about other positions. Vico intends his "Reprehension" to be a genuine one in the sense that he is posing a new position that is radically different from that which dominates modern thought. This "new" position or new science is in reality an attempt, like that of St. Augustine, to confront, together in one metaphysics, the Greco-Roman world and the Judeo-Christian world, to recover the problems of ancient metaphysics' confrontation with myth in a world that is governed by history.

Appendix

Vico's Writings in English Translation

The renaissance in Vico studies in the last decades of the twentieth century and that continues today owes a profound debt to the excellent translations of the *New Science* and the *Autobiography* by Thomas Goddard Bergin and Max Harold Fisch that first appeared in the 1940s and have undergone numerous editions and reprintings. They made Vico available to English-speaking scholars in all fields of the humanities and the social sciences. These and subsequent translations of Vico's works into English have done much to spread interest in Vico worldwide.

1692/1693. Poem: "Affetti di un disperato" [Feelings of one in despair]: Two translations (both retain the Italian title):
  (1) H. P. Adams. *The Life and Writings of Giambattista Vico.* London: Allen and Unwin, 1935, 223–26.
  (2) Thomas Goddard Bergin. *Forum Italicum* 2 (1968): 305–9.

1693. Poem: "Canzone in morte di Antonio Carafa" [Canzone on the death of Antonio Carafa]. See below, 1716, *Carafa.*

1699. Oration before the Palatine Academy:
  "On the Sumptuous Dinners of the Romans." Translated by George A. Trone. *New Vico Studies* 20 (2002): 79–89.

1699–1707. The six university inaugural orations:
  On Humanistic Education (Six Inaugural Orations, 1699–1707). Translated by Giorgio A. Pinton and Arthur W. Shippee, with an introduction by Donald Phillip Verene. Ithaca, N.Y.: Cornell University Press, 1993.

1709. The seventh university inaugural oration (delivered 1708):
  On the Study Methods of Our Time. Translated with an introduction by Elio Gianturco. Indianapolis, Ind.: Bobbs-Merrill, 1965. Reissued, with a preface

and a translation of "The Academies and the Relation between Philosophy and Eloquence" by Donald Phillip Verene. Ithaca, N.Y., Cornell University Press, 1990.

Partial translation, in *Vico: Selected Writings*. Edited and translated by Leon Pompa. Cambridge: Cambridge University Press, 1982, 33–45.

1710. On the Most Ancient Wisdom of the Italians:

On the Most Ancient Wisdom of the Italians Unearthed from the Origins of the Latin Language, Including the Disputation with the "Giornale de' letterati d'Italia." Translated with an introduction by Lucia M. Palmer. Ithaca, N.Y.: Cornell University Press, 1988.

Partial translation, in *Vico: Selected Writings*, 49–78.

1711. Textbook of rhetoric:

The Art of Rhetoric (Institutiones Oratoriae, 1711–1741). Edited and translated by Giorgio A. Pinton and Arthur W. Shippee. Amsterdam: Rodopi, 1996.

1711–1712. Disputation concerning the *Most Ancient Wisdom* in the *Giornale de' letterati d'Italia:*

See above, 1710, *Ancient Wisdom*, 113–87.

1713. University inaugural oration (full text lost, but probably delivered in 1713; partially quoted as a digression in the *Autobiography*):

See below, 1725–1728, *Autobiography*, 123–25.

1715. Letter to Adriano Carafa [25 September 1715]:

See below, 1716, *Carafa*.

1716. *De rebus gestis Antonii Caraphaei* (On the life and deeds of Antonio Carafa). Translated and edited by Giorgio A. Pinton under the title *Statecraft: Leopold I of Austria and Antonio Carafa*. New York: Peter Lang, 2004. Includes translations of Vico's "Canzone in morte di Antonio Carafa" (1693) and his letter to Adriano Carafa (1715).

1719. University inaugural oration (text lost, but its argument is quoted in the *Autobiography*):

See below, 1725–1728, *Autobiography*, 156.

1720. Postface from a lost manuscript on jurisprudence; "To the Equable Readers" ("Ad lectores aequanimos"):

"Vico's Address to His Readers from a Lost Manuscript on Jurisprudence: Commentary and Translation" by Donald Phillip Verene. *New Vico Studies* 19 (2001): 161–68.

1720–1722. *Universal Law* ("Synopsis" and first book, 1720; second book, 1721; third book of notes and dissertations, 1722): Two complete translations:

(1) Translated and edited by Giorgio A. Pinton and Margaret Diehl under the title *Universal Right*. Amsterdam: Rodopi, 2000.

(2) *Universal Law* (in three issues of *New Vico Studies*):

"Synopsis of Universal Law." Translated by Donald Phillip Verene. *New Vico Studies* 21 (2003): 1–22.

Vico's Writings in English Translation

Book 1. *On the One Principle and One End of Universal Law.* Translated by John D. Schaeffer. *New Vico Studies* 21 (2003): 23–274.

Book 2. *On the Constancy of the Jurisprudent,* including *Notae.* Translated by John D. Schaeffer. *New Vico Studies* 23 (2005): 1–308.

Book 3. *Dissertations.* Translated by John D. Schaeffer. *New Vico Studies* 24 (2006): 1–80.

1720–1725. Correspondence between Vico and Bernardo Maria Giacco, and between Vico and Jean Le Clerc, including a letter from Aniello Spagnuolo to Vico:

See above, 1720–1722, *Universal Right,* 714–28.

Part of the letter of Jean Le Clerc to Vico (8 September 1711) is quoted by Vico in the *Autobiography.* See below, 1725–1728, *Autobiography,* 159.

1721. Poem: "Giunone in danza" [Juno in Dance]:

"Juno to Apollo" (lines 195–299). Translated by Joseph Tusiani. *Rivista di studi italiani* 1 (1983): 106–9.

1725. *The First New Science:*

[*The First New Science*] *The principles of a new science of the nature of nations leading to the discovery of the principles of a new system of the natural law of the gentes. The First New Science.* Translated and edited by Leon Pompa. Cambridge: Cambridge University Press, 2002.

Partial translation in *Vico: Selected Writings,* 81–156 (superseded by the above complete translation of *The First New Science*).

1725–1729. Correspondence concerning the *First New Science:*

Letter of 25 October 1725 to Fr. Bernardo Maria Giacco. Translated by Max Harold Fisch. See below, 1725–1728, Introduction to *Autobiography,* 14–16.

"Four Letters of Giambattista Vico on the *First New Science*." Translated by Giorgio A. Pinton. *New Vico Studies* 16 (1998): 31–58. (1) 25 October 1725 to Fr. Bernardo Maria Giacco (also see above, the translation of this letter by Fisch); (2) Early January 1726 to Luigi Esperti; (3) 20 January 1725 to Edoardo de Vitry; (4) 12 January 1729 to Francesco Saverio Estevan.

1725. Letter on Dante and true poetry:

[Letter of 26 December 1725] "To Gherardo degli Angeli: On Dante and on the Nature of True Poetry." Translated by Maggie Günsberg. In *Dante: The Critical Heritage.* Edited by Michael Caesar. London: Routledge, 1989, 348–55.

1725–1728. The *Autobiography:*

The Autobiography of Giambattista Vico. Translated by Max Harold Fisch and Thomas Goddard Bergin. Ithaca, N.Y.: Cornell University Press, 1944 (Great Seal Books edition, 1963; Cornell Paperbacks edition, 1975), 111–73 (portion of the autobiography published during Vico's lifetime).

1727. Oration on the Death of Donn'Angela Cimmino:

"On the Death of Donn'Angela Cimmino, Marchesa of Petrella." Translated by Robin L. Thomas. *New Vico Studies* 25 (2007): 11–33.

1728/1729. Discovery of the true Dante ("Discovery of the True Dante" is Nicolini's title in the Laterza edition of Vico's works): Three translations: (1) "Discovery of the True Dante." Translated by Irma Brandeis, in *Discussions of the Divine Comedy*. Edited by Irma Brandeis. Boston: Heath, 1961, 11–12.
(2) " 'The Discovery of the True Dante' or 'New Principles in Dante Criticism.' Concerning the commentary of an anonymous writer on the *Comedy*." Translated by Maggie Günsberg. See above, 1725, *Dante: The Critical Heritage*, 348–55.
(3) "Discovery of the True Dante." Translated by Cristina Mazzoni, in *Critical Essays on Dante*. Edited by Giuseppe Mazzotta. Boston: G. K. Hall, 1991: 58–60.

1729. *Vici vindiciae* ("Vindication[s] of Vico"; Vico's reply to the false book notice on the *First New Science* published in the Leipzig *Acta Eruditorum*): "Vico's Reply to the False Book Notice: The *Vici vindiciae:* Translation and Commentary." Translated by Donald Phillip Verene. *New Vico Studies* 24 (2006): 129–75.
Partial translation: "A Factual Digression on Human Genius, Sharp, Witty Remarks, and Laughter." Translated by A. Illiano, J. D. Tedder, and P. Treves. *Forum Italicum* 2 (1968): 310–14 [a translation of the first ten paragraphs of the "Digression"].

1729. Letter to the Leipzig Academy of Sciences concerning the above false book notice; 19 October 1729 to Johann Burkhard Mencken (not sent, but included by Vico in his continuation of the *Autobiography*): See below, 1731, *Autobiography*, 190.

1730. Vico's advice to the reader in the second edition of the *New Science:* "[The *Second New Science*, 1730] Giambattista Vico to the Reader." Translated by Leon Pompa. In *Vico: Selected Writings*, 269–70. This passage comes at the end of the "Idea of the Work" in the 1730 edition; it does not appear in the 1744 edition (see Laterza edition, vol. 4, pt. 2, pars. 1131–38).

1730. Reply to Spinelli on errors in the *New Science;* December. Letter to Francesco Spinelli, thanking him for his analysis of several errors in the *New Science*. Included in the continuation of the autobiography: See below, 1731, *Autobiography*, 195–97.

1731. Vico's continuation of the *Autobiography:* "Continuation by the Author [1731]." Translated by Max Harold Fisch and Thomas Goddard Bergin. *Autobiography*, 173–200.

1731. Additions to the 1730 edition of the *New Science*, which Vico prepared for inclusion in his third edition but which remained in manuscript: "Giambattista Vico's 'Reprehension of the Metaphysics of René Descartes, Benedict Spinoza, and John Locke': An Addition to the *New Science* (Translation and Commentary)" by Donald Phillip Verene. *New Vico Studies* 8 (1990): 2–18 (Laterza edition, vol. 4., pt. 2, pars. 1212–17).

"Practic of the New Science." Translated by Thomas Goddard Bergin and Max Harold Fisch. In *Giambattista Vico's Science of Humanity*. Edited by Giorgio Tagliacozzo and Donald Phillip Verene. Baltimore: Johns Hopkins University Press, 1976, 451–54. Reprinted in *The New Science of Giambattista Vico* (1984), 427–30 (Laterza edition, vol. 4., pt. 2, pars. 1405–11).

"Ragionamento primo" (concerning whether the Law of Twelve Tables were Roman in origin), and "Ragionamento secondo" (concerning the Royal Law of Tribonian). Translated by Giorgio A. Pinton, with Notes and Comments. *New Vico Studies* 19 (2001): 87–160 (Laterza edition, vol. 4, pt. 2, pars. 1412–59).

"How All the Other Sciences Must Take Their Principles from This [Science of Divination]." Translated by Donald Phillip Verene. *New Vico Studies* 22 (2004): 101–4 (Laterza edition, vol. 4, pt. 2, pars. 1199–1211).

1732. University inaugural oration on the heroic mind:
Two translations:
(1) "On the Heroic Mind." Translated by Elizabeth Sewell and Anthony C. Sirignano. *Social Research* 43 (1976): 886–903. Reprinted in *Vico and Contemporary Thought*. Edited by Giorgio Tagliacozzo, Michael Mooney, and Donald Phillip Verene. Atlantic Highlands, N.J.: Humanities Press, 1979: 2:228–45.
(2) "On the Heroic Mind." Translated by Paul J. Archambault. *New Vico Studies* 22 (2004): 85–99.

1737. Inaugural oration to the Academy of Oziosi on philosophy and eloquence:
"The Academies and the Relation between Philosophy and Eloquence." Translated by Donald Phillip Verene. See above, 1709, *Study Methods*, 85–90.

1744. *The New Science*, third edition:
Two complete translations:
(1) *The New Science of Giambattista Vico*. Translated by Thomas Goddard Bergin and Max Harold Fisch. Ithaca, N.Y.: Cornell University Press, 1948; rev. ed. 1968, 1984. Abridged ed.: Garden City, N.Y.: Doubleday Anchor Books, 1961; reprint, Ithaca, N.Y.: Cornell Paperbacks, 1970.
(2) *New Science: Principles of the New Science Concerning the Common Nature of Nations*. Translated by David Marsh, with an introduction by Anthony Grafton. London: Penguin, 1999. Reprint 2001.
A principal difference between these two translations of Vico's major work is the way in which each treats Vico's terminology. Where possible, Bergin and Fisch translate Vico's major terms with their English cognates; Marsh generally does not. For example, Bergin and Fisch render Vico's *favola* as "fable," Marsh as "myth"; Bergin and Fisch render Vico's *caratteri poetici* as "poetic characters," and Marsh, variously, as "poetic symbols"

or "archetypes"; Bergin and Fisch render Vico's *lingua comune mentale* as "common mental language," Marsh as "conceptual language"; Bergin and Fisch render Vico's *barbarie della riflessione* as "barbarism of reflection," Marsh as "barbarism of calculation," but revised in the reprinting of 2001 as "this calculating barbarism of reflection" (see par. 1106). In Vico's original there is no term corresponding to "calculation" or "calculating."

For a discussion of these terminological differences, see Donald Phillip Verene, "On Translating Vico: The Penguin Classics Edition of the *New Science,*" *New Vico Studies* 17 (1999): 85–107.

Some partial translations of the *New Science:*

"The Third Book of Vico's *Scienza nuova:* On the Discovery of the True Homer." Translated by Henry Nelson Coleridge. In Coleridge, *Introductions to the Study of the Greek Classic Poets: Designed Principally for the Use of Young Persons at School and College,* 2nd ed. London: Murray, 1834, 73–98; 3rd ed. 1846, 63–84.

"[Selections from] the *Scienza nuova.*" Translated by E. F. Carritt. In Carritt, *Philosophies of Beauty from Socrates to Robert Bridges: Being the Sources of Aesthetic Theory.* Oxford: Clarendon Press, 1931, 73–74.

"[*The Third New Science*] *Principles of a new science concerning the common nature of nations.*" Translated by Leon Pompa. In *Vico: Selected Writings,* 159–267.

Index

Index

Index

Index

Index

THE EDITORS

Thora Ilin Bayer is chair of the Department of Philosophy and RosaMary Foundation Professor of Liberal Arts at Xavier University of Louisiana in New Orleans. She is the author of *Cassirer's Metaphysics of Symbolic Forms* and of essays and articles in the history of philosophy and philosophy of culture. She is an associate editor of *New Vico Studies*.

Donald Phillip Verene is Charles Howard Candler Professor of Metaphysics and Moral Philosophy and director of the Institute for Vico Studies at Emory University. His previous books include *Vico's Science of Imagination, The New Art of Autobiography: An Essay on the "Life of Giambattista Vico Written by Himself," Philosophy and the Return to Self-Knowledge, The Art of Humane Education,* and *Knowledge of Things Human and Divine: Vico's New Science and Finnegans Wake.* He is a fellow of the Accademia Nazionale dei Lincei, Rome. He is the editor of *New Vico Studies.*